THE BOOK OF
GOLF
QUOTATIONS

PAT SULLIVAN

EBURY
PRESS

First published as *Inside Golf* in the USA by Atheneum 1985

First published in Great Britain by Stanley Paul & Co. Ltd 1987

This edition published in Great Britain 2006

1 3 5 7 9 10 8 6 4 2

Text © Pat Sullivan 2006

Ebury Press, an imprint of Ebury Publishing.
Random House, 20 Vauxhall Bridge Road, London SW1V 2SA

Random House Australia (Pty) Limited
20 Alfred Street, Milsons Point, Sydney, New South Wales 2061, Australia

Random House New Zealand Limited
18 Poland Road, Glenfield, Auckland 10, New Zealand

Random House (Pty) Limited
Isle of Houghton, Corner of Boundary Road and Carse O'Gowrie,
Houghton, 2198, South Africa

Random House Publishers India Private Limited
301 World Trade Tower, Hotel Intercontinental Grand Complex,
Barakhamba Lane, New Delhi 110 001, India

The Random House Group Limited Reg. No. 954009

www.randomhouse.co.uk

A CIP catalogue record for this book is available from the British Library.

Cover design by 2 Associates
Typeset by Textype

ISBN 9780091912048 (after Jan 2007)
ISBN 0091912040

Papers used by Ebury Press are natural, recyclable products made from wood grown in sustainable forests.

Printed and bound in Great Britain by Bookmarque Ltd, Croydon, Surrey

Contents

For Bonnie Kay, my partner in life

Also for Jim Sullivan, Mary Maloney, J. P. O'Shea,
John Strege, the staff at AAF/Ziffren Library, Los Angeles,
and Ward Clayton, Director of Editorial Services,
PGA Tour, for inspiration and assistance.

Introduction

The year was about AD 1100. The setting was a knoll in Scotland, perhaps next to one of the king's archery ranges. A sewn spheroid packed with feathers – the first golf ball – was whacked for the first time in history. Moments later, someone probably made a comment, perhaps what teaching professional Bob Toski calls the saddest words in golf:

'You're still away.'

It is the nature of golf that a lot more words – of wit, of truth and of mirth – are spoken than rounds played. This book contains a collection of utterances on golf – famous and newly discovered – gems of insight, random thoughts, and pointed statements that in sum, we trust, will inspire the reader to a finer appreciation of the game. And if we have achieved our purpose, perhaps the reader will find some advice contained within these nuggets to shave a stroke or two off his own game. Then we can all retire to the clubhouse.

Not long after golf was invented, it became evident that the game had a peculiar hold on those who played it. Worried that the game was distracting the populace from its compulsory archery practice, the Scottish Parliament of

James II in 1457 issued a proclamation: 'Golfe be utterly cryed down and not be used.'

By 1600, Parliament had backed down somewhat, forbidding golf only during the Sunday hours of 'devine services'. By the middle of the eighteenth century, golf's reputation among the educated classes hadn't improved much. 'It is unjust to claim the privileges of age,' remarked Dr Samuel Johnson on the game, 'and retain the playthings of childhood.' Finally, in the twentieth century, Canadian economist and humorist Stephen Butler Leacock put the game in its proper perspective. 'Golf may be played on Sunday,' he wrote, 'not being a game within the view of the law, but being a form of moral effort.'

Today some of our finest golf is played on Sundays, the traditional day of the final round every week on the magnificent professional golf tours. But it was on a Friday during the second round of the Western Open that Lee Trevino was struck and seriously injured by lightning. When asked if golf clubs didn't serve as lightning rods, he struck back with his own wit. 'Even God,' said Trevino, 'couldn't hit a one-iron.'

When it comes to mishitting the ball, one would think the memorable comments would come from hackers; but that's not the case. George Bayer, a powerful driver who would hit the ball so far – and so wildly – that he once asked Arnold Palmer how to *reduce* his length, would understand Jim Dent's comment, 'I can airmail the ball, but sometimes I don't put the right address on it.' Or consider Miller Barber's dilemma in trying to find the proper fairway: 'I don't say my game is bad,' he said, 'but if I grew tomatoes they'd come up sliced.'

Beauty, grace, balance, harnessed energy, self-control and deep concentration are all elements of the golf swing. The problem – and golf's paradox – is that such perfection can never be sustained. Out of that conflict flows the words. Baseball, a game of similar eloquence, allows a career for a man who hits the ball well – a base hit – just one out of four times, the .250 hitter. In this respect baseball resembles golf, where a man can shoot seventy and still have delivered only a dozen well-stroked balls in the round.

But for some of us, even a mediocre round can be saved by playing with the right people, for the well-turned phrase can give us as much pleasure as the well-hit ball. And golf seems to provide the phrases, for as writer John Hogben said in his book, *On the Green*: 'It seems that the most reticent of men on other subjects no sooner takes to golf than eloquence descends upon him.'

These quotations, arranged by subject, are taken from a variety of sources: magazines, newspapers, radio, television, books and the press tent; they are, in effect, chip shots, the chip shot being defined by the *Encyclopedia of Golf* as 'a short approach'. We hope with these chip shots to encourage the reader to explore the richness of golf literature, an area that the late golf historian Herbert Warren Wind said '... far surpasses any other game's for sheer quantity', and of which author George Plimpton says, 'No other sport can offer such fine reading.'

The new material in this edition is dedicated to the memory of the late Bob Chieger, the driving force behind our original collaboration. Bob was a visionary editor and writer who at first sought to become a modern John Bartlett (*Familiar Quotations*, first published in 1855). Persuaded by editors to break down his research into subjects, Bob published quotation books on baseball, then love, sex and romance, then the original golf book, bringing me in as a co-editor and also renewing a friendship first started at *Rolling Stone* Magazine/Straight Arrow Books in the early 1970s.

In *The Book of Golf Quotations,* I have strived to stay true to Bob's vision. I hope you, dear reader, enjoy the newest words of golf as much as I know Bob would have enjoyed working to gather them.

Pat Sullivan
February 2006

1 ● Amateurs and Duffers

Out on the course each morning you could see represen-
tatives of every nightmare style that was ever invented. There
was the man who seemed to be attempting to deceive his ball
and lull it into a false security by looking away from it and
then making a lightning slash in the apparent hope of
catching it off its guard.

P. G. WODEHOUSE, *The Heart of a Goof*, 1923

Even in foursomes where fifty yards is reckoned a good shot
somebody must be away.

P. G. WODEHOUSE, *Chester Forgets Himself*, 1923

I won't try to describe A.R.'s game, beyond saying the way he
played it would have taken him three years of solid practice
to work up to where he could be called a duffer.

PAUL GALLICO, *Golf Is a Nice Friendly Game*, 1942

If I were a man I wouldn't have half a dozen Tom Collinses before going out to play golf, then let profanity substitute for proficiency on the golf course.
PATTY BERG, *Ladies' Home Journal*, **1945**

Under an assumed name.
DUTCH HARRISON, his advice to a hacker on how to play a shot during a pro-am

As I burst into the clubhouse to tell everyone, news came that Lindbergh had flown the Atlantic. Guess who's remembered?
HERB GRAFFIS, golf editor, on his first ace, **1950**

Give me golf clubs, the fresh air and a beautiful partner and you can keep my golf clubs and the fresh air.
JACK BENNY

Every time I have the urge to play golf I lie down until the urge passes.
SAM LEVENSON, humorist

A golfer might as well turn in his clubs if he can't find some excuse for his own duffery.
MILTON GROSS, *Eighteen Holes in My Head*, **1959**

The cross-handed grip is used principally by left-handed golfers who have purchased right-handed clubs by mistake (or vice-versa) and is too special for discussion here.
REX LARDNER, *Out of the Bunker and Into the Trees*, **1960**

This will give the duffers a bit of heart.
ARNOLD PALMER, as he took a twelve on the final hole of the Los Angeles Open, **1961**

Any golfer serious enough about his game to want to break 120 must learn to stop worrying about the last ten or twenty missed strokes.
STEPHEN BAKER, *How to Play Golf in the Low 120's,* **1962**

Nothing goes down slower than a golf handicap.
BOBBY NICHOLS, *Never Say Never,* **1965**

If you pick up a golfer and hold it close to your ear, like a conch shell, and listen – you will hear an alibi.
FRED BECK, *89 Years in a Sand Trap,* **1965**

The average golfer doesn't play golf. He attacks it.
JACKIE BURKE

Your financial cost can best be figured out when you realize that if you were to devote the same time and energy to business instead of golf, you would be a millionaire in approximately six weeks.
BUDDY HACKETT, *The Truth About Golf and Other Lies,* **1968**

I am the world's foremost master at the topped shot. Not everyone can learn to play this delicate little line drive around the green with finesse.
JIM MURRAY, *The Sporting World of Jim Murray,* **1968**

You were hitting some shots out there that weren't making any *noise.*
DAVE MARR, to George Plimpton at the Bing Crosby National Pro-Am

The biggest liar in the world is the golfer who claims that he plays the game merely for exercise.
TOMMY BOLT, *How to Keep Your Temper on the Golf Course,* **1969**

I had always suspected that trying to play golf in the company of big-time pros and a gallery would be something like walking naked into choir practice.
DAN JENKINS on pro-ams,
The Dogged Victims of Inexorable Fate, **1970**

Mulligan: Invented by an Irishman who wanted to hit one more twenty-yard grounder.
JIM BISHOP, syndicated column,**1970**

Like all Saturday foursomes it is in difficulties. One of the patients is zigzagging about the fairway like a liner pursued by submarines.
P. G. WODEHOUSE, *P. G. Wodehouse on Golf,* **1973**

I have three-putted in forty countries.
FRED CORCORAN, former PGA executive director,
Golf Digest, **1977**

How about that guy? He gives me a stroke a side and I still have to shoot a sixty-eight to beat him. The lousy sandbagger.
BOB HOPE

The loudest sound you hear on the golf course is the guy jangling coins to distract the player he bets against.
JIM MURRAY, *Los Angeles Times* sports columnist

Bob Newhart to Suzanne Pleshette: It was a great dude ranch. I shot an eighty-three.
The Bob Newhart Show, NBC-TV, **1980**

I may be the only golfer never to have broken a single putter, if you don't count the one I twisted into a loop and threw into a bush.
THOMAS BOSWELL, sportswriter, *Golf Digest,* **1980**

As of this writing, there are approximately 2,450 reasons why a person hits a rotten shot, and more are being discovered every day.
JAY CRONLEY, *Playboy*, **1981**

Hell is standing on the most beautiful golf course that's ever been made and not having a set of clubs.
JIM MEYERS, radio station general manager,
San Francisco Chronicle, **1982**

The flags on the greens ought to be at half-staff.
AL MALATESTA, amateur golfer, on his game,
San Francisco Examiner, **1982**

If I died ... it meant I couldn't play golf. No way was I giving up golf, so I gave up drinking.
BOB HOPE, *Los Angeles Times*, **1982**

I call him the PGA hit man. But it's wonderful being able to get back some of that money I gave to the government.
BOB HOPE, on President Gerald R. Ford,
San Jose Mercury News, **1982**

Bob says I have made golf a combat and contact sport.
GERALD R. FORD, on Bob Hope, *People*, **1983**

And the name that is synonymous with Ford – Fore!
VIN SCULLY, *Bob Hope Classic*, NBC-TV, **1984**

My tournament lineup would include ... anyone who never finished a par-five hole with the same ball he started it with.
JIM MURRAY, *Los Angeles Times*, **1983**

If you used these pin placements on a Saturday afternoon with municipal players, they'd be out here two weeks.
LEE TREVINO, *Isuzu-Andy Williams San Diego Open*,
NBC-TV, **1983**

When you're looking at the scores, start at the bottom.
FRANK DILL, San Francisco radio personality, playing in the
Bing Crosby National Pro-Am, **1983**

Frank will be with us in a minute. He's on his eighth phone call in the first three holes. His over-and-under number today is thirty for eighteen holes.
DAN JENKINS, *Fairways and Greens*, **1994**

The only tournaments for amateurs nowadays are these scrambles, and that's no kind of competition. You can't find anyone who's ever hit a bad shot in a scramble. You just get in a cart, eat a cheeseburger, burp a couple of times and hit it. And if you cold-top it, it doesn't matter, because four other guys get a crack at it from the same spot.
JACKIE BURKE JR., *Vegasgolfer*, **2000**

Tuesday, I'm leaving for the Northeast Amateur. Talk about a buzz-kill. Nothing against the Northeast Amateur. It's a great tournament, but . . .
MATT EVERY, low amateur at the US Open, *GolfWorld*, **2005**

2 ● Brains and Flakes

Never saw one who was worth a damn.
HARRY VARDON, asked about left-handed golfers, **1900**

I sure am glad we don't have to play in the shade.
WALTER HAGEN, when told at a match in Florida that it was
105 degrees in the shade, **1926**

The trick is to know when that one time is about to happen.
WALTER HAGEN, after betting ten dollars on a hole-in-one, a one
in 100,000 shot, and making it

How in the world did they ever get that? I never been to
New York in my life.
SAM SNEAD, when shown a picture of himself in the
New York papers after winning the Oakland Open, **1937**

I never could hit that fairway.
LADDIE LUCAS, after he crash-landed his Spitfire next to the ninth
fairway at Prince's Club, Kent, during the Battle of Britain, **1940**

What are you trying to do, man? You had ten birdies today. Why, the officials are still inside talking about it. They're thinking of putting a limit on you.

JIMMY DEMARET, when he saw Ben Hogan practising after Hogan shot a record sixty-four in the Rochester Open, **1941**

Not necessarily. It simply seems to require more skill than I have at the moment.

BEN HOGAN, when asked if the twelfth hole at Augusta was impossible

What did he go out in?

SAM SNEAD, upon hearing on election day that Thomas Dewey was leading, **1948**

Have you ever noticed that most of the young guys who come out here are pretty big? Most of them are built like a truck driver. And did you notice they can all putt? Well, the trouble with you is, you're built like a hairdresser and you've got a touch like a truck driver.

CLAYTON HEAFNER, to Charles Price, **1948**

What are you gonna do, build a bonfire?

GEORGE LOW, club professional, when a member dipped in for tees

Excuse me, madam, would you mind either standing back or closing your mouth – I've lost four balls already.

TED RAY, comedian, to a spectator at a charity match in Scotland, **1952**

Hey, Lindbergh got eight days of confetti for less than this.

JIMMY DEMARET, on a bumpy flight to Japan for the World Cup

The valleys are so narrow that the dogs have to wag their tails up and down.
SAM SNEAD, on his birthplace in the mountains of Virginia, *The Education of a Golfer*, **1962**

Typically, for a man who might spend three-quarters of an hour shaving, the Haig spent more than six years of his retirement writing his autobiography, five of which were devoted to searching for just the right title.
CHARLES PRICE, *The World of Golf*, **1962**

In February 1949, Ben Hogan had his famous motor accident – it is an interesting reflection that had he been wearing a seat belt at the time he would now have been dead some sixteen years.
HENRY LONGHURST, *Highlights of the Ryder Cup*, **1965**

The University of Houston, better known as the 'University of Golf', where, that gag goes, the entrance requirements are a sixty-four on an accredited course and a sound short game.
JIM MURRAY, *The Best of Jim Murray*, **1965**

Fifteen years ago Houston had the three best teams in the country – the five guys that made it and the ten that missed it.
MIKE HOLDER, Oklahoma State golf coach, *Sports Illustrated*, **1984**

Three of the happiest years of my life were in the second grade.
JOE KIRKWOOD, Australian-born professional, **1967**

Hey, Arnie, how 'bout letting us play through.
CHI CHI RODRIGUEZ, to Arnold Palmer and his Army at the Masters, **1970**

Where the ##%&+&@ are the marshalls!
TOMMY BOLT, as deer twice ran across the fairway at the Bing
Crosby National Pro-Am, **1970**

My family was so poor they couldn't afford any kids. The
lady next door had me.
LEE TREVINO, *Sports Illustrated,* **1971**

If you don't shut up, I'm going to tell where you swam across
the border.
DOUG SANDERS, to Lee Trevino at the Masters

The hardest thing was being young and coming onto the
tour right out of high school and a very close home environment. I think the thing I miss most is my mother's home-
made soup.
AMY ALCOTT, aged twenty-one, *New York Times,* **1977**

I was born in the southeastern part of Oklahoma. Ever hear
of Idabel? . . . It was so far back in the sticks, they had to pipe
daylight in there.
TOMMY BOLT, *Golf Digest,* **1977**

I only use glasses when I want to see. I even keep them close
to my bed so I can see my dreams.
TOM KITE, *Golf Digest,* **1978**

Did you ever smell your golf bag after you carried a tuna
sandwich around in the hot sun?
AL GEIBERGER, on why he chose peanut butter, *Golf Digest,* **1978**

When I left the course after a round this year, a lady told me that my biorhythms were off. I told her my golf game was off.
JACK NICKLAUS, *Golf Digest,* **1978**

I looked down the list of competitors there and I was the only person I'd never heard of.
PETER MCEVOY, British Amateur champion, at the
World Series, **1978**

I like cowboy-and-Indian books. I read that night until I forgot about my problems and started worrying about the Indians.
SEVE BALLESTEROS, at the British Open, **1979**

I started in engineering and switched to business for my major. If I had stayed for my junior year, I'd have had to switch to basket weaving. It was getting tough.
NANCY LOPEZ, *Golf Digest,* **1979**

I'm playing better now than I ever have in my career. I don't know what's happened, but I'm not going to search for the answer.
RAYMOND FLOYD, after winning the Doral-Eastern Open, **1981**

On the 18th hole, a par 4, I first thought of using my 4-wood on my second shot. But, you see, my 4-wood is actually a 5-wood and my 3-wood is actually a 4-wood. Realizing my 4-wood would wind up short – that's actually my 5-wood – I went instead to my 3-wood, actually my 4-wood. So, the shot put me closer to the hole and I could 2-putt. I used my head. For a Puerto Rican, that's pretty good thinking.
CHI CHI RODRIGUEZ, *San Jose Mercury News,* **1981**

Too frequently their idea of great art is a painting of the Quarry Hole at Merion. Their literature seems to consist of the Rules of Golf or Ben Hogan's fundamentals.
ART SPANDER, on professional golfers, *Golf Magazine,* **1981**

There's a full moon, and I'll tell you I've been affected. I'm pulling energy from all over the world. Friends from all over, from Tokyo, California, everywhere, are pulling for me. And I'm pulling in the vibes.
MUFFIN SPENCER-DEVLIN, *The Sporting News,* **1982**

I never did see the sense in keeping my head down. The only reason I play golf at all is to see where the ball goes.
CHARLES PRICE, *Golfer-At-Large,* **1982**

I thought you had to be dead to win that.
JOANNE CARNER, on winning the Bob Jones Award for sportsmanship, *Sports Illustrated,* **1982**

It's this way. I'd start for my economics class and wind up at a driving range.
ROGER MALTBIE, on why he didn't finish college,
Golf Magazine, **1982**

By the time I was five I was out in the fields, too. I thought hard work was just how life was. I was twenty-one years old before I knew Manual Labor wasn't a Mexican.
LEE TREVINO, *They Call Me Super Mex,* **1982**

That ball had more bite on it than any other during the round.
J. C. SNEAD, as a dog grabbed his ball at the US Open,
San Francisco Examiner, **1982**

Why do I love kids so much? Because I was never a kid myself. I was too poor to be a child, so I never really had a childhood. The biggest present I ever got was a marble.
CHI CHI RODRIGUEZ, *Golf Digest*, **1983**

I'm really fifteen years younger than my birth certificate shows. In Virginia, we don't count the years you go barefoot.
SAM SNEAD, *Golf Magazine*, **1983**

Is that right? How long are decades nowadays?
SAM SNEAD, on being told he has won tournaments in six different decades, *Sports Illustrated*, **1983**

I love to sweat and heave and breathe and hurt and burn and get dirty. . . There's something good about getting all dirty and grimy and nasty and then showering; you feel twice as clean.
JAN STEPHENSON, *Playboy*, **1983**

It's funny. You need a fantastic memory in this game to remember the great shots, and a very short memory to forget the bad ones.
GARY MCCORD, at the Bing Crosby National Pro-Am, *Sports Illustrated*, **1984**

I don't trust doctors. They are like golfers. Every one has a different answer to your problem.
SEVE BALLESTEROS, *Seve: The Young Champion*, **1984**

College? I thought it was just somewhere where guys played football. . . If I'd gone to college, though, I probably wouldn't have liked it. Everybody's too damned serious for me.
LEE TREVINO, *Golf Magazine*, **1984**

I didn't need to finish college to know what golf was all about. All you need to know is to hit the ball, find it and hit it again until it disappears into the hole in the ground.
FUZZY ZOELLER, *Golf Magazine,* **1984**

Reporter: What's it like to be Jack Nicklaus's son?
Nicklaus II: I don't know. I've never had anybody else for a father.
JACK NICKLAUS II, *San Francisco Chronicle,* **1984**

They're ripping it at the flag – of course I guess that's where the hole is.
KEN VENTURI, *'Doral-Eastern Open',* CBS-TV, **1984**

In Japan, player who scores hole-in-one while leading tournament always lose. It's proven jinx.
AYAKO OKAMOTO, *PGA Magazine,* **1984**

Reporter: How hot is it out there on the course?
Zoeller: It's as hot as my first wrist watch.
FUZZY ZOELLER, **1984**

God must watch over left-handers, because nobody else does.
FURMAN BISHER, *Atlanta Journal* sports columnist, **1984**

I am not impressed with Magnolia Lane. Hell, I've seen better drives in northwestern Connecticut.
KEN GREEN, US tour pro, on his first Masters experience, **1986**

About a hundred and twenty years.
SANDY LYLE, on the difference between winning the Tournament Players Championship and the Open, **1987**

You can't birdie all eighteen holes if you don't birdie the first three.
NICK FALDO, **1987**

Vicente Fernandez walks with a slight limp; the reason being he has one leg shorter than the rest!
RODDY CARR, commentator, **1988**

Some of the players told me not to expect too much this week. They said I'd come down out of the clouds. But it worked the opposite for me. I stayed in the clouds.
SHERRI TURNER, on back-to-back victories on the LPGA Tour, **1988**

I played crap. He played crap. He just out-crapped me.
WAYNE GRADY, after losing an extra-holes match to
Greg Norman, **1990**

I've never played it.
SANDY LYLE, asked his opinion of Tiger Woods, **1991**

Golf is the only sport in which you move from the general to the specific, in an ideal number of discrete moves. Each move is a correction. The first stroke is kind of a leap of faith that the hole is out there. The second stroke corrects that, and the third corrects that, and by then, hopefully, you're on the green. And with any luck, at a par-four hole, you can place that ball in a four-and-a-quarter-inch diameter circle . . . What you did is find it in the landscape. You found the hole.
CHUCK CLOSE, American artist, likening golf to the process by which he creates a painting, *Men's Journal*, **1994**

The par here at Sunningdale is seventy and anything under that will mean a score in the sixties.
STEVE RIDER, BBC TV sportscaster, *The Sporting Word*, **1994**

I became the best in the world and I thought I had to change everything to stay the best. I tried to change my swing and that was a load of rubbish. I went to a sports psychologist and that was a load of crap. I'm a natural.
IAN WOOSNAM, **1996**

I've got manure for brains. I feel like a rank amateur.
CRAIG PARRY, after final-round mistakes caused him to lose the Australian PGA, **1999**

I wish I could see the light at the end of the tunnel but somebody turned the light off.
LEE WESTWOOD, during a slump, *Golf Weekly*, **2001**

I'm going to be playing in a lot of events that I usually watch on television.
TODD HAMILTON, whose 2003 Open victory brought invitations to the Grand Slam of Golf, Nedbank Million Dollar Challenge and Target World Challenge, *GolfWorld,* **2004**

I'm not sure that too many people who play golf professionally are necessarily brainy golfers.
PETER THOMSON, *GolfWorld*, **2005**

I was at the past champions dinner the other night, and I was sitting there thinking, 'You know, it's true. I really was good once.'
MARK CALCAVECCHIA, 1989 British Open champion,
Boston Globe, **2005**

Every time I try to play smart, I do something stupid.
CHRISTINA KIM, women's tour pro, *GolfWorld*, **2005**

I had no golf balls. What can I say? It was embarrassing.
Australian-born pro MARK HENSBY, on why he walked off the
course after hitting his tee shot O.B. on the eighteenth hole at
Bay Hill, *Boston Globe*, **2005**

You mean no one ever made four?
ARJUN ATWAL, India-born pro, after being told he was the
seventeenth player to make three eagles in a single round in a
PGA Tour event, *San Diego Union-Tribune*, **2006**

3 ● Caddies

The player may experiment about his swing, his grip, his stance. It is only when he begins asking his caddie's advice that he is getting on dangerous ground.
SIR WALTER SIMPSON, *The Art of Golf,* **1887**

The caddie must be kept in his place.
CLARENCE MACQUOID, *Punch,* **1888**

Vardon: What on earth shall I take now?
Caddie: Well, sir, I'd recommend the 4:05 train.
HARRY VARDON, playing poorly and uncertain about his
club selection

Aye, but I'll get sober. T'aint nothin' ye can do aboot that gowff game of yours.
LANG WILLIE, legendary St Andrews caddie, to an R&A member
who accused him of being drunk on the course

I have been playing golf three hundred and seventy-five (expletive deleted) years and after all that time I reach the day where I ask a twenty-five-year-old caddie what club to use.
BOBBY CRUICKSHANK, after a double bogey at the US Open, **1924**

There were three things in the world that he held in the smallest esteem – slugs, poets, and caddies with hiccups.
P. G. WODEHOUSE, *Rodney Fails to Qualify,* **1924**

I think it is slightly straight, Mr Faulkner.
MAD MAC, caddie, advising Briton Max Faulkner on a putt

When I ask you what kind of club to use, look the other way and don't answer.
SAM SNEAD, to his caddie before a tough match

I've been caddying for him for ten years and he's never had a bad lie yet.
SKEETS, caddie for Bob Hope, c. **1950s**

I asked [my caddie] what had been so important to require a phone call after the starter had summoned us to the tee. 'I wanted to call the wife to tell her not to wait for dinner,' he said wistfully, 'and to kiss the kids goodnight for me.'
MILTON GROSS, *Eighteen Holes in My Head,* **1959**

Why ask me? You've asked me two times already and paid no attention to what I said. Pick your own club.
DOW FINSTERWALD'S CADDIE, at the US Open, **1960**

We work as a team – I hand him the clubs and he makes the shots.
NATHANIEL (IRONMAN) AVERY, Arnold Palmer's caddie

When Mr Palmer's gettin' ready to make his move, he jerks at that glove, pulls up his britches and starts walkin' fast. When he do that, everybody better watch out. He gonna stampede anything that gets in his way.

NATHANIEL (IRONMAN) AVERY, at the Masters, **1962**

Sarazen: I'm sorry, Joe. I went to church last Sunday and I prayed.

Caddie: Well, boss, I don't know what you folks pray about when you go to church, but when I go to church I keep my head down.

GENE SARAZEN AND CADDIE, at qualifying for the US Open,
Daily Telegraph, **1963**

Shor, after shooting a 211: What should I give the caddie?

Gleason: Your golf clubs.

TOOTS SHOR AND JACKIE GLEASON

Never let him tell you anything more than how deep the hole is and what time it is.

JIM MURRAY, on caddies, *The Sporting World of Jim Murray,* **1968**

I am going to win so much money this year my caddie will make the top twenty money-winners' list.

LEE TREVINO, *Sports Illustrated,* **1973**

If a caddie can help you, then you don't know how to play golf.

DAN JENKINS, *Dead Solid Perfect,* **1974**

One caddie was explaining why he couldn't loan out any more money. 'I sent my Crosby check to my wife, my Inverrary check to my grandmother, my Citrus check to my girlfriend, and I already bet this one on the Boston Celtics.'
DAN GLEASON, *The Great, The Grand and the Also-Ran,* **1976**

Cart paths at Pebble Beach? What next? Astro Turf greens at St Andrews?
ART SPANDER, *Golf Digest,* **1977**

We just prayin' we're both still out here when Roy's pants come back in style.
LEE TREVINO on a caddie, *Golf Digest,* **1978**

Girls, of course, excel as caddies in Japan . . . Sam Snead had to be deterred from leaving his clubs behind and bringing his caddie home in the bag in their place.
HENRY LONGHURST, *The Best of Henry Longhurst,* **1978**

My game is so bad I gotta hire three caddies – one to walk the left rough, one for the right rough, and one down the middle. And the one in the middle doesn't have much to do.
DAVE HILL, *Golf Digest,* **1979**

My own experience as a caddie imparted lasting knowledge to me in only two areas – sex and poker.
LARRY SHEEHAN, *Great Golf Humor from Golf Digest,* **1979**

He'd rather go to the beach. I think the only reason he puts up with caddying is because he has to eat. Angelo has basically been retired since he was twenty-one.
JACK NICKLAUS, on his caddie Angelo Argea, **1979**

There's something haunting about getting up at dawn and walking a golf course, checking pin placements. It's easy to lose track of reality.
ERNEST (CREAMY) CAROLAN, caddie, *Sports Illustrated,* **1981**

My caddie said today on the thirteenth hole, 'Hit the tee shot over the third hump.' I did. We went out and the ball was fifteen yards into waist-high grass. I said, 'What happened?' 'Wrong hump, governor,' he apologized.
RAY FLOYD at the British Open, *Washington Post,* **1981**

I don't know why that putt hung on the edge. I'm a clean liver. It must be my caddie.
JOANNE CARNER, *Golf Digest,* **1981**

Caddies are a breed of their own. If you shoot 66, they say, 'Man, *we* shot sixty-six!' But go out and shoot 77 and they say, 'Hell, *he* shot seventy-seven!'
LEE TREVINO, *They Call Me Super Mex,* **1982**

Don't worry about it. Everybody has bad days. The chairman of the board has bad days. Multi-millionaires have bad days. The Pope has bad days.
HERMAN MITCHELL, caddie, consoling Lee Trevino, **1982**

You get either the youngest caddie or the oldest golf car – and neither works.
RICHARD HASKELL, Massachusetts Golf Association executive director, *Golf Digest,* **1982**

He told me just to keep the ball low.
CHI CHI RODRIGUEZ, putting advice from his caddie,
The Sporting News, **1982**

I was lying 10 and had a 35-foot putt. I whispered over my shoulder, 'How does this one break?' And he said, 'Who cares?' That's the greatest line from a caddie I ever heard.
JACK LEMMON, playing the Bing Crosby National Pro-Am,
San Jose Mercury News, **1983**

When he gets the ball into a tough place, that's when he's most relaxed. I think it's because he has so much experience at it.
DON CHRISTOPHER, caddie for Jack Lemmon,
San Jose Mercury News, **1983**

Once when I'd been in a lot of bunkers, my caddie told me he was getting blisters from raking so much.
JOANNE CARNER, *San Francisco Examiner,* **1983**

He looks like he had his hair done in a pet shop.
DAVE MARR on a caddie, *'British Open'*, ABC-TV, **1984**

The only time I talk on a golf course is to my caddie – and only then to complain.
SEVE BALLESTEROS, *GolfWorld,* **1984**

I always know which side a putt will break; it slopes towards the side of the green Herman is standing on.
LEE TREVINO, making reference to his overweight caddie
Herman Mitchell

You under-clubbed me. Do that again and I fire you. Get out.
SEVE BALLESTEROS, to his caddie during the US Open,
1986

I'm not carrying that bloody thing any more. You're a naturally gifted golfer. Stop mucking about.
DAVE MUSGROVE, Sandy Lyle's caddie, referring to Lyle's long-shafted putter, **1990**

I give you one job to do and you can't even get that right.
IAN WOOSNAM, to his caddie at the Open after being hit with a two-stroke penalty for carrying fifteen clubs, one over the limit, **2001**

In Ireland, when a caddie says, 'Yer too farty,' he does not mean that you're excessively flatulent but rather that you're 240 yards from the green.
STEVE RUSHIN, writer, *Sports Illustrated*, **2003**

I'm not as popular as I probably could be with the fans because I know what it takes for Tiger to play in his best environment, and I can definitely piss a lot of people off. But that's making his job easier for him and . . . that's what counts.
STEVE WILLIAMS, Tiger Woods' caddie, on his run-ins with fans and photographers, *GolfWorld*, **2004**

Realistically, I think I've got thirteen more years. I can't see myself still doing this at 90. But who knows?
MARTY LARKIN, seventy-seven-year-old regular caddie at Cypress Point when asked how much longer he plans to work, *Monterey County (Calif.) Herald*, **2005**

4 ● Celebrities

The fun you get from golf is in direct ratio to the effort you don't put into it.
BOB ALLEN, comedian, **1950**

I can't say for sure, but I'd like to have that much footage along Wilshire Boulevard.
PHIL HARRIS, when asked if his birdie putt really travelled
ninety feet, at the Bing Crosby National Pro-Am, **1951**

Obviously she has seen you tee off before and knows that the safest place to be when you play is right down the middle.
JACKIE GLEASON, to writer Milton Gross when a deer
wouldn't leave the fairway

Who plays golf anymore? I've gone in for gambling now. At the tables I only lose my money. On the course I lose my mind.
JACKIE MILES, comic

He would rather win a golf match than an Oscar.
BING CROSBY, on Bob Hope, *New York Herald Tribune*, **1953**

Two of my favourites out there . . . are comedian Bing
Crosby and singer Bob Hope. Or is it the other way around?
I always forget which one thinks he's funny and which one
thinks he can sing.
JIMMY DEMARET, *My Partner, Ben Hogan*, **1954**

The hardest shot is a mashie at ninety yards from the green,
where the ball has to be played against an oak tree, bounces back
into a sandtrap, hits a stone, bounces on the green and then rolls
into the cup. That shot is so difficult I have only made it once.
ZEPPO MARX

I find it to be the hole-in-one.
GROUCHO MARX, when asked about the most difficult shot

And now here's Jack Lemmon, about to hit that all-impor-
tant eighth shot.
JIM MCKAY, on Lemmon playing the fourteenth hole at Pebble
Beach, *'Bing Crosby National Pro-Am'*, ABC-TV, **1959**

Jack's getting more footage here today than he had in his last
three films.
BING CROSBY, *'Bing Crosby National Pro-Am'*, ABC-TV, **1959**

I would rather play Hamlet with no rehearsal than play golf
on television.
JACK LEMMON

Jack Lemmon has been in more bunkers than Eva Braun.
PHIL HARRIS

Phil is the only man I know who keeps his left arm straight all day, and bent all night.
PAUL HAHN, trick-shot golfer, on Phil Harris

Hope: Okay, what's wrong with my game?
Palmer: If you're talking about golf, that's *not* your game.
ARNOLD PALMER AND BOB HOPE,
'*Chrysler Presents a Bob Hope Special*', NBC-TV, **1963**

My subject tonight will be golf. At least we have that in common, Bob. I play the game, too. I don't have to tell you what my handicap is – you told me when I tried to join your club.
FLIP WILSON, to Bob Hope at a celebrity roast

My handicap is that I am a one-eyed Negro.
SAMMY DAVIS JR

What a foolish thing for her to do. Now she'll have to play all her drives off the back tees.
BING CROSBY, on hearing of a sex-change operation

Murray: Have I got a shot to the green?
Caddie: Mr Murray, I'd say you have several shots to the green.
JAN MURRAY, comic

I think I've got the idea now.
HOAGY CARMICHAEL, composer, after an ace at Pebble Beach

Be funny on a golf course? Do I kid my best friend's mother about her heart condition?
PHIL SILVERS, comedian

One day, I called Dean Martin and said, 'Dean, do you want to play golf?' And he said, 'Sorry, Buddy, we already have three.'
BUDDY HACKETT, *The Truth About Golf and Other Lies,* **1968**

He played so poorly [in the 1967 Bing Crosby National Pro-Am] that his singing teacher quit him, he was cancelled out of $160,000 worth of bookings and before he got back to the hotel at Carmel, they gave his room away to a better player.
BUDDY HACKETT on Robert Goulet,
The Truth About Golf and Other Lies, **1968**

Vic Damone would be a fine player, but he's too busy looking in the grass to see if he can find a mirror.
DON RICKLES

Johnny Carson plays fantastic golf on television when he stands in front of the camera with his funny little swing. On the golf course, the man has trouble walking against the wind.
DON RICKLES

I never pray on the golf course. Actually, the Lord answers my prayers everywhere except on the course.
REV. BILLY GRAHAM, *Golf Magazine,* **1970**

How could a guy who won the West, recaptured Bataan and won the battle of Iwo Jima let himself be defeated by a little hole in the ground?
JAMES EDWARD GRANT, screenwriter, on John Wayne giving up golf, *Golf Digest,* **1973**

There is a certain romance in futility pursued. A golfer always loses on the golf course.
EFREM ZIMBALIST JR, actor

Not only are three-putt greens probable. At times they're an achievement.
CHARLEY PRIDE, country singer, **1978**

I only see Charley when we get to the greens. Charley hits some good woods – most of them are trees.
GLEN CAMPBELL, on playing with Pride

I am a victim of circumference. When I stand close enough to the ball to reach it, I can't see it. When I see it, I can't reach it.
TOOTS SHOR, restaurateur

You know you're not going to wind up with anything but grief, pal, but you can't resist the impulse.
JACKIE GLEASON, comparing golf to an unpromising woman, *Golf Digest,* **1977**

I love to play with Andy, but he can be very distracting. Have you ever tried to pitch over a water hazard while your partner is humming 'Moon River'?
BOB HOPE on Andy Williams, *Golf Digest,* **1981**

I do a lot of humming out on the course. I tend to stick with one song . . . I shot a sixty-six to 'Moon River'.
JACK NICKLAUS

Par is anything you want it to be. For instance, this hole here is a par forty-seven. And yesterday I birdied the sucker.
WILLIE NELSON, country singer, on the course he purchased near Austin, Texas, **1981**

If that's true, I'm the first dead man to make six double bogeys on the back nine on the day of his funeral.
VICTOR MATURE, actor, when his death was erroneously reported on radio, *Golf Digest,* **1982**

If this was a prize fight, they'd stop it.
BOB HOPE on his golf game, *San Jose Mercury News,* **1982**

The toughest part about matches with Crosby was collecting.
BOB HOPE, *Golf Magazine,* **1983**

Telly Savalas, struggling under an eighteen handicap, now needs a three axe to get out of this trouble.
VIN SCULLY, *'Bob Hope Classic',* NBC-TV, **1984**

The typical day in the life of a heavy-metal musician consists of a round of golf and an AA meeting.
BILLY JOEL, American rock & roll singer

Me and Bob never talked about comedy or rock and roll. We talked about golf.
ALICE COOPER, heavy-metal musician and ten-time participant in the Bob Hope Chrysler Classic, *GolfWorld,* **2004**

The best thing I do all year is Pebble Beach. There's 18 greens and 18 tees. That's like 36 shows – and that's just the formal room.
BILL MURRAY, actor-comedian, on his antics at the AT&T Pebble Beach Pro-Am, *GolfWorld,* **2005**

I'll stick to playing the sax. I know when I play, there are not 150 guys trying to take my gig away from me. This is a hard life out here.

KENNY G, saxophone-playing pop star, after shooting 82–83 on a sponsor's exemption at a Nationwide Tour tournament, *San Diego Tribune*, **2005**

5 ● Character and the Mind

If profanity had an influence on the flight of the ball, the game would be played far better than it is.
HORACE G. HUTCHINSON, *Hints on the Game of Golf,* **1886**

Golf has some drawbacks. It is possible by too much of it to destroy the mind; a man with a Roman nose and a high forehead may play away his profile.
SIR WALTER SIMPSON, *The Art of Golf,* **1887**

It is better to smash your clubs than to lose your temper.
LORD BALFOUR, **1890**

In the actual playing of the game, the golfer cannot keep a great amount of theory in mind and have any attention left to bestow upon the ball.
JOHN DUNN, British professional, **1916**

After taking the stance, it is too late to worry. The only thing to do then is to hit the ball.
BOBBY JONES, *Vanity Fair,* **1929**

I'm going to miss at least seven shots in every eighteen holes, so if I'm going to be angry, I might as well start right on the first tee.

WALTER HAGEN

Give me a man with big hands, big feet and no brains and I will make a golfer out of him.

WALTER HAGEN

I say this without any reservations whatsoever. It is impossible to outplay an opponent you can't out-think.

LAWSON LITTLE, American professional

In a gin'ral way, all I can say about it is that it's a kind iv game iv ball that ye play with ye'er own worst inimy, which is ye'ersilf.

FINLEY PETER DUNNE, American humorist

Good golfing temperament falls between taking it with a grin or shrug and throwing a fit.

SAM SNEAD

Golf is a funny game. It's done much for health, and at the same time has ruined people by robbing them of their peace of mind. Look at me, I'm the healthiest idiot in the world.

BOB HOPE

The most advanced medical brains in the universe have yet to discover a way for a man to relax himself, and looking at a golf ball is not the cure.

MILTON GROSS, *Eighteen Holes in My Head,* 1959

The most exquisitely satisfying act in the world of golf is that of throwing a club. The full backswing, the delayed wrist action, the flowing follow-through, followed by that unique whirring sound, reminiscent only of a passing flock of starlings, are without parallel in sport.
HENRY LONGHURST, '***********!', 1965

I've thrown or broken a few clubs in my day. In fact, I guess at one time or another I probably held distance records for every club in the bag.
TOMMY BOLT, *How to Keep Your Temper on the Golf Course*, 1969

Why, during those early days Palmer was on tour, he threw them. I have to say that he was the very worst golf-club thrower I have ever seen. He had to learn to play well, he'd have never made it as a thrower.
TOMMY BOLT, *The Hole Truth*, 1971

About the only thing left for me is acupuncture – in the brain.
GEORGE ARCHER, walking off the final green at the Hawaiian Open, *Golf Magazine*, 1974

I tell the lady scorekeepers that if they can hear me cuss, they're standing too close. They've got to realize they're not at a church social.
DAVE HILL, 1975

I buried a few in the ground, you know. It took two men to get one of them out.
DAVE HILL, *Teed Off*, 1977

Golf is a game of expletives not deleted.
DR IRVING A. GLADSTONE, *Confessions of a Golf Duffer*, 1977

I looked around for any generals or corporation presidents I might recognize in the throng, reached for my cigarettes, dropped them, picked them up, stuck one in my ear and set fire to my nose.

DAN JENKINS, playing a pro-am, *Golf Digest,* **1979**

Like one's own children, golf has an uncanny way of endearing itself to us while at the same time evoking every weakness of mind and character, no matter how well hidden.

W. TIMOTHY GALLWEY, *The Inner Game of Golf,* **1979**

Let's face it, ninety-five per cent of this game is mental. A guy plays lousy golf, he doesn't need a pro, he needs a shrink.

TOM MURPHY, touring professional

After an abominable round of golf, a man is known to have slit his wrists with a razor blade and, having bandaged them, to have stumbled into the locker room and inquired of his partner, 'What time tomorrow?'

ALISTAIR COOKE, journalist

As every golfer knows, no one ever lost his mind over one shot. It is rather the gradual process of shot-after-shot watching your score go to tatters . . . knowing that you have found a different way to bogey each one.

THOMAS BOSWELL, *Golf Digest,* **1980**

When I play my best golf, I feel as if I'm in a fog . . . standing back watching the earth in orbit with a golf club in your hands.

MICKEY WRIGHT, *Golf Digest,* **1981**

Your ego is everything. And if you don't get that pumped up regularly, you can't last.

DAVE MARR

To succeed at anything, you must have a huge ego. I'm not talking about confidence. Confidence is self-assurance for a reason. Ego is self-assurance for no good reason.
FRANK BEARD, *Golf Magazine,* **1981**

When you reflect on the combination of characteristics that golf demands of those who would presume to play it, it is not surprising that golf has never had a truly great player who was not also a person of extraordinary character.
FRANK D. (SANDY) TATUM JR, *The US Open Book,* **1982**

Golf is a non-violent game played violently from within.
BOB TOSKI, *Golf Digest,* **1982**

I actually feel that the unconscious mind has much better control than the conscious mind. The mind uses words, and the muscles don't understand English.
W. TIMOTHY GALLWEY, *Golf Magazine,* **1982**

Every day I try to tell myself this is going to be fun today. I try to put myself in a great frame of mind before I go out – then I screw it up with the first shot.
JOHNNY MILLER, *Golf Magazine,* **1984**

It was stupid. I learned a lesson. When you have a fight with a club, the club always wins.
PATTI HAYES, on kicking her club and injuring her foot at the Samaritan Turquoise Classic, **1984**

This is the hardest game in the world, believe me. There is no way a golfer can think he is really something, because that's when the game gets you.
BEN CRENSHAW, *San Jose Mercury News,* **1984**

I would like to knock it on every green and two-putt, but that's not my style of living.
MUFFIN SPENCER-DEVLIN, *Seattle Times,* **1984**

I don't have any particular hang-ups about superstitions. I did try them all, but they didn't work.
KATHY WHITWORTH, after her eighty-sixth career win,
Safeco Classic, **1984**

If you're stupid enough to whiff, you should be smart enough to forget it.
ARNOLD PALMER, at the US Senior Open, *Sports Illustrated,* **1984**

Golf is really a mind game. The more you keep your mind out of it, the better off you are.
BOB BRUE, US senior-tour pro, **1989**

Screw it! Golf is just a game – and an idiotic game most of the time.
MARK CALCAVECCHIA, after becoming the first defending
British Open champion for fourteen yearsto miss the cut, **1990**

I can't shoot sixty-six every time. I'm not God, you know.
SEVE BALLESTEROS, on his final-round seventy-five
in the British Masters, **1991**

I'm a mental basket case. I have the mind of a twelve-year-old, a total waste of space. Disgusting, absolutely disgusting. It's disheartening. I've got the yips on my putts and the yips on my chips. I was just trying to hit the thing at the pin, an eight-iron, for crying out loud, from the middle of the fairway and I hit a 125-yard duck hook.
MARK CALCAVECCHIA, on botching the final hole
at the Colonial tournament, **1991**

When you've had a three-year dry spell, fear is always around the corner.
SANDY LYLE, upon breaking that spell with a victory, **1991**

It seems like the harder I try, the worse I get.
BETSY KING, **1994**

Golf is like bicycle shorts. It reveals a lot about people.
RICK REILLY, *Sports Illustrated*, **1995**

If you think positively and keep your mind on what's right, it gives you a better attitude. If you moan and groan and are disgusted, you play miserably, too.
BERNHARD LANGER, after winning in inclement conditions,
1997

My mind was always keen to play but unfortunately my body was saying 'no' today.
COLIN MONTGOMERIE, after a loss in the World Match Play
Championship, **1997**

I used to get very upset at myself and then I thought, 'What's the point of shouting and screaming at myself?' So over the years I have become a much calmer person as a result of playing golf, I suspect.
PRINCE ANDREW, *The Times*, **2001**

When you finish second seven times in a season all sorts of terrible things go through your mind, and that word 'choker' would be top of the pile. You wonder if you will ever win, you wonder what you did wrong, whether it was your bad golf or someone else's brilliant golf.
PADRAIG HARRINGTON, *Guardian*, **2001**

I'm not really interested in sports psychology. It makes me feel like a crazy person.
MICHELLE WIE

I'm happy out of my mind. I like beating a lot of people.
MICHELLE WIE, after winning the US Women's Amateur
Public Links, 2003

6 ● Course Design and Places

If I had my way, I'd never let the sand be raked. Instead, I'd run a herd of elephants through them every morning.
CHARLES BLAIR MACDONALD, American course architect

A golf course is the epitome of all that is purely transitory in the universe, a space not to dwell in, but to get over as quickly as possible.
JEAN GIRAUDOUX, *The Enchanted,* 1933

Alaska would be an ideal place for courses – mighty few trees and damn few ladies' foursomes.
REX LARDNER, *Out of the Bunker and Into the Trees,* 1960

A great golf hole is one which puts a question mark into the player's mind when he arrives on the tee to play it.
MACKENZIE ROSS, British course architect

Anyone who criticizes a golf course is like a person invited to a house for dinner who, on leaving, tells the host that the food was lousy.
GARY PLAYER

A good golf course is like good music. It is not necessarily a course which appeals the first time one plays it.
ALISTER MACKENZIE, British course architect

Golf in and around Los Angeles tends to be – like the rest of the landscape – unreal . . . part Royal and Ancient, part Disneyland. The Good Ship Lollipop with four-irons.
JIM MURRAY, *Golf in Disneyland,* **1973**

I try to make players worry.
TOM SIMPSON, British course architect

Every hole should be a demanding par and a comfortable bogey.
ROBERT TRENT JONES, American course architect,
Golf Magazine, **1976**

'The man who hates golfers' is what they call me. They couldn't be more wrong. I design holes that are fun to play.
ROBERT TRENT JONES

Saw a course you'd really like, Trent. On the first tee you drop the ball over your left shoulder.
JIMMY DEMARET

The first golf course architect was a fifteen-handicapper with a whippy swing from Scotland named Father Nature.
MARK MULVOY and ART SPANDER, in
Golf: The Passion and the Challenge, **1977**

The real trick of golf course architecture is to lure the golfer into a false sense of security.
PETER DYE, *Golf Digest,* **1979**

Pebble Beach is so exclusive that even the Samaritans have an unlisted number.
PETER DOBEREINER,
National Amateur Championship programme, **1981**

That's how architects make their money, always going back to fix what they don't do right in the first place.
LEE TREVINO, *Golf Digest,* **1981**

All truly great golf courses have an almost supernatural finishing hole, by way of separating the chokers from the strokers.
CHARLES PRICE, *Golf Magazine,* **1981**

There's no such thing as a bad course. Courses are like people – each course has its own personality. You have to challenge each one as it comes along.
BARBARA MIZRAHIE, *Golf Digest,* **1982**

Dye's true hallmark is the use of railroad ties, telephone poles or planking to shore up greens, sand traps and the banks of water hazards. He uses so much wood that one of his courses may be the first ever to burn down.
BARRY MCDERMOTT on architect Peter Dye,
Sports Illustrated, **1982**

There was no doubt a few professionals watching who were hoping that the water was ten feet deep and neither could swim. Especially Dye.
RON COFFMAN, when Jerry Pate threw Peter Dye in the water at the Tournament Players Championship, *GolfWorld,* **1982**

Are you sure he's really building a golf course out here? He's already spent $1.5 million and I don't have anything that looks like a golf course.
JOE WALSER, president of Oak Tree, on Peter Dye,
Golf Digest, **1983**

There is no denying that golf has put Hilton Head Island on the map. After all, how many homes can you build around a tennis court?
CHARLES PRICE, golf writer

It's pretty, but too golfy.
HOLLIS STACY, on Hilton Head Island,
San Francisco Examiner, **1983**

There are no straight lines on my courses. The good Lord never drew a straight line.
JACK NICKLAUS, *Golf Digest,* **1983**

If I were designing one for myself, there'd be a dogleg right on every hole and the first hole wouldn't count. That would be a warm-up hole.
LEE TREVINO, *Golf Digest,* **1983**

Some players would complain if they were playing on Dolly Parton's bedspread.
JIMMY DEMARET, *Golf Magazine,* **1983**

Great golf courses should have at least one silly hole.
FRANK HANNIGAN, USGA director

It is easier to tell a man that there's something wrong with his wife and child than with his golf course.
FRANK HANNIGAN, *Chicago Tribune,* **1984**

We come from the same backgrounds, more or less, where growing up next to a golf course didn't mean a 10,000-square-foot house and gold faucets in the bathrooms.
LEE TREVINO, on Seve Ballesteros, **1984**

You can treat them [the flowers] as a water hazard and drop your ball to one side. Otherwise, you can try to play it out. However, if you do, you never will be permitted to play Sentry World again.
ROBERT TRENT JONES, on his new course in Wisconsin,
Golf Digest, **1984**

Every course needs a hole that puckers your rear end.
JOHNNY MILLER, on the seventeenth at the TPC at Sawgrass,
'*Tournament Players Championship*', CBS-TV, **1984**

I know that I have had previous lives from experiences in my therapy and in my dreams. I have had some of my most vivid dreams of fighting in the Civil War – in and around where this course is now.
MUFFIN SPENCER-DEVLIN, on winning an LPGA tournament
at Portsmouth Sleepy Hole GC, Portsmouth, Va., **1986**

Believe me, man, I don't play golf for pleasure. Hey, did you ever see a dentist in his office on his day off? No way. And you want me to remember holes? Ha! Let me ask you – do you remember the girl or girls you were dating back in 1966? No you don't. Well, I forget golf courses.
LEE TREVINO, *US Open Official Magazine*, **1987**

European courses require more imagination, and that's why our tour has more character. There are a hell of a variety of courses and weather, and there's no use complaining about the greens one week because they'll probably be worse the next week.
NICK FALDO, *Golf Illustrated*, **1991**

The rough is so tough on me. Thank God for fairways.
FRED FUNK, on the course set-up at Bellerive CC for the PGA Championship, **1992**

I can't imagine any course that doesn't favor Tiger [Woods]. It doesn't matter what course you put him on, he'll play well.
JACK NICKLAUS, *Sports Illustrated*, **2000**

To chop down more than 17,000 Monterey pines for golf is akin to cutting down the Amazon forest for hamburger.
MARK MASSARA, California Sierra Club official, an opponent of a new course planned by the Pebble Beach Co., Knight Ridder, **2005**

At night it's just us, the rabbits and the drunks on the beach. It's a wonderful place to be.
EUAN GRANT, head greenkeeper at St Andrews, on working at night to prepare the Old Course for the Open, BBC, **2005**

I don't have a clue where to put a fairway bunker any more. I hate the fact that we have to build courses longer every day just to keep pace with equipment. I'm tired of fighting it.
JAY MOORISH, golf course architect, *GolfWorld*, **2005**

I like to think courses are like Scotch whisky. There aren't bad ones out there; just some are better than others.
ANGUS MACKENZIE, LPGA Tour official,
San Diego Union-Tribune, **2005**

I don't want to say anything bad about the hole, but it's the worst one on the course.

MARK CALCAVECCHIA, critiquing Harding Park GC, San Francisco, *GolfWorld,* **2005**

7 ● Diet, Exercise and Injuries

If your adversary is a hole or two down, there is no serious cause for alarm in his complaining of a severely sprained wrist . . . Should he happen to win the next hole, these symptoms will in all probability become less troublesome.
HORACE G. HUTCHINSON, *Hints on the Game of Golf,* **1886**

It is ridiculous to suggest, as some people do, that golf is a dangerous game. I myself have only been struck three times this season!
W. T. LINSKILL, founder, Cambridge University Golf Club, c. **1900**

A fifth at night, a sixty-eight in the morning.
WALTER HAGEN

Ben, you old sonofabitch. Just because I beat you in a play-off, you didn't have to get so mad that you tried to run a bus off the road.
JIMMY DEMARET, to Hogan after his highway accident, **1949**

I'm going to handle it just like a round of golf. I'm going to play it one shot at a time.
BEN HOGAN, recovering from injuries, **1949**

His legs weren't strong enough to carry his heart around.
GRANTLAND RICE, on Hogan's comeback at the Los Angeles Open, **1950**

I understand you have a weight problem. As you know, I have kept my weight exactly the same for years. I will be glad to send you my diet.
JACKIE GLEASON, telegram to Arnold Palmer, **1960s**

To really lose weight playing golf, the best place to play is in Mexico. Go to any Mexican golf course, stop at every hole and drink water. Within a week you'll have reached your desired weight.
BUDDY HACKETT, *The Truth About Golf and Other Lies,* **1968**

If you're hungry, you're more alert. You're like a hungry lion. All your senses are sharpened for the kill.
BILLY CASPER, on why he began skipping breakfast, **1970**

Five bogeys will give a guy a stomach ache every time.
MILLER BARBER, on why Casper skips breakfast, **1970**

Q: How's the food here, Roberto?
A: Like Jack Nicklaus. Very good, and very slow.
ROBERTO DE VICENZO, at a restaurant

I missed a bunch of tournaments; but considering all the hospitalization insurance I carry, I figure I wound up leading money winner.
LEE TREVINO, on his surgery, *Golf Digest,* **1977**

Somebody asked me if I run, and I said, 'Not unless some-body's after me.'
SAM SNEAD, *Golf Digest,* **1977**

Give me a banana. I'm playing like a monkey. I might as well eat like one.
CHI CHI RODRIGUEZ, *Golf Digest,* **1977**

I'd probably be the fat lady in a circus right now if it hadn't been for golf. It kept me on the course and out of the refrigerator.
KATHY WHITWORTH, *Golf Digest,* **1982**

With glasses I can see ants on the ground, but for some reason the ball looks too big to go in the hole.
DICK MAYER, *Sports Illustrated,* **1982**

There was a thunderous crack like cannonfire and suddenly I was lifted a foot and a half off the ground . . . Damn, I thought to myself, this is a helluva penalty for slow play.
LEE TREVINO, on his lightning incident in 1975,
They Call Me Super Mex, **1982**

They say your whole life passes before you at that moment and, believe me, it does. Hey, I never knew I was so bad! I saw a lot of old girlfriends.
LEE TREVINO, *They Call Me Super Mex,* **1982**

For the first time in your life, don't be afraid of a bunker.
LEE TREVINO, on how to avoid lightning, 'The Tonight Show',
NBC-TV, **1982**

We don't want to get anybody killed. Of course, if we could pick which ones, it might be a different story.
HORD HARDIN, Augusta National chairman, postponing
play in the Masters because of lightning, **1983**

I didn't like being fat, and that's exactly what I was – fat! I used to say it was because I was big-boned, but I knew better.
NANCY LOPEZ, *Golf Magazine,* **1983**

No. The golf course got in the way.
CALVIN PEETE, when asked if an injury had contributed to this third-round eighty-six in the Masters, **1983**

I've injured both my hands playing golf and they're OK now, but my brain has always been somewhat suspect.
BOB MURPHY, *San Jose Mercury News,* **1984**

I'm on a grapefruit diet. I eat everything but grapefruit.
CHI CHI RODRIGUEZ, at the Everett Open, **1984**

I like to smoke and drink and I'm lazy. It's past time for me to train. I enjoy doing absolutely nothing and I'm pretty darn good at it.
DON JANUARY, *GolfWorld,* **1984**

The difference between us and the pros is that we skull wedges and they wedge skulls.
JACK O'LEARY, golf writer, on Ben Crenshaw beaning himself
with his club, requiring three stitches on the back of his head,
Boston Herald, **1986**

I was just too heavy. It got so bad I couldn't bend over to tie my shoes. I was just about to get some loafers with spikes in them.
LEE TREVINO, on slimming from 202 lbs to 185, **1989**

These are *my* boys. I can go into a locker room and bum a cigarette. You go inside on the other Tour and all they are doing is drinking orange juice and eating bananas.
LEE TREVINO, about his new playing colleagues on the
Senior Tour, **1990**

I've paid my dues. I've slept in my car and eaten two hot dogs for a dollar at 7-Eleven. I've done it all.
JOHN MAGINNES, US tour pro, after his first victory,
San Francisco Examiner, **1994**

We have a gym at home gathering dust. Just goes to show that after all the hard work I've done in the gym this winter, my right arm is definitely stronger.
DARREN CLARKE, noted non-teetotaller, **2000**

It feels like I have a different body. I'm not used to being supple, but if I'm going to play on the seniors' tour, I have to do it.
IAN WOOSNAM, then forty-six, on his exercise programme,
GolfWorld, **2004**

That was Jack [Nicklaus]. This is all original equipment.
ARNOLD PALMER, to an autograph seeker, when asked about
hip-replacement surgery he never had, *GolfWorld*, **2004**

When you have a good hangover, sometimes you're all loosey-goosey, you can play good golf.
JOHN DALY, *San Francisco Chronicle*, **2005**

I didn't bring a coat or anything. I'm not into the dinners, man. You can't get a coat and tie on this fat boy.
JOHN DALY, when asked why he didn't attend the past
champions' dinner at the British Open, *Boston Globe*, **2005**

I'm not day-to-day. I'm hole-by-hole.
LEE TREVINO, age sixty-six, three months after back surgery,
GolfWorld, **2005**

If you go out for a meal in this country, you're lucky if you
find anything without half a pound of cheese on it. I've never
seen so much cheese in my life. You go into a supermarket
and there's a whole aisle of cheese.
MARK JAMES, Englishman on the US Champions Tour,
GolfWorld, **2005**

I lost 45 [pounds] in 30 days years ago, and I couldn't hit the
ball out of my shadow. I don't eat that bad. It's when I ice
down my bad back from the inside, like with vodka. That's
calories.
MARK CALCAVECCHIA, to columnist Bob Verdi, *GolfWorld,* **2006**

8 ● Equipment

It's good sportsmanship to not pick up lost golf balls while they are still rolling.

MARK TWAIN

Do not be tempted to invest in a sample of each golfing invention as soon as it makes its appearance. If you do, you will only complicate and spoil your game – and encumber your locker with much useless rubbish.

HARRY VARDON

Honey, why don't you quit kidding yourself? It just can't be entirely the clubs. Your trouble is *you*!

LOUISE NELSON, advising husband Bryon, **1936**

Laddie, throw me that ball. I thought so. The bugger isn't round.

ARTHUR LEES, British pro, after missing a thirty-foot putt,

c. **1940s**

The trouble that most of us find with the modern matched sets of clubs is that they don't really seem to know any more about the game than the old ones did!
ROBERT BROWNING, *A History of Golf,* **1955**

'How are you getting on with your new clubs?' asked the golfer when he walked into the bar and saw a friend of his. 'Fine,' replied the friend. 'They put twenty yards on my slice.'
DAI REES, *Dai Rees on Golf,* **1959**

Talk to the ball. 'This isn't going to hurt a bit,' I tell the ball under my breath. 'Sambo is just going to give you a nice little ride.'
SAM SNEAD, *The Education of a Golfer,* **1962**

George, you look perfect . . . That beautiful knitted shirt, an alpaca sweater, those expensive slacks. . . You've got an alligator bag, the finest matched irons, and the best woods money can buy. It's a damned shame you have to spoil it all by playing golf.
LLOYD MANGRUM, to comedian George Burns

A professional will tell you the amount of flex you need in the shaft of your club. The more the flex, the more strength you will need to break the thing over your knees.
STEPHEN BAKER, *How to Play Golf in the Low 120s,* **1962**

Once when I was golfing in Georgia I hooked the ball into the swamp. I went in after it and found an alligator wearing a shirt with a picture of a little golfer on it.
BUDDY HACKETT, *The Truth About Golf and Other Lies,* **1968**

I've been a test pilot for Foot Joy forever. I test their $65 alligator models to see if standing in them for long periods of time in a bar brings them any serious harm. What effect spilling beer has on them.
GEORGE LOW, former touring professional, **1970**

You know the old rule. He who have fastest cart never have to play bad lie.
MICKEY MANTLE, *Esquire,* **1971**

I'd give up golf if I didn't have so many sweaters.
BOB HOPE, **1972**

Never wear hand-me-downs, freebies, borrowed togs or Christmas presents.
DOUG SANDERS, on how to become a better dresser,
Come Swing With Me, **1974**

Bing Crosby, who once lived on the 'slice' side of the fourteenth fairway at Pebble Beach, was reported never to have had to buy a ball in his life.
HENRY LONGHURST, *The Best of Henry Longhurst,* **1978**

I was gonna buy me one of them Johnny Miller leisure suits . . . but the dude said the fire marshall took 'em off the racks! They don't make no medium dumpy anyway.
LEE TREVINO, *Golf Digest,* **1978**

Where'd you get this ugly thing? Man, this is one of them airport drivers. That's right! You hit this thing for two days, miss the cut and go to the airport!
LEE TREVINO, as above

I don't like Number Four balls. And I don't like fives, sixes, or sevens on my cards.

GEORGE ARCHER, on his superstitions, **1979**

I had a letter from this bloke in Scotland the other day. 'Don't worry,' he wrote, 'it's not your fault. It's the ball's.' He went on for ten pages explaining that no two golf balls had the same centre of gravity and that's why my putts veer away.

TONY JACKLIN, *The Sunday Times*

Willis' Rule of Golf: You can't lose an old golf ball.

JOHN WILLIS, television sportscaster, **1980**

I wear black. I loved Westerns and the cowboys always looked good in black.

GARY PLAYER

I'm a traditionalist. I want to play a white ball. But a manufacturer wouldn't have to offer me a million dollars to change my mind.

CHI CHI RODRIGUEZ, *Golf Magazine,* **1982**

I have seen mink headcovers, bamboo shafts, concave sand wedges, the twelve-wood, the seven-and-a-half iron, floating balls, linoleum shoes, dome-shaped tees, distance measurers, girdles that keep your elbows together . . . and putters as ugly as Stillson wrenches. But the silliest thing I have ever seen in golf is the headcover that goes with the ball retriever.

CHARLES PRICE, *Golfer-At-Large,* **1982**

There is one more important characteristic: it must have a large and smooth area for advertising material. That, above all, is the purpose of golf hats.

PETER DOBEREINER, *Golf Digest,* **1982**

Never, never, never, never, will I ever be able to force myself to hit a pink golf ball. After all, the line has to be drawn somewhere.

PETER DOBEREINER, *Golf Digest,* **1983**

I used to use three a round, but since I bought the company I only use one.

JACK NICKLAUS, on MacGregor golf gloves,
Golf Digest, **1983**

My tournament line-up would include ... any guy who just bought a new club called a Birdie-Seeker or FlagJammer or a putter that looks like something you'd fix the plumbing with.

JIM MURRAY, *Los Angeles Times,* **1983**

How about knickers? Can you imagine anything sillier than a man wearing knickers? That's like putting Bermuda shorts on an alligator.

CHARLES PRICE, *Golf Digest,* **1983**

I feel like Spiderman.

FUZZY ZOELLER, on his rubber-spiked golf shoes,
Golf Digest, **1984**

Those clubs have no idea how old Lee is.

JACKIE BURKE, on Trevino's new clubs and improved play,
USA Today, **1984**

Did you know that a seven-iron thrown into a water hazard begins to rust after only forty-eight hours? Do you call that workmanship?

PETER ANDREWS, *Golf Digest,* **1984**

The old one didn't float too well.
CRAIG STADLER, when asked why he was using a new putter
during the US Open, *GolfWorld*, **1993**

It's not the strength of the players. My good friend John Daly
hits the ball 30 yards farther in 2005 than he did in 1991.
Now John will be the first one to tell you he hasn't done too
many push-ups in the last 15 years.
PETE DYE, *Golfweek*, **2005**

You know, downwind [the wooden driver] was okay. But
anything into the wind, or any crosswind, it was a joke. You
couldn't put any spin on it, and it would just nose dive. You
had to hit the ball hard, and put spin on it. These modern
balls don't spin.
DAVIS LOVE III, *Golfweek*, **2005**

Not naming names, but a lot of players say we need to do
something about the ball, then they come on a TV commercial
and say, 'Look how far I hit my new so-and-so.'
DAVIS LOVE III, *GolfWorld*, **2005**

I hear guys saying you can't work the ball anymore. Not the
one I'm playing. When I hit it crooked, it goes crooked.
JUSTIN LEONARD, *GolfWorld*, **2005**

Keep the ball, keep the glove. But I don't want to see them
on eBay tomorrow.
JACK NICKLAUS, to son and caddie, Jackie, after his final
competitive round at the Masters, *GolfWorld*, **2005**

9 ● Famous Last Words

It's a shame, but he'll never make a golfer – too much temper.
ALEX SMITH, Scottish professional, on Bobby Jones, **1915**

You'll never get anywhere fooling around those golf courses.
CLARA HOGAN, to son Ben at age sixteen, **1929**

Mister Gene, you got to hit the three-wood if you want to clear that water.
STOVEPIPE, caddie of Gene Sarazen, before his 220-yard four-wood for a double eagle at the Masters, **1935**

Hey, hurry up, Gene, I got a date tonight.
WALTER HAGEN, to Sarazen before his famous shot, **1935**

If I didn't have to throw that tomato for a living, I'd take this game up in a serious way and win all the championships. And this is one course I'd tear wide open.
DIZZY DEAN, St Louis Cardinals pitcher, on Oakmont, site of the US Open, **1935**

Would you like to know how to sink those putts? Just hit the ball a little closer to the hole.
VALERIE HOGAN, to husband Ben during the
Los Angeles Open, **1937**

Pick the ball up, have the clubs destroyed, and leave the course:
VISCOUNT CASTLEROSSE, British columnist, to his caddie after topping three straight shots, c. **1930s**

If I'da cleared the trees and drove the green, it woulda been a great tee shot.
SAM SNEAD, **1954**

His type come and go every year.
CHARLES PRICE, quoting his editors at the *Saturday Evening Post* who refused a feature story on Arnold Palmer, **1955**

Yes, a lot more people beat me now.
DWIGHT D. EISENHOWER, when asked if his game had changed since leaving the White House

I can beat the fat kid the best day he ever had.
ARNOLD PALMER, after losing the US Open play-off to
Jack Nicklaus, **1962**

No matter how hard I try, I just *can't* seem to break sixty-four.
JACK NICKLAUS

I'm not afraid of Jack. If you play better than he does, you can beat him.
TOM WEISKOPF

He was standing too close to my ball.
BARRY M. GOLDWATER, after beaning a spectator
thirty yards off the tee at the Phoenix Open pro-am, **1965**

Do Janie a favour. Tell her to get off the tour. Nobody who
swings like Shirley Temple can make a living in this game.
RICHIE FERRARIS, father of Jan Ferraris, on
Jane Blalock, **1969**

I can't win anything but money.
FRANK BEARD, leading the tour in money-winnings without
having won a tournament, **1969**

I figure on going for another six years until I'm forty. Then
I'll try the pro golf circuit. I'm as good right now as any of
them.
EVEL KNIEVEL, stunt man, *Sports Illustrated,* **1972**

Well, I guess all those years of practice finally paid off.
JACK NICKLAUS II, aged nine, after breaking fifty for nine holes,
1973

You want to be out there because you are a good golfer, not
because you are wearing something. I don't think a good
player has to dress differently or stop wearing make-up to
win tournaments.
LAURA COLE, winless in eleven years on the LPGA Tour,
Golf Magazine, **1981**

He looks like a pretty good player indeed. But what do I
know? I'm the guy who said Lee Trevino would never make
it out here!
RAYMOND FLOYD on Tim Norris, *Golf Magazine,* **1982**

Now that I'm a high school graduate, all kinds of opportunities should open up for me next year.
CALVIN PEETE, a millionaire on the tour, on passing his high school equivalency test, *Sports Illustrated,* **1982**

Those guys don't intimidate me. I can beat them.
JODIE MUDD, within two strokes of the lead at the Masters, shot a final-round eighty-six, **1983**

During the seventies, I wasn't a good striker of the ball at all. Oh, I won a lot of tournaments.
JACK NICKLAUS, who won eight majors in the seventies, *The New Yorker,* **1983**

I always thought the game was silly. Who wants to chase a little ball around under the hot sun?
CALVIN PEETE, on why he didn't take up golf at an early age, *San Francisco Chronicle,* **1983**

I was stubborn. I knew the four-iron was the right club.
BEN CRENSHAW, on knocking three balls in the water for an eleven at the fourteenth hole, Sea Pines Heritage Classic, **1983**

I shoot at the stick.
MANCIL DAVIS, on how he has scored forty-two aces, *Golf Magazine,* **1983**

Don't be bloody silly.
SIR MICHAEL BONALLACK, first reaction to the idea that he might some day become Secretary of the Royal and Ancient Golf Club of St Andrews, a position he held from 1984–1999

I was worried about the people behind me getting mad because we would play so slow.
KAREN DISABELLA, a twenty-three-year-old secretary
from Stonington, Connecticut, who aced the first
hole she ever played, **1984**

I know I'm getting better at golf because I'm hitting fewer spectators.
GERALD R. FORD, **1984**

There's no word for it. Germans don't have 'yips'.
BERNHARD LANGER about his getting the dreaded 'yips' in the **1970s**

Done, through, washed up.
TOM MCCOLLISTER, golf writer, in a pre-Masters story on Jack Nicklaus, prior to his victory at the age of forty-six, Atlanta Constitution, **1986**

And don't come back without the Cup.
PRESIDENT GEORGE H. W. BUSH to the US Ryder Cup team before their departure to Britain, **1989**

If we can't beat Paraguay, we might as well go home.
COLIN MONTGOMERIE, prior to Scotland's loss at the Alfred Dunhill Cup, **1993**

I think I can win. I've got nothing better to do this weekend.
DAVID FEHERTY, an also-ran at the Open at Turnberry GL, **1994**

Education always has been my first priority. That's why I chose Stanford. Golf is secondary. Even if I win three [US] Amateur titles, I'll stay in school to get my degree in business.
TIGER WOODS, *USA Today*, **1994**

The Far Eastern countries have improved dramatically over the last ten years. They can compete as well as anyone and proved that today.

COLIN MONTGOMERIE, after Scotland's loss to China in the Alfred Dunhill Cup, **1998**

Even if I shoot 90 tomorrow I'm going to enjoy it. Maybe people will say 'Oh, he blew it' or whatever. Maybe I'm going to blow it; it's the first time I've been there. What do you expect? You know I'm not number one in the world. My knees are going to touch each other on the first tee tomorrow. But let me tell you, I'm going to enjoy it.

JEAN VAN DE VELDE, French pro, on the eve of his final-round collapse in the Open at Carnoustie, **1999**

10 ● Fans

My gallery at the end consisted of my two opponents, three caddies, and some guy who was in the Army with me and wanted to borrow ten bucks.

CARY MIDDLECOFF, en route to a seventy-eight, **1949**

I say, are those your old school colours or your own unfortunate choice?

BERNARD DARWIN, playing at St Andrews, when he
spotted a flashily dressed fan, **1955**

No doubt the public knows less about the inside intricacies of first-class golf than of any other sport. It seems to be their particular delight to watch a famous golfer miss a shot and then hold him up to ridicule.

TOMMY ARMOUR, US professional

In a stroke-play tournament, with so much going on all over the course simultaneously, more often than not an observer finds himself stationed intently just where nothing is happening.

HERBERT WARREN WIND, *Nine Strokes in 27 Holes,* **1961**

I'm a hot-dog pro. That's when someone in the gallery looks at his pairing sheet and says, 'Here comes Joe Baloney, Sam Sausage, and Chi Chi Rodriguez. Let's go get a hot dog.'

CHI CHI RODRIGUEZ, at the PGA, **1964**

It is a gallery that revels in disaster. 'Palmer just took an eight!' will ring through it from time to time, and the town criers who hurry from fairway to fairway with the bad news are as happy as an old maid reporting a new divorce.

JIM MURRAY, on the Los Angeles Open,
The Sporting World of Jim Murray, **1968**

If the crowd won't applaud for me, I'll do it myself.

LEONARD THOMPSON, after hitting a good sand wedge, **1974**

If I had been in the gallery, I'd have gone home.

JOHNNY MILLER, after a thirty-nine on the front side at the
Bing Crosby National Pro-Am, **1975**

Rule One: Whenever a spectator seeks out a really good vantage point and settles down on shooting stick or canvas chair, the tallest and fattest golf watcher on the course will take up station directly in front.

PETER DOBEREINER, *GolfWorld,* **1975**

The crowds are so large, especially around the name players, that one can travel eighteen holes and never see a shot. But it's the finest tournament you'll ever hear.

MARK MULVOY and ART SPANDER, on the Masters,
Golf: The Passion and the Challenge, **1977**

The hero-worshippers in his gallery ought to appreciate that somebody has to play along with Arnold to keep his score if nothing else.

DAVE HILL, *Teed Off,* **1977**

I drew a big gallery today. I was paired with Palmer.

GENE LITTLER

I don't like to watch golf on television. I can't stand whispering.

DAVID BRENNER, comic, **1978**

Heck, I wish they'd make the gallery ropes out of bounds. We're the only sport that plays in the audience.

LEE TREVINO, *Sports Illustrated,* **1979**

Watching golf on TV is one thing. Trying to watch a golf tournament in person is like trying to cover a war on foot.

JAY CRONLEY, *Playboy,* **1981**

I told 'em, 'If you want to laugh, you have two choices: either go to a circus or I'll bury this eight-iron in your head.'

DAVID GRAHAM, to fans at the British Open, **1981**

A woman had me autograph a five-dollar bill once and told me she would keep it for the rest of her life. A half-hour later, I bought some drinks with a twenty. The change came back, and the five was in it.

LEE TREVINO, *Detroit Free Press,* **1982**

I can't figure out where they all came from – even Thursday and Friday. I thought people worked during the week.
CAROL RISSEL, Bing Crosby National Pro-Am executive committee, *San Francisco Examiner,* **1982**

A number of years ago, it dawned on me that the biggest seller at golf tournaments were those periscopes.
DEANE BEMAN, PGA Tour Commissioner, on the origin of stadium golf, *Golf Digest,* **1983**

Golf fans have a remarkable sixth sense that tells them what is happening elsewhere on the course, often a mile away. Some sort of telepathic wizardry takes place that not even the Soviet Union's KGB could figure out.
DAN HRUBY, *San Jose Mercury News,* **1983**

Galleries understand the game and are very respectful. In my opinion, it's the last civilized country left in the world.
TOM WATSON about the British fans, **1983**

I was naturally unhappy at what happened to the lady but I still feel I should have won.
IAN WOOSNAM, whose ball caromed out of bounds at the Cannes Open after hitting a woman spectator, sending her to hospital, **1990**

I remember when I used to win a match in Britain, people would cheer me. The Ryder Cup isn't like that any more. Make a birdie now and they boo.
LEE TREVINO, *Daily Mail,* **1993**

The galleries were applauding Nicklaus for breathing, which slowed things up a bit.
COLIN MONTGOMERIE, on playing in the group behind Jack Nicklaus's at the Masters, **1998**

As [Jose Maria Olazabal] was walking up the hill, the spectators were chanting, 'Kill him, kill him, kill him!' I was quite shocked. It was not 'Beat him', it was not 'Win this match' or 'Come on, keep going', it was 'Kill him' like in the Roman gladiator circus.

SERGIO GOMEZ, Olazabal's manager, on fans' behaviour at the Ryder Cup, Brookline, Mass., *Sunday Times*, **2001**

Say what you like about the Scots, but they recognize tripe when they see it.

DEREK LAWRENSON, golf writer, on the sparsely attended Dunhill Links Championship, *Daily Mail*, **2001**

Any golfer . . . who tells you he doesn't like signing autographs is a liar. When it's not there, you miss it like crazy.

BRIAN BARNES, whose career was curtailed by rheumatoid arthritis, *GolfWorld*, **2004**

My entourage is a bunch of drunks having a good time.

JOHN DALY, *San Francisco Chronicle*, **2005**

11 ● Friendly Matches

If golfers keep on playing so slowly, on the green particularly, one way to correct the situation is to knock your ball into the SOBs. There will be a slight delay while you have a hell of a fight, but from that point on you will move faster.

HORACE G. HUTCHINSON, *Hints on the Game of Golf,* **1886**

Remember, they were friends. For years they had shared each other's sorrows, joys, and golf balls, and sliced into the same bunkers.

P. G. WODEHOUSE, *A Woman Is Only a Woman,* **1919**

The least thing upset him on the links. He missed short putts because of the uproar of butterflies in the adjoining meadows.

P. G. WODEHOUSE, *The Unexpected Clicking of Cuthbert,* **1921**

It is a law of nature that everybody plays a hole badly when going through.

BERNARD DARWIN, *Playing the Like,* **1934**

Man, to threesome: Mind if I play through? My wife's having a pretty tricky operation and I'd like to get to the hospital as soon as I can.

DAVID LANGDON, cartoon in *The New Yorker,* **1952**

You must expect anything in golf. A stranger comes through, he's keen for a game, he seems affable enough, and on the eighth fairway he turns out to be an idiot.

ALISTAIR COOKE, journalist, **1957**

It's a funny thing, Bob. I've just lent Bolivia millions of dollars, but I only have one buck on me to pay with.

DWIGHT D. EISENHOWER, paying off a golfing bet with
Bob Hope

I confess that I have played rounds where the other three players in the foursome became total strangers to me in the long distances between tee and green.

MILTON GROSS, *Eighteen Holes in My Head,* **1959**

You don't much care in the mixed game whether you win or lose. All you want to do is make a jackass out of your male opponent and get his partner to flare up at him, which can sometimes be amusing.

REX LARDNER, *Out of the Bunker and Into the Trees,* **1960**

Many a golf course and many a big gambler would have eaten me up if I hadn't eaten them first by having a mean frame of mind.

SAM SNEAD, *The Education of a Golfer,* **1962**

You can imagine my consternation when I was invited to play at this place . . . Usually, I play golf with the kind of people who rob banks not own them.
JIM MURRAY, on playing at the Los Angeles Country Club, *The Sporting World of Jim Murray,* **1968**

I used to play to a six handicap and now I play to a twelve. Not only that, it now takes me five and a half hours to complete a round.
DON WALKER, Florida neighbour of Jack Nicklaus and Dr Cary Middlecoff

I play with friends, but we don't play friendly games.
BEN HOGAN, *Golf Digest,* **1970**

Gimme: An agreement between two losers who can't putt.
JIM BISHOP, syndicated column, **1970**

There's no better game in the world when you are in good company, and no worse game when you are in bad company.
TOMMY BOLT, *The Hole Truth,* **1971**

Give me a millionaire with a bad backswing and I can have a very pleasant afternoon.
GEORGE LOW

I never lied about my handicap; I just let my opponents talk themselves into a trap.
BOBBY RIGGS, *Court Hustler,* **1973**

The only difference I was aware of between Democrats and Republicans was that Republicans seemed to have lower handicaps and more sets of clubs while Democrats like to bet more — and paid off quicker.
DAN JENKINS. *Dead Solid Perfect,* **1974**

Somebody asked me one time why I didn't turn pro. Man, I can't afford it.
DICK MARTIN, Texas golf hustler

Never bet with anyone you meet on the first tee who has a deep suntan, a one-iron in his bag and squinty eyes.
DAVE MARR

It's amazing how many people in the world almost walk around looking to be hustled.
DAVE HILL, *Teed Off*, **1977**

Some guys get so nervous playing for their own money, the greens don't need fertilizing for a year.
DAVE HILL, *Teed Off*, **1977**

I've just heard that soon he might be well enough to play golf. Hasn't the man suffered enough?
PAUL HARVEY, radio commentator, on artificial-heart-transplant patient Barney Clark, *Golf Digest*, **1983**

Seve, I wouldn't give my mother two strokes a side.
TOMMY BOLT, to Seve Ballesteros, on a television ad for golf clubs, **1984**

They play for big bucks at private clubs, too, but there's a difference. They can afford to lose.
HALE IRWIN, *Golf Digest*, **1984**

My car absolutely will not run unless my golf clubs are in the trunk.
BRUCE BERLET, golf writer, *Hartford Courant*, **1984**

You don't necessarily have to bring your clubs to play golf — just lie about your score.
LON SIMMONS, Oakland A's broadcaster

There's an old saying: If a man comes home with sand in his cuffs and cockleburs in his pants, don't ask him what he shot.
SAM SNEAD, *USA Today,* **1984**

My worst day on the golf course still beats my best day in the office.
JOHN HALLISEY, *Monterey Peninsula-Herald* golf writer, **1984**

At least it keeps me out of the pub.
GEOFFREY OWEN, 90-year-old resident of Buckinghamshire,
on his twice-weekly playing schedule, *GolfWorld*, **2004**

Gamesmanship in golf is usually subtle, but if you don't have the brains to shut your eyes and ears when you're playing seriously, then you deserve what you get.
PETER THOMSON, *GolfWorld*, **2005**

12 ● Golf: General Thoughts

Golf always makes me so damned angry.
KING GEORGE V

I do not remember having met any golfer who did not consider himself on the whole a remarkably unlucky one.
HORACE G. HUTCHINSON, *Hints on the Game of Golf*, 1886

Human nature is so funny, it is a thousand pities that neither Aristotle nor Shakespeare was a golfer. There is no game that strips the soul so naked.
HORACE G. HUTCHINSON, as above

Excessive golfing dwarfs the intellect. And is this to be wondered at when we consider that the more fatuously vacant the mind is, the better for play.
SIR WALTER SIMPSON, *The Art of Golf*, 1887

Golf is a good walk spoiled.
MARK TWAIN

The wit of man has never invented a pastime equal to golf for its healthful recreation, its pleasurable excitement, and its never ending source of amusement.
LORD BALFOUR

I am quite certain that there has never been a greater addition to the lighter side of civilization than that supplied by the game of golf.
LORD BALFOUR

A tolerable day, a tolerable green and a tolerable opponent supply – or ought to supply – all that any reasonably constituted human being should require in the way of entertainment.
LORD BALFOUR

Golf, like art, is a goddess whom we would woo in early youth if we would win her.
SIR HENRY RIDER HAGGARD, novelist

Golf is an indispensable adjunct to high civilization.
ANDREW CARNEGIE, American industrialist, on leaving $200,000 to Yale to build a golf course

Golf is so popular simply because it is the best game in the world at which to be bad. . . At golf it is the bad player who gets the most strokes.
A. A. MILNE, *Not That It Matters,* **1919**

The uglier a man's legs are, the better he plays golf. It's almost a law.
H.G. WELLS, author

Golf is twenty per cent mechanics and technique. The other eighty per cent is philosophy, humour, tragedy, romance, melodrama, companionship, camaraderie, cussedness, and conversation.

GRANTLAND RICE, sportswriter, **1920**

Golf is the only game where the worst player gets the best of it. He obtains more out of it as regards both exercise and enjoyment, for the good player gets worried over the slightest mistake, whereas the poor player makes too many mistakes to worry over them.

DAVID LLOYD GEORGE

It was a morning when all nature shouted 'Fore!' The breeze, as it blew gently up from the valley, seemed to bring a message of hope and cheer, whispering of chip-shots holed and brassies landing squarely on the meat.

P. G. WODEHOUSE, *The Heart of a Goof,* **1923**

I guess there is nothing that will get your mind off everything like golf will. I have never been depressed enough to take up the game, but they say you can get so sore at yourself that you forget to hate your enemies.

WILL ROGERS

Golf is like a love affair: if you don't take it seriously, it's not fun; if you do take it seriously, it breaks your heart.

ARNOLD DALY, *Reader's Digest,* **1933**

Golf may be . . . a sophisticated game. At least, it is usually played with the outward appearance of great dignity. It is, nevertheless, a game of considerable passion, either of the explosive type, or that which burns inwardly and sears the soul.

BOBBY JONES

The terrible thing about a missed shot in golf is that the thing is done, irrevocably, irretrievably. Perhaps that is why golf is so great a game; it is so much like the game of life. We don't have the shots over in either.

O. B. KEELER, Atlanta sportswriter

Golf is the Esperanto of sport. All over the world golfers talk the same language – much of it nonsense and much unprintable – endure the same frustrations, discover the same infallible secrets of putting, share the same illusory joys.

HENRY LONGHURST, *Round in Sixty-Eight,* **1953**

Like life, golf can be humbling. However, little good comes from brooding about mistakes we've made. The next shot, in golf or in life, is the big one.

GRANTLAND RICE, *The Tumult and the Shouting,* **1954**

It is this constant and undying hope for improvement that makes golf so exquisitely worth the playing.

BERNARD DARWIN, British golf writer

I've been around golf courses all my life. They are the Demaret answer to the world's problems. When I get out on that green carpet called a fairway and manage to poke the ball right down the middle, my surroundings look like a touch of heaven on earth.

JIMMY DEMARET, *My Partner, Ben Hogan,* **1954**

If you watch a game, it's fun. If you play it, it's recreation. If you work at it, it's golf.

BOB HOPE, *Reader's Digest,* **1958**

Golf does strange things to other people, too. It makes liars out of honest men, cheats out of altruists, cowards out of brave men and fools out of everybody.
MILTON GROSS, *Eighteen Holes in My Head,* **1959**

One reward golf has given me, and I shall always be thankful for it, is introducing me to some of the world's most picturesque, tireless and bald–faced liars.
REX LARDNER, *Out of the Bunker and Into the Trees,* **1960**

Golf is essentially an exercise in masochism conducted out-of-doors; it affords opportunity for a certain swank, it induces a sense of kinship in its victims, and it forces them to breathe fresh air, but it is, at bottom, an elaborate and addictive rite calculated to drive them crazy for hours on end and send them straight to the whisky bottle after that.
PAUL O'NEIL, *Life,* **1962**

If you don't succeed at first, don't despair. Remember, it takes time to learn to play golf; most players spend their entire lifetime finding out about the game before they give it up.
STEPHEN BAKER, *How to Play Golf in the Low 120s,* **1962**

Golf is the greatest game in the world. It is frustrating. It is rewarding. It is humbling. It is exhilarating. It can send you into the depths of despair. It can rocket you into an orbit of incomparable satisfaction and joy. It teaches. It puts a man's character to the anvil and his richest qualities – patience, poise, restraint – to the flame.
BILLY CASPER, in *My Million Dollar Shots,* **1970**

Gentlemen play golf. And if you aren't a gentleman when you start, after the crushing events of the game, you surely become one.
BING CROSBY

It was named by drunken Scots after listening to barking dogs. Golf is played by twenty million mature American men whose wives think they are out there having fun.

JIM BISHOP, syndicated column, **1970**

It is sometimes said that only when he stands at the altar on his wedding day does a man experience quite the same sensation of impending doom as he feels each week on the first tee of a Sunday morning.

NORMAN MAIR, *Of Games and Golf*

Golf should not be taught in schools. It encourages children to be selfish and makes them pig-headed and conceited.

CYRIL STAFFORD-NORTHCOTE, headmaster,
St Bede's School, Staffordshire, *Sun*, **1971**

There are now more golf clubs in the world than Gideon Bibles, more golf balls than missionaries and, if every golfer in the world, male and female, were laid end to end, I for one would leave them there.

MICHAEL PARKINSON, president, Anti-Golf Society,
Sunday Times, **1975**

Golf is an open exhibition of overweening ambition, courage deflated by stupidity, skill soured by a whiff of arrogance. . . These humiliations are the essence of the game.

ALISTAIR COOKE

It is a wonderful tribute to the game or to the dottiness of the people who play it that for some people somewhere there is no such thing as an insurmountable obstacle, an unplayable course, the wrong time of the day or the year.

ALISTAIR COOKE, *Golfers and Other Strangers,* **1975**

Golf is the only sport where a man [of] sixty can play with the best. That's why golf is such a great game. And no one has ever licked it.
SAM SNEAD, *Golf Digest,* **1975**

The game was easy for me as a kid, and I had to play a while to find out how hard it is.
RAYMOND FLOYD, after winning the Masters, **1976**

Golf is like art; it's impossible to be perfect.
SANDRA PALMER, *Golf Magazine,* **1977**

Indeed, the highest pleasure of golf may be that on the fairways and far from all the pressures of commerce and rationality, we can feel immortal for a few hours.
COLMAN MCCARTHY, *The Pleasures of the Game,* **1977**

Good golf isn't a matter of hitting great shots. It's finding a way to make your bad ones not so bad. If I hadn't learned to do that, you'd still be thinking 'Trevino' is Italian.
LEE TREVINO, *Golf Digest,* **1979**

A hundred years of experience has demonstrated that the game is temporary insanity practised in a pasture.
DAVE KINDRED, *Washington Post,* **1979**

Golf is a science, the study of a lifetime, in which you may exhaust yourself but never your subject.
DAVID R. FORGAN, of the Forgan club-making family

To see one's ball gallop two hundred and more yards down the fairway, or to see it fly from the face of an eight-iron clear across an entire copse of maples in full autumnal flare, is to join one's soul with the vastness that, contemplated from another angle, intimidates the spirit, and makes one feel small.
JOHN UPDIKE, *Updike's Adventures in Golf's Wonderland,* **1982**

The golfer has more enemies than any other athlete. He has 14 clubs in his bag, all of them different; 18 holes to play, all of them different, every week; and all around him are sand, trees, grass, water, wind and 143 other players. In addition, the game is fifty per cent mental, so his biggest enemy is himself.
DAN JENKINS, *Sports Illustrated,* **1982**

Good night, this game teaches you a lot about yourself. You can tell by the way a guy walks how he's doing.
BEN CRENSHAW, *Golf Digest,* **1983**

Golf combines two favourite American pastimes: taking long walks and hitting things with a stick.
P. J. O'ROURKE, *Modern Manners,* **1983**

In golf, finally, it all gets down to the player, the club and the ball, and no other people.
PETER ALLISS, in *The Who's Who of Golf,* **1983**

This game is great and very strange.
SEVE BALLESTEROS, after winning the British Open, **1984**

Golf is like fishing and hunting. What counts is the companionship and fellowship of friends, not what you catch or shoot.
GEORGE ARCHER, *Golf Digest,* **1984**

Good companionship? Have you ever actually listened to golfers talking to each other? 'Looked good starting out.' 'Better direction than last time.' 'Who's away?' It sounds like a visitors' day at a home for the criminally insane.
PETER ANDREWS, *Golf Digest,* **1984**

Golf is the cruellest of sports. Like life, it's unfair. It's a harlot. A trollop. It leads you on. It never lives up to its promises. It's not a sport, it's bondage. An obsession. A boulevard of broken dreams. It plays with men. And runs off with the butcher.
JIM MURRAY, *Los Angeles Times,* **1985**

It's a faithless love, but you hit four good shots and you've started your day right.
DINAH SHORE, **1989**

Golf is not a game, it's a punishment. Clubs are enemies, courses are haunted houses or torture chambers, tournaments are where one guy is happy and 150 are sad.
JIM MURRAY, *Los Angeles Times,* **1990**

The best year of my life was when I was eleven. I got straight As, had two recesses a day, and the cutest girlfriend, and won thirty-two tournaments that year. Everything's been downhill since.
TIGER WOODS, *Las Vegas Review-Journal,* **2000**

When I was young, it wasn't cool to play golf. And there certainly wasn't anything cool to wear to play golf. I love it. It's all changing around.
TIGER WOODS, *Daily News Record,* **2000**

If God had wanted man to play golf, He would have given him an elbowless left arm, short asymmetrical legs with side-hinged knees, and a trapezoid rib cage from which diagonally jutted a two-foot neck topped by a three-eyed head.
ALAN COREN, *The Times*, 2001

The sweet swinger will always beat the strong-arm player.
PETER THOMSON, *GolfWorld*, 2005

13 ● Golf and Other Sports

It's just the old-fashioned pool hall moved outdoors, but with no chairs around the walls.
WILL ROGERS, on golf

Golf tournaments are lonely. In baseball there's eight other guys to keep me company.
WALTER HAGEN, when asked why he wanted to play baseball instead of golf, 1913

When I hit a ball, I want someone else to go chase it.
ROGERS HORNSBY, baseball player

In other games you get another chance. In baseball you get three cracks at it; in tennis you lose only one point. But in golf the loss of one shot has been responsible for the loss of heart.
TOMMY ARMOUR

Yeah, no more golf for me. But I tell you, Buchanan, maybe if you aren't busy tomorrow we could meet on the first tee at nine tomorrow morning, because if I'm going to quit I might as well get in one more game.
BABE RUTH, to Florida pro J. A. Buchanan

I think golf is good for boxing, but the reverse is far from being the case.
MAX BAER, former heavyweight champion, **1937**

In tennis you seldom have a chance, once things get going, to get shaky. You're too busy running around like a race horse. But in golf – hell, it makes me nervous just to talk about it. That little white ball just sits there. A man can beat himself before he ever swings at it.
ELLSWORTH VINES, tennis champion who later became a professional golfer

In golf, when we hit a foul ball, we got to go out and play it.
SAM SNEAD, to Ted Williams

I just shook a hand that felt like five bands of steel.
TED WILLIAMS, upon meeting Ben Hogan, **1951**

The pay is great, and the only way you can get hurt playing golf is by getting struck by lightning.
TED WILLIAMS, on professional golf

One of the advantages bowling has over golf is that you seldom lose a bowling ball.
DON CARTER, professional bowler

The only reason I ever played golf in the first place was so I could afford to hunt and fish.
SAM SNEAD, hinting about retirement, *Sports Illustrated*, **1968**

One point on which all golfers can immediately agree is that, whatever else golf may be, it is not a game. How much simpler life would be if it were just a game, like tennis.
PETER DOBEREINER, *The Glorious World of Golf,* **1973**

My best score ever is 103. But I've only been playing fifteen years.
ALEX KARRAS, former NFL defensive lineman

Thanks a lot for curing my slice. Now what can you do for my hook?
JIM PALMER, baseball pitcher, to pro Dave Stockton,
Golf Digest, **1977**

It took me seventeen years to get 3,000 hits in baseball. I did it in one afternoon on the golf course.
HANK AARON

I'd do better if the ball were two feet off the ground and moving.
STAN MUSIAL, *Golf Digest,* **1978**

I played mixed doubles with a whole new foursome yesterday and I explained that golf was really my game. Of course, I told my golfing foursome today that tennis was really my game.
DINAH SHORE, *Golf Magazine,* **1981**

Too bad there aren't water hazards in baseball like there are in golf. We could lose all the balls and go home.
LON SIMMONS, Oakland A's announcer, during a dull game, **1981**

Hitting a golf ball correctly is the most sophisticated and complicated manoeuvre in all of sport, with the possible exception of eating a hot dog at a ball game without getting mustard on your shirt.

RAY FITZGERALD, *Golf Digest,* **1981**

The larger the ball, the less the writing about the sport. There are superb books about golf, very good books about baseball, not many good books about football, and very few good books about basketball. There are no books about beach balls.

GEORGE PLIMPTON, **1982**

The first time he ever let himself get talked into a celebrity golf tournament, he shot a score of 115. It was his own fault. He counted all his strokes.

BOB UECKER, on pitcher Bob Gibson, *Catcher in the Wry,* **1982**

He could hit a ball farther off line than any man I ever knew. When Sandy practised he would blanket three fairways, three hundred yards out and three hundred yards wide. He was like a one-man hailstorm.

MAC HUNTER, Riviera Country Club professional, on former pitcher Sandy Koufax, *Golf Digest,* **1982**

Why shouldn't he [infielder Pete O'Brien] have a good attitude? He was raised in Pebble Beach. Wouldn't you have a good attitude if your biggest decision every morning was whether to play Spyglass Hill or Cypress Point?

DOUG RADER, Texas Rangers manager, **1983**

In football . . . some coaches have stated, 'When you throw a pass, three things can happen, two of them are bad.' In golf, there is no limit.

MARINO PARASCENZO, *Golf Magazine,* **1983**

Everybody survives slumps . . . except maybe boxers. If they have a bad streak, they get knocked on their cans.
TOM WATSON, *Sports Illustrated,* **1984**

I think golf is the hardest sport to play. . . One day you're up on Cloud Nine and the next day you couldn't scratch a whale's belly.
SAM SNEAD, *San Francisco Chronicle,* **1984**

I was winning golf tournaments when John McEnroe was five years of age and I'll be winning tournaments, if I stay healthy, when I'm fifty-five and sixty years of age. Not many tennis players will be doing that.
GARY PLAYER, in an interview, **1984**

I think if I'd had some coaching I could have played county cricket as a bowler. Luckily, I didn't have any coaching.
NICK FALDO, **1990**

Baseball players quit playing and they take up golf. Basketball players quit, take up golf. What are we supposed to take up when we quit?
LEE TREVINO, **1990**

The world's No. 1 tennis player spends ninety per cent of his time winning, while the world's No. 1 golfer spends ninety per cent of his time losing. Golfers are great losers.
DAVID FEHERTY

Show me a basketball coach who's a good golfer and I'll show you a coach whose team I want to schedule.
STU JACKSON, basketball coach, University of Wisconsin, *GolfWorld,* **1993**

Shorts are for tennis or yard work. Anklets are for the LPGA. Do you like losing to a guy who wears shorts and anklets? For that matter, do you even like being in the same foursome where the other three guys are wearing shorts and anklets?
DAN JENKINS, *Fairways and Greens*, **1994**

Baseball is a game you play when you are young, strong and on steroids. Golf is a more venerable venture.
PETER JACOBSEN, *GolfWorld*, **2005**

It's not like I'm hitting bad putts. I'm hitting good putts. There's a goalkeeper in there and he's playing great.
PAUL MCGINLEY, *Los Angeles Times*, **2005**

I would rather go golfing before games than go out after games and get smashed.
RHEAL CORMIER, Philadelphia Phillies pitcher, *GolfWorld*, **2005**

If any sport evokes passion that continues for a lifetime, it's golf. Unlike some other sports, golfers play golf until they die. And most would be happy to die on the golf course.
BOB GREENWAY, senior VP of the Golf Channel, at its tenth anniversary celebration, *GolfWorld*, **2005**

14 ● Golf and Politics

I find it difficult to squeeze in the claims of both golf and politics into the twenty-four hours.
LORD BALFOUR

I did not see the sense in chasing a little white ball around a field.
CALVIN COOLIDGE, on why he never played golf

You get to know more of the character of a man in a round of golf than you can get to know in six months with only political experience.
DAVID LLOYD GEORGE, *Observer,* 1924

No man has mastered golf until he has realized that his good shots are accidents and his bad shots good exercise.
EUGENE R. BLACK, American government official

Rail-splitting produced an immortal President in Lincoln, but golf hasn't produced even a good A-1 Congressman.
WILL ROGERS, American humorist

Here you are, the greatest golfer in the world, being introduced by the worst one.

JAMES J. WALKER, Mayor of New York, at a City Hall ceremony honouring Bobby Jones, **1930**

If I had my way, any man guilty of golf would be ineligible for any public office in the United States, and the families of the breed would be shipped off to the white slave corrals of the Argentine.

H. L. MENCKEN, American journalist

Golf is a game whose aim is to hit a very small ball into an even smaller hole, with weapons singularly ill-designed for the purpose.

SIR WINSTON CHURCHILL

If Macmillan thinks he can keep Ike off the golf course he has made the biggest miscalculation in political history.

SIR WINSTON CHURCHILL, on Dwight D. Eisenhower, first dispatch from the Bermuda Conference

Playing the game, I have learned the meaning of humility. It has given me an understanding of the futility of human effort.

ABBA EBAN, Israeli ambassador

Augusta is the course Ike Eisenhower usually plays on. That's proof enough for me that he is a man with good taste.

JIMMY DEMARET, *My Partner, Ben Hogan,* **1954**

President Eisenhower has given up golf for painting – it takes fewer strokes.

BOB HOPE

Did you read where Arnold Palmer has been talking about the governorship of Pennsylvania? Man, I think that hip injury must be moving up to his *head*.
DAVE MARR, **1968**

The last time I played a round with Vice President Agnew he hit a birdie – an eagle, a moose, an elk and a Mason.
BOB HOPE

Sanders won $200 in the tournament, and that just paid for the medical attention he required.
SPIRO T. AGNEW, after Agnew's errant shot hit Doug Sanders in the Bob Hope Desert Classic, *Golf Digest,* **1970**

At least he can't cheat on his score – because all you have to do is look back down the fairway and count the wounded.
BOB HOPE, on Spiro T. Agnew, **1971**

I said a few unprintable words under my breath and called it a Mulligan.
ALAN SHEPARD, on his missed six-iron on the moon, **1971**

Golf acts as a corrective against sinful pride. I attribute the insane arrogance of the later Roman emperor almost entirely to the fact that, never having played golf, they never knew that strange chastening humility which is engendered by a topped chip shot.
P. G. WODEHOUSE, *P. G. Wodehouse on Golf,* **1973**

I'm aware that golf is probably some kind of a mental disorder like gambling or women or politics.
DAN JENKINS, *Dead Solid Perfect,* **1974**

Golf is a humbling game, yes, but with one solid stroke of the ball a pro can imagine himself a colossus, greater than Einstein, Rockefeller, and all the generals of the armies.
AL BARKOW, *Golf's Golden Grind,* **1974**

If I swung the gavel the way I swung that golf club, the nation would be in a helluva mess.
TIP O'NEILL, Speaker of the House, *Golf Digest,* **1980**

Somebody asked me the other day about this Parkinson woman some of the [House] members are supposed to be involved with. I told them that at my stage of life the greatest thrill a guy gets is sinking a forty-foot putt.
TIP O'NEILL, *Golf Digest,* **1981**

It's one of those years. Jimmy Carter had four of 'em, so I don't feel so bad.
LEE TREVINO, having a bad year, **1981**

The other day my golf-loving friend Bob Hope asked me what my handicap was, so I told him – the Congress.
RONALD REAGAN, **1982**

Golf, a game kings and presidents play when they get tired of running countries.
CHARLES PRICE, *Golf Magazine,* **1982**

Golf, in my opinion, is a game for deposed Latin American dictators in plaid pants; it allows them to putter away their exile until God's extradition.
JOHN LEONARD, *New York Times,* **1982**

President Ford waits until he hits his first drive to know what course he's playing that day.
BOB HOPE, *San Francisco Chronicle,* **1983**

When Andrei Gromyko gets down to disarmament talks, the first item on his agenda is taking away Gerald Ford's golf clubs.
BOB HOPE, **1984**

He doesn't know he can't hit the ball through the trunk of a tree.
JACK NICKLAUS, on Ford, **1984**

The difference between golf and government is that in golf you can't improve your lie.
GEORGE DEUKMEJIAN, Governor of California, *Golf Digest,* **1984**

A Tiger Woods candidacy would bring me out of retirement. He would capture the country.
FRANK LUNTZ, veteran political campaign strategist, when
asked what would happen if Tiger Woods ran for President,
Travel & Leisure Golf, **2004**

15 ● Hazards

There are no bunkers in the air.
WALTER HAGEN, on why he hits the ball high, **1920**

The object of a bunker or trap is not only to punish a physical mistake, to punish lack of control, but also to punish pride and egotism.
CHARLES BLAIR MACDONALD, golf course architect,
The American Golfer, **1924**

Did I make it look hard enough, son?
WALTER HAGEN, to Norman von Nida after hitting out of the rough to the green, **1929**

The difference between a sand trap and water is the difference between a car crash and an airplane crash. You have a chance of recovering from a car crash.
BOBBY JONES

When they start hitting back at me, it's time to quit.
HENRY RANSOM, when his shot from the beach at Cypress Point's
sixteenth hole rebounded from the cliff and hit him in the
stomach, c. **1955**

And don't send your Son down. This is a man's job.
BERNARD DARWIN, golf writer, swearing to God in a bunker

I've lost balls in every hazard and on every course on which
I've tried, but when I lose a ball in the ball washer it's time to
take stock.
MILTON GROSS, *Eighteen Holes in My Head,* **1959**

If the tree is skinny, aim right at it. A peculiarity of golf is that
what you aim at you generally miss . . . the success of the shot
depending mainly, of course, on your definition of 'skinny'.
REX LARDNER, *Out of the Bunker and Into the Trees,* **1960**

If he takes the option of dropping behind the point where
the ball rests, keeping in line with the pin, his nearest drop is
Honolulu.
JIMMY DEMARET, on Arnold Palmer on the rocks at the
seventeenth hole at Pebble Beach, **1964**

Hey, is this room out-of-bounds?
ALEX KARRAS, after hitting his tee shot through the clubhouse
window at Red Run Country Club, Royal Oak, Michigan

Only bullfighting and the water hole are left as vestigial
evidence of what a bloody savage man used to be. Only in
golf is this sort of contrived swindle allowed.
TOMMY BOLT, *How to Keep Your Temper on the Golf Course,* **1969**

The last time I left the fairway was to answer the telephone. And it was a wrong number.
CHI CHI RODRIGUEZ, **1970**

What's over there? A nudist colony?
LEE TREVINO, after his three playing partners drove into the woods, **1970**

Water creates a neurosis in golfers. The very thought of this harmless fluid robs them of their normal powers of rational thought, turns their legs to jelly, and produces a palsy of the upper limbs.
PETER DOBEREINER, *The Glorious World of Golf,* **1973**

I spent so much time in the rough, my playing partner Buddy Allin thought I was part of the gallery. I walked so much I had to replace my cleats.
LEE TREVINO, at the US Open, **1974**

The sand was heavier than I thought, and it only took me four swings to figure it out.
JOHNNY MILLER, at the US Open, **1974**

It is not unusual to find strange objects in municipal sand traps, even bones. Some players think that the rake by the side of the trap is a hazard itself and that it is a two-stroke penalty if you touch it.
JAY CRONLEY, *Golf Digest*

The number one thing in trouble is: Don't get into more trouble!
DAVE STOCKTON, *Golf Magazine,* **1977**

Check the diaper: if it's wet you get relief from casual water.
BOB MURPHY, when his partner's ball landed in a baby carriage,
Golf Digest, **1978**

I must live with the dishonour they now call 'The Sands of
Nakajima'.
TOMMY NAKAJIMA, Japanese pro, after needing four swings to
escape the Road Bunker en route to a nine at St Andrews'
seventeenth during the Open, **1978**

I have discovered one important thing about the course,
though – those big pine trees don't move.
FUZZY ZOELLER, at the Masters, *Des Moines Register,* **1979**

I didn't realize how windy it was yesterday until I came out
today and got a look at Tom Watson. The wind had blown
fourteen freckles off Tom's face. Now man, that's windy.
JERRY MCGEE, at the Andy Williams–San Diego Open,
Golf Digest, **1979**

A rough should have high grass. When you go bowling they
don't give you anything for landing in the gutter, do they?
LEE TREVINO, *Golf Digest,* **1979**

I love rotten weather. The founders of the game accepted
nature for what it gave, or what it took away. Wind and rain
are great challenges. They separate real golfers. Let the seas
pound against the shore, let the rains pour.
TOM WATSON, *San Francisco Chronicle,* **1981**

If this was an airport, it would have been closed.
LARRY ZIEGLER, on a windy and rainy day,
Golf Magazine, **1982**

I've joked about how I survived being struck by lightning. 'I'm a reject,' I said. 'The Lord didn't want me.'
LEE TREVINO, *They Call Me Super Mex*, **1982**

I'm too young to get fried up out here – I don't like the game that much.
FUZZY ZOELLER, walking off the course during a thunderstorm, **1983**

Golf is the strangest game in the world. It involves a lot of luck. And when your ball starts rattling in the trees, then it's all luck.
REX CALDWELL, *San Francisco Chronicle*, **1983**

My Turn-Ons: big galleries, small scores, long drives, short rough, fat pay cheques, and skinny trees.
PETER JACOBSEN, *Golf Magazine*, **1983**

They say that trees are no problem because trees are ninety per cent air.
JOHN BRODIE, *'Women's Kemper Open'*, NBC-TV, **1983**

I didn't get much tan this week.
STEVE MELNYK, playing in the trees,
'Colonial National Invitation', NBC-TV, **1983**

My tournament line-up would include . . . any guy who never got out of a sand trap in fewer than six strokes.
JIM MURRAY, *Los Angeles Times*, **1983**

I never saw a good player from the trees.
BYRON NELSON, *'Doral-Eastern Open'*, CBS-TV, **1984**

On the scenic and infamous par-five eighteenth, he had one last chance, but from the way he struck his tee shot it appeared as if he were trying to hit the ocean in regulation.
DAN JENKINS, on Crosby winner Hale Irwin's shot that bounced off the rocks and back on the fairway at Pebble Beach, **1984**

It's only my career, folks.
FUZZY ZOELLER, to spectators at the US Open when he was in trouble, *Sports Illustrated,* **1984**

The last time I was this cold was when I climbed the Alps.
NICK FALDO, at the Bing Crosby National Pro-Am, **1984**

The possibility of having to battle the elements holds a strong appeal for the eccentric side of the English character.
HERBERT WARREN WIND, in *Following Through,* **1985**

You and I would play in weather in Scotland that would keep us by the fire at home.
DICK TAYLOR, writer and editor, *GolfWorld,* **1985**

My, my, it looks like a couple of Shetland ponies have been mating in there.
PETER ALLISS, BBC television commentator, on a player's several botched shots in the Road Bunker, **1986**

Two balls in the water. By God, I've got a good mind to jump in and make it four!
SIMON HOBDAY, Senior PGA Championship, **1994**

I get pissed off. I simply do not understand someone who hits a ball that lands behind a tree and can look at it and say 'Well, that's golf.'
SIMON HOBDAY

When it's wet, bet on the Welsh.
JOHN HUGGAN, on the WGC–Algarve World Cup victory in
rainy Portugal by relatively unknown pros Bradley Dredge and
Stephen Dodd, *GolfWorld*, **2005**

My marriages don't last this long.
JOHN DALY, during a rain delay at the Nissan Open,
GolfWorld, **2005**

I don't want to say [the US players] are spoiled. . . We were
out today in hail, sleet and mud, and I couldn't help thinking
if this was taking place in the US, the kids would walk off.
BUTCH HARMON, swing coach, at a junior event in Scotland,
The Times, **2005**

16 ● The International Game

Golf is a typical capitalist lunacy of upper-class Edwardian England.

GEORGE BERNARD SHAW

Individually, they are pretty nice folks. But get them together and they are about as miserable a bunch of people as you could ever have the misfortune to run into in a supposedly civilized world.

TOMMY BOLT, on the British, *Los Angeles Times,* 1957

'Are those mosquitoes dangerous?' I asked the hotel manager. 'Not if you've had spotted fever, malaria, and dengue fever,' he said.

SAM SNEAD, in the Belgian Congo,
The Education of a Golfer, 1962

I only came here because I heard the Irish hate the British as much as I do.

DAVE HILL, playing in Dublin

Everyone is studying golf technique like mad. Every young lad now aspires to be another Palmer or another Nicklaus. We may go centuries before we produce another playwright.
JOE CARR, Irish amateur, *The New Yorker,* **1967**

It has been estimated that more golf poetry exists in Scotland than heather.
DAN JENKINS, *The Dogged Victims of Inexorable Fate,* **1970**

What else is there to do over there? Wear a skirt?
GEORGE LOW, on golf in Scotland

We [Americans] invented wind and rough, hooks and slices, bunkers and doglegs, and we were just getting ready to invent the over-lapping grip when Henry Vardon, an Englishman, beat us to it.
DAN JENKINS, in *The Dogged Victims of Inexorable Fate,* **1970**

We had to eat everything with our fingers, except a piece of fish. They gave me a toothpick to eat that. Hell, I've got a cat back home in Texas who eats with a fork!
LEE TREVINO, at the British Open, Muirfield, **1972**

A stroke may be played again if interrupted by gunfire or sudden explosion.
LOCAL CLUB RULE, Rhodesia, **1972**

After all these years, it's still embarrassing for me to play on the American golf tour. Like the time I asked my caddie for a sand wedge and he came back ten minutes later with a ham on rye.
CHI CHI RODRIGUEZ, Puerto Rican touring pro

Certainly they [the greens] are the greenest, which is hardly surprising in a country where housewives habitually peep out of their cottage windows and observe that it is a beautiful day for hanging the washing out to rinse.
PETER DOBEREINER on Ireland, *The Glorious World of Golf,* 1973

Man, in this country there are no strangers. Even to a coloured guy like me, everybody is a friend.
RABBIT DYER, American caddie of Gary Player at the
British Open, 1974

I had this prejudice against the British, until I discovered that fifty per cent of them were female.
RAYMOND FLOYD, *Golf Digest,* 1977

The key to British links golf is the word 'frustration'. You can hit the perfect shot and, all of a sudden, it will bounce straight right or, for no apparent reason, jump beyond the hole. . . If I played over here four straight weeks I'd be a raving lunatic.
TOM WATSON, in *The Sunday Times,* 1977

All I could think of was those movies and what Texans did to strangers they didn't like. Nine out of ten they get lynched. I really was afraid I might get lynched.
BRUCE CRAMPTON, Australian professional, playing in the
Houston Open in 1957, *Golf Digest,* 1978

I love it here in the United States. In Japan I have no privacy. In the States I can have a hole in my jeans and nobody will notice.
AYAKO OKAMOTO, *The Sporting News,* 1984

Every round I play I shorten my life by two years.
TOMMY NAKAJIMA, on the tough tour courses in the
United States, 1984

In Britain, you skip the ball, hop it, bump it, run it, hit under it, on top of it and then hope for the right bounce.
DOUG SANDERS, *Sports Illustrated*, **1984**

Birkdale Golf Club, Royal, Southport

At fifteen, we put down my bag to hunt for a ball – found the ball, lost the bag.
LEE TREVINO, *Sports Illustrated*, **1983**

The clubhouse looks like the main terminal of the Entebbe Airport.
PETER RYDE, *Times* writer

Carnoustie Golf Club, Carnoustie

I've got a lawn mower back in Texas. I'll send it over.
BEN HOGAN, at the British Open, **1953**

A good swamp, spoiled.
GARY PLAYER, *GolfWorld*, **1975**

Tom Watson likens Carnoustie to an ugly old woman who at least is honest with you: when you add up your score after your round, she tells you what she thinks of you.
HERBERT WARREN WIND, *The New Yorker*, **1981**

The weather was dreadful. It was gray and mean and awful – blowy and cold as it so often is in the United Kingdom. And it was July!
BEN WRIGHT, on his first visit, *Good Bounces and Bad Lies*, **1999**

Dornoch Golf Club, Royal, Dornoch, Sutherland

When you play it, you get the feeling you could be living just as easily in the eighteen-hundreds, or even the seventeen-hundreds. If an old Scot in a red jacket had popped out from behind a sand dune, beating a feather ball, I wouldn't have blinked an eye.
PETER DYE, golf course architect, *The New Yorker,* **1964**

'Dornoch's simply too far out of the way,' he explained. 'I've no reason to go anyplace near there. I have all the Shetland sweaters I need.'
HERBERT WARREN WIND, quoting a British friend in
The New Yorker, **1964**

Muirfield, East Lothian

When there is no wind and rain, this course is like a lady without a dress on – no challenge for a guy.
TOM WATSON, **1987**

Prestwick Golf Club, Prestwick, Ayrshire

The green was there, all right, as are all of the greens at Prestwick, but you never see them until you are on them, which is usually eight or ten strokes after leaving the tee.
DAN JENKINS, *The Dogged Victims of Inexorable Fate,* **1970**

You would like to gather up several holes from Prestwick and mail them to your top ten enemies.
DAN JENKINS, as above

Royal Lytham and St Annes, St Annes

Fourteen is where the back nine begins.
EDDIE BIRCHENOUGH, club pro, *Independent on Sunday*, **2001**

The Lytham greens are harder to read than *Finnegans Wake*.
MARK REASON, during the Open, *Sunday Telegraph*, **2001**

St Andrews, Old Course, Fife

You can play a damned good shot there and find the ball in a damned bad place!
GEORGE DUNCAN, British professional, *The American Golfer,* **1923**

Say, that looks like an old, abandoned golf course. What did they call it?
SAM SNEAD, upon first seeing St Andrews, **1946**

You have to study it, and the more you study, the more you learn; the more you learn, the more you study it.
BOBBY JONES, **1958**

There's nothing wrong with the St Andrews course that a hundred bulldozers couldn't put right.
ED FURGOL, American touring professional

The Old Course needs a dry clean and press.
ED FURGOL

The only place over there that's holier than St Andrews is Westminster Abbey.
SAM SNEAD, *The Education of a Golfer,* **1962**

So many Britons know each bunker by its designated name and could probably walk out blindfolded from the first tee to any one you mentioned.
HERBERT WARREN WIND, in *The New Yorker,* **1962**

Know what I really feel about St Andrews? I feel like I'm back visiting an old grandmother. She's crotchety and eccentric, but also elegant and anyone who doesn't fall in love with her has no imagination.
TONY LEMA, American professional, **1964**

I don't know whether you have ever played St Andrews in the wind, but it has been known to make scratch players switch to tennis.
CHARLES PRICE, in *The American Golfer,* **1964**

Those greens on St Andrews used to be so crisp that you could hear the crunch your spikes made when they cut into the turf. Oh, they were fast!
BOBBY JONES, in *The New Yorker,* **1968**

In the galleries, there were lots of dogs, which never barked, and lots of children, who didn't howl or fuss, which is the way it is in Scotland.
HERBERT WARREN WIND, *The New Yorker,* **1970**

The Road Hole, the seventeenth, is the most famous and infamous hole . . . As a planner and builder of golf holes worldwide, I have no hesitation in allowing that if one built such a hole today you would be sued for incompetence.
PETER THOMSON, *Golf Digest,* **1984**

The reason the Road Hole is the greatest par-four in the world is because it's a par-five.
BEN CRENSHAW, *Sports Illustrated,* **1984**

I hate its arrogant lumps and bumps and the times you must play shots with one leg up in the air.

NEIL COLES, **1984**

There is no place in the world that I would rather win a championship.

JACK NICKLAUS, **1984**

My first impression of St Andrews was one of strange ambiguousness. I didn't like it, nor, for that matter, did I hate it. I've never been so puzzled after a first practice round in my life.

TOM WATSON, in *Golf Magazine,* **1984**

It's sickening to drive dead straight and see some fairway hump divert the ball into a bunker or the whins.

PETER ALLISS, **1984**

It finds you out. If there is one part of your game not right, no matter how you try to hide it – to protect it – the Old Course will find it during the championship.

PETER THOMSON, **1984**

In St Andrews the spirit of golf fills the air as nowhere else. To be in the old grey town when a crackling good Open is being played – what more can one ask?

HERBERT WARREN WIND, in *Following Through,* **1985**

It's a great golf hole. It gives you a million options, not one of them worth a damn.

TOM KITE about the thirteenth at St Andrews, **1990**

It's a dashed good job it's there otherwise, in this weather and with the clubs these guys are using, this place would be no more than a pitch and putt course.
Unnamed policeman about the Road Hole during the
British Open, **1990**

My most common mistake at St Andrews is turning up.
MARK JAMES

You must never get mad at St Andrews. You must be willing to accept exactly what you get. Then you must keep on trying. Keep a clear mind all the time. For there are so many humps and hollows that it is easy to allow your mind to become tangled with frustration. Once you start seeking excuses, St Andrews has got you beat.
GERALD MICKLEM, British golf administrator, handwritten
advice to a then twenty-year-old Nick Faldo in 1978,
Nick Faldo: Driven, **2001**

St George's, Royal, Kent

A fine spring day, with the larks singing as they seem to sing nowhere else; the sun shining on the waters of Pegwell Bay and lighting up the white cliffs in the distance; this is as nearly my idea of heaven as is to be attained on any earthly links.
BERNARD DARWIN, golf writer

Augusta National Golf Club, Augusta, Georgia

There isn't a hole out there that can't be birdied if you just think. But there isn't one that can't be double-bogeyed if you stop thinking.
BOBBY JONES

The greens *are* the course. . . They are faster than a fart in a hot skillet.
DAVE HILL, *Teed Off,* **1977**

The only difference is at Augusta the divots tear loose on dotted lines.
JOHN UPDIKE, *Thirteen Ways of Looking at The Masters,* **1980**

We could make them [the greens] so slick we'd have to furnish ice skates on the first tee.
HORD HARDIN, Augusta National chairman,
Golf Digest, **1981**

Amen Corner looks like something that fell from heaven, but it plays like something straight out of hell.
GARY VAN SICKLE, *Milwaukee Journal,* **1981**

They say position is required at Augusta and it's true. Put it 320 yards from where you're standing and you're perfect.
HOWARD TWITTY, on the need for length,
Golf Magazine, **1983**

There is a saying around north Georgia that the Augusta National Golf Club is the closest thing to heaven for a golfer – and it's just about as hard to get into.
JOE GESHWILER, *San Francisco Examiner,* **1983**

I kept telling Tom, 'Let's go ahead and hit before they suspend play.' That's one hole you don't want to wake up to.
MARK LYE, to Tom Kite on the par-three twelfth hole, **1984**

I was shocked at where Augusta National was. I thought it was in the middle of nowhere. Nobody told me it was across the street from a shopping plaza.
PAUL AZINGER, *GolfWorld,* **1991**

The biophilia of Augusta is so beautiful. Then, suddenly, the course mutilates you. And you haven't done anything wrong. It's like a black widow. It seduces you, entices you – and then it stings you, kills you emotionally.

MAC O'GRADY, *Golf Magazine*, **1993**

Driving down Magnolia Lane melts down your spikes. You can't tee off quick enough.

GREG NORMAN, *GolfWorld*, **1993**

I remember the first time I went to the range at Augusta National and took a divot. I looked down and the dirt was green. I couldn't believe it.

KENNY KNOX, US pro, *GolfWorld*, **1993**

If it weren't for the greens, this course would be nothing.

STEVE SCOTT, US amateur, after shooting a seventy-nine to miss the cut in the Masters, **1997**

I think it took Prince Andrew a little while to get acclimated to Southern hospitality. In the UK, you don't exactly approach the royal family . . . Augusta, Georgia, was sort of a different world for him.

FRED RIDLEY, USGA president and Augusta National member, after hosting Prince Andrew at the Masters, *GolfWorld*, **2004**

Bel-Air Golf Club, Los Angeles, California

W.C. Fields was fond of playing the course sideways with his pal, Oliver Hardy. He liked being in the trees where he could drink without scandalizing the natives.

JIM MURRAY, *Golf Digest,* **1973**

Butler National Golf Club, Oak Brook, Illinois

If the USGA ever got its hands on this course, it would be all over.
DAVE STOCKTON, on the 75.34 course rating, **1975**

I used to dream that I could be a waiter in a place like this.
CHI CHI RODRIGUEZ, *San Francisco Examiner,* **1983**

Colonial Country Club, Fort Worth, Texas

Colonial is the halter-top capital of the world.
TOM BROOKSHIER, sports commentator, *Texas Monthly,* **1977**

If you don't like what you see at Colonial, you're too old to be looking.
NORM ALDEN, Fort Worth disc jockey, *Texas Monthly,* **1977**

The Country Club, Brookline, Massachusetts

To me, the ground here is hallowed. The grass grows greener, the trees bloom better, there is even a warmth to the rocks. I don't know, gentlemen, but somehow or other the sun seems to shine brighter on The Country Club than any other place that I have known.
FRANCIS OUIMET, **1932**

Cypress Point Golf Club, Pebble Beach, California

Cypress Point is a dream . . . so bewilderingly picturesque that it seems to have been the crystallization of the dream of an artist who has been drinking gin and sobering up on absinthe.
O. B. KEELER, *The American Golfer,* **1929**

Cypress Point is the Sistine Chapel of golf.
FRANK (SANDY) TATUM, former USGA president

Cypress – what a course that is. It has the looks of Christie
Brinkley and the tenderness of Tokyo Rose.
BOB HOPE, *Golf Magazine,* **1983**

Cypress Point is so exclusive that it had a membership drive
and drove out forty members.
BOB HOPE

Firestone Country Club, South Course, Akron, Ohio

The Winner at Firestone? Par!
Headline, *Golf Magazine,* **1976**

I just can't play this course. It eats my lunch. Firestone's a
long-iron course. I'd just as soon pull a rattlesnake out of my
bag as a two-iron.
LEE TREVINO, *Golf Digest,* **1979**

Harbour Town Golf Club, Hilton Head Island,
South Carolina

Harbour Town is so tough even your clubs get tired.
CHARLES PRICE, *Golf Magazine,* **1970**

I like to putt the Harbour Town greens. They're so bumpy the
gallery can't tell when I have the yips.
LARRY ZIEGLER, *Golf Digest,* **1978**

Hazeltine Golf Club, Chaska, Minnesota

The greens resembled Indian burial mounds more than anything else. And their horses had been buried along with the Indians.

DAVE HILL, *Teed Off,* **1977**

Houston Country Club, Houston, Texas

The Houston Country Club has gold dust instead of sand in the traps and the greens are irrigated with oil. It is home base for those hackneyed caricatures, the Texas zillionaire and his lady hung with ice cubes.

RED SMITH, A *Hundred and Four Years Old,* **1964**

Kemper Lakes GC, Hawthorn Woods, Illinois

Classy golf courses are not named after insurance executives. Trust me on this. I didn't make it up. Nowhere in the lore of golf is there talk of Kemper Beach, Kemper Valley, St Kemper, Royal Kemper, Kemperhurst No. 2, Kempercock Hills, Winged Kemper, Cypress Kemper. Classy golf courses are named for oaks, rivers, creeks, forests, monts and rols.

DAN JENKINS, on the naming of the course for James Kemper, CEO of Kemper Insurance, *Golf Digest,* **1989**

Lakeside Country Club, Los Angeles, California

A requirement at Lakeside was that you be able to hold your booze. That was the club of the hard-drinking Irish and the gag, standard for admission, was that you had to be able to kill a fifth in nine holes.

JIM MURRAY, *Los Angeles Times*

Los Angeles Country Club, North Course, Los Angeles, California

The eight hundred members comprise the elite of California and legend has it that when one member proposed a movie star for membership once, they not only turned the star down, they threw out the guy who proposed him.
JIM MURRAY, *The Sporting World of Jim Murray,* **1968**

Medinah Country Club, Number Three, Medinah, Illinois

Golf architects dream about creating such a hole. Players dream about boiling architects in oil.
JOHN MARSHALL, resident pro, on the tough par-three seventeenth hole

Melbourne Golf Club, Royal, Melbourne, Victoria

If you can imagine a hole halfway down the bonnet of a Volkswagen Beetle, and then you have to putt it from the roof.
NICK FALDO, describing the putting surfaces, **1990**

Merion Golf Club, East Course, Ardmore, Pennsylvania

If you hit this green with your second shot, you heave a sigh so deep that it is usually audible a mashie shot away.
ROBERT TRENT JONES, on the par-four eleventh hole 'Merion'

I didn't beat Merion. I just compromised with her, like a wife, trying not to let her have her way too often.
LEE TREVINO, upon winning the US Open, **1971**

That course doesn't even belong in the top 200! They have to grow rough up to your rear end to make it playable for the Open.

SAM SNEAD, *Golf Digest*, **1981**

Merion wouldn't alter that course for the Second Coming, let alone another golf championship.

CHARLES PRICE, *Golf Magazine*, **1981**

Muirfield Village Golf Club, Dublin, Ohio

The Muirfield Village golf course near Columbus, Ohio, site of last week's tournament, was in such immaculate condition that people would sooner have dropped cigarette butts on their babies' tummies.

DAN JENKINS, *Sports Illustrated*, **1977**

They should have slippers at every hole and pass a rule that you have to take off your shoes before going to the green. They shouldn't be walked on with cleats.

LEE TREVINO

Do you realize water comes into play on eighteen shots? That's *eighteen shots*!

TOM WEISKOPF

Oakland Hills Country Club, South Course, Birmingham, Michigan

The course is playing the players instead of the players playing the course.

WALTER HAGEN, at the US Open, **1951**

I am glad to have brought this monster to its knees.
BEN HOGAN, at the presentation ceremonies of the
US Open, **1951**

I don't want to make it a lady's course, but I don't want every
hole to play like the last one I'm ever going to play.
LIONEL HEBERT, aged fifty-three, at the US Senior Open,
San Francisco Examiner, **1981**

Oakmont Country Club, Oakmont, Pennsylvania

You gotta sneak up on these holes. If you clamber and clank
up on 'em, they're liable to turn around and bite you.
SAM SNEAD, **1953**

This is a course where good putters worry about their
second putt before they hit the first one.
LEW WORSHAM, Oakmont club professional

You could have combed North Africa with it, and Rommel
wouldn't have gotten past Casablanca.
JIMMY DEMARET, on the special rake designed for the traps,
Golf Magazine, **1983**

Pebble Beach Golf Links, Pebble Beach, California

Pebble Beach is Alcatraz with grass.
BOB HOPE, at the Bing Crosby National Pro-Am, **1952**

It's like fighting Rocky Marciano . . . every time you step
onto the course, you're a cinch to take a beating.
JACKIE BURKE, C. **1950s**

If you moved Pebble Beach fifty miles inland, no one would have heard of it.
JIMMY DEMARET

Pebble Beach is the world's leading argument for indoor golf.
DAN JENKINS, sportswriter

This here is a pivotal hole. If you're five over par when you hit this tee, it's the best place in the world to commit suicide.
LEE TREVINO, at the sixth hole, *Golf Digest,* **1978**

The only thing gonna stick around that hole is a dart! Yesterday I was on in three, off in four! They oughta put one of them miniature windmills on this thing and charge fifty cents to play it.
LEE TREVINO, at the fourteenth hole, *Golf Digest,* **1978**

I thought the course treated me rather cruelly. I'm not an obnoxious guy. I don't throw clubs. I'm nice to galleries. I don't deserve some of the things Pebble Beach did to me.
WILLIAM ISRAELSON, Minnesota professional,
San Francisco Examiner, **1982**

I've heard of unplayable lies, but on the tee?
BOB HOPE, *Confessions of a Hooker,* **1985**

Pinehurst Country Club, Number Two, Pinehurst, North Carolina

The man who doesn't feel emotionally stirred when he golfs at Pinehurst beneath those clear blue skies and with the pine fragrance in his nostrils is one who should be ruled out of golf for life.
TOMMY ARMOUR, C. **1960s**

I've been asked many times, what's the hardest golf course I've ever played? Now I have the answer.

LEE JANZEN, *GolfWorld*, **2005**

Pine Valley Golf Club, Clementon, New Jersey

Tell me, do you chaps actually play this hole – or just photograph it?

EUSTACE STOREY, British amateur, on his first look at the second hole, c. **1920s**

You don't make 'recoveries' at Pine Valley, except of course from the sand traps – you merely push your way into the undergrowth and endeavour to knock your ball out through the bushes to where it ought to have been in the first place.

HENRY LONGHURST, *It Was Good While It Lasted*, **1941**

It has no rough, in the accepted sense of the term, and no semi-rough. Your ball is either on the fairway, in which case it sits invitingly on a flawless carpet of turf, or it is not. If it is not, you play out sideways till it is.

HENRY LONGHURST

In all my travels, I do not think I've seen a more beautiful landscape. This is as thrilling as Versailles or Fontainbleau.

LOWELL THOMAS, American radio news commentator, early **1950s**

'You ever play Pine Valley?' I asked her. 'There's a tough course! Texas with bunkers!'

REX LARDNER, *Out of the Bunker and Into the Trees,* **1960**

Pine Valley is the shrine of American golf because so many golfers are buried there.
ED SULLIVAN, American television personality,
Philadelphia Bulletin, **1966**

Pine Valley . . . a weekend in a mental ward.
CHARLES PRICE, *Golf Digest,* **1983**

Here is the ultimate expression of sado-masochistic golf, the supreme example of the penal school of architecture. A Philadelphia businessman, George Crump, conceived the idea, possibly during a nightmare.
PETER DOBEREINER, *Down the Nineteenth Fairway,* **1983**

Pine Valley has been described as one huge bunker dotted with eighteen greens, eighteen tees and about that many more target areas.
MIKE BRYAN, *Golf Magazine,* **1983**

It looks as though a squad of Marines ought to be raising a flag over it.
CHARLES PRICE, on the second green atop a hill,
International Magazine, **1987**

Preston Trail Golf Club, Dallas, Texas

If I were ever tempted to get a big head, all I'd have to do is go out and play a round at Preston Trail. Every guy out there can buy and sell me ten times. It puts things in perspective real quick.
LANNY WADKINS, *Golf Digest,* **1983**

Rancho La Costa, Carlsbad, California

Arnold Palmer had no trouble at all taking a twelve there last year although I must say if he played it a little smarter he could have made a nine.

JIM MURRAY, on the ninth hole,
The Sporting World of Jim Murray, **1968**

Riviera Golf Club, Pacific Palisades, California

Very nice course. But tell me, where do the members play?
BOBBY JONES, c. **1930s**

Where's the rest of the fairway? Who stole half of your hole?
GARY PLAYER, upon seeing the narrow par-four eighth hole,
c. **1950s**

Sawgrass Golf Club, Ponte Vedra Beach, Florida

This is the first time I ever withdrew while my ball was still airborne.
CESAR SANUDO, walking off the course after hitting three balls
in the water on the ninth hole at the Tournament Players
Championship, **1977**

We call him [the alligator] Mr Sawgrass, or sometimes Sir. But like everyone else here he doesn't spend a great deal of time on the fairways.
JIM BLANKS, Sawgrass associate professional,
Golf Digest, **1977**

Southern Hills Country Club, Tulsa, Oklahoma

This hole is 614 yards. The person I played my practice round with said you don't need a road map for this one, you need a passport.
JAY CRONLEY, on the fifth hole, *Golf Digest,* **1977**

Speidel Golf Club, Wheeling, West Virginia

When you get to your ball, you're too tired to hit it.
ROBYN DUMMETT, touring professional, c. **1970s**

Spyglass Hill Golf Club, Pebble Beach, California

Pebble Beach and Cypress Point make you want to play, they're such interesting and enjoyable layouts. Spyglass Hill – that's different; that makes you want to go fishing.
JACK NICKLAUS, *The Greatest Game of All,* **1969**

Not long ago two doctors started out with three dozen golf balls. They had to send the caddie in for a new supply after six holes.
CAL BROWN, *Golf Digest,* **1971**

They ought to hang the man who designed this course. Ray Charles could have done better.
LEE TREVINO, *San Francisco Chronicle,* **1985**

Torrey Pines Golf Club, La Jolla, California

I always play better on the North Course. It's cooler over there, closer to the North Pole.
GARY MCCORD, *San Jose Mercury News,* **1984**

Tournament Players Club at Eagle Trace, Coral Springs, Florida

I like the balance of the course – I shot 41–41.
JACK NICKLAUS, *Golf Digest,* **1984**

Tournament Players Club at Sawgrass, Ponte Vedra Beach, Florida

It's too early to rate this course. It's like trying to rate girls when they're born. They get better later.
JERRY PATE, *San Jose Mercury News,* **1982**

If you birdie the eighteenth, do you win a free game?
JOHN MAHAFFEY, *San Francisco Examiner,* **1982**

It's *Star Wars* golf. The place was designed by Darth Vader.
BEN CRENSHAW, *Sports Illustrated,* **1982**

I've never been very good at stopping a five-iron on the hood of a car.
JACK NICKLAUS, *Sports Illustrated,* **1982**

To play well on this course you have to be both skilful and lucky, and if you are both skilful and lucky your name is Jack Nicklaus.
CHI CHI RODRIGUEZ, *Golf Digest,* **1983**

The only way to improve it would be to put the green on a barge and have it float around the lagoon.
DALE HAYES, on the island-green seventeenth hole,
Golf Digest, **1984**

It's the easiest par-five on the course.
JOHN MAHAFFEY, on the par-three seventeenth,
Golf Digest, **1984**

Winged Foot Golf Club, Mamaroneck, New York

To match par on this course you've got to be luckier than a
dog with two tails.
SAM SNEAD

A motorist attempting to leave the Winged Foot Golf Club
takes a wrong turn and accidentally drives across the first
green. He does no damage at all. The green holds up like
asphalt.
DICK SCHAAP, *Massacre at Winged Foot,* **1974**

Putting on these greens is like playing miniature golf without
the boards.
HALE IRWIN, at the US Open, **1974**

Spectator: C'mon, Johnny, hit it close.
Miller: On this course, it doesn't do any good to get it close.
JOHNNY MILLER, at the US Open, **1974**

Winged Foot has the toughest eighteen finishing holes in
golf.
DAVE MARR, *'US Open',* ESPN-TV, **1984**

17 ● The Majors

British Open

Their only fault is that they give no possible excuse for a missed putt.

BOBBY JONES, on the greens at Hoylake, **1930**

I should have played that hole in an ambulance.

ARNOLD PALMER, on his ten strokes at the seventeenth hole at St Andrews, **1960**

What did I want with prestige? The British Open paid the winner $600 in American money. A man would have to be two hundred years old at that rate to retire from golf.

SAM SNEAD, on why he hesitated going to Scotland in 1946, *The Education of a Golfer,* **1962**

If I could have had the periscope, the lost-ball, and the hay concessions, I think I'd be the leading money-winner now.

DOUG SANDERS, American professional, at the British Open, **1966**

Any golfer worth his salt has to cross the sea and try to win the British Open.
JACK NICKLAUS, **1970**

I thought I'd blown it at the seventeenth green when I drove into a trap. God is a Mexican.
LEE TREVINO, eventual winner at Muirfield, **1972**

Wind is part of the British Open. It is an examination and it took me a long time to pass the examination. Eighty per cent of the fellows out there have not passed the test.
GARY PLAYER, **1974**

How do you do, Mr Prime Minister – ever shake hands with a Mexican before?
LEE TREVINO, meeting Prime Minister Edward Heath,
Sport, **1978**

The winner, Severiano Ballesteros, chose not to use the course but preferred his own, which mainly consisted of hay fields, car parks, grandstands, dropping zones and even ladies' clothing.
COLIN MACLAINE, Chairman of the Championship Committee, **1979**

I guess it was inevitable. Remember all those good breaks I had here in 1972? Well, Muirfield just caught up with me.
LEE TREVINO, **1980**

I'm disappointed. They have us playing American golf. I didn't come to play American golf. I came here to play British golf.
TOM WATSON, on the faster pace than usual, **1981**

When Ballesteros triumphed at the British Open in 1979, for his first major win, he hit so few fairways off the tee that he was often mistaken for a gallery marshall.
DAN JENKINS, *Sports Illustrated,* **1983**

All my life I wanted to play golf like Jack Nicklaus, and now I do.
PAUL HARVEY, news commentator, after Nicklaus shot an eighty-three at Royal St George's, **1981**

I had my second-place speech all prepared.
TOM WATSON, after Nick Price collapsed in the final round, **1982**

I'm a serious contender this week. How can they beat me? I've been struck by lightning, had two back operations and been divorced twice.
LEE TREVINO, at Royal Birkdale, *Sports Illustrated,* **1983**

Actually, my plan was to be twenty under par after two days but it didn't work.
LEE TREVINO, leading at the halfway mark, **1984**

The romance has gone out of it as far as American players go. It's the bottom line. Everyone wants to make a buck.
PETER JACOBSEN, American professional, on why many of his countrymen passed up the Open, **1985**

To me, the Open is the tournament I would come to if I had to leave a month before and swim over.
LEE TREVINO, **1985**

Is winning the Open worth a million pounds? Well, it's worthwhile winning it – I would recommend it to anybody!
SANDY LYLE, defending Open champion, Turnberry, **1986**

I never felt I could be a complete professional without having won the British Open. It was something you had to do to complete your career.

ARNOLD PALMER, **1990**

I never thought I'd live to see golf played so well.

GENE SARAZEN, on Greg Norman's victory in the
Open at Royal St George's, *Daily Mail*, **1993**

In 1982 I had my left hand on this trophy. In 1988 I had my right hand on the trophy. Now finally I have it in both hands.

NICK PRICE, after winning the Open at Turnberry GL, **1994**

C'mon, I'm the guy who's retiring, not you.

JACK NICKLAUS, after Tom Watson became teary-eyed during
their practice round at St Andrews prior to Nicklaus's final Open,
LIFE, **2005**

I think they would allow a trained monkey to play in the Open just to create attention.

KATHRYN MARSHALL, Scottish LPGA player, on the R&A's
removal of a male-only requirement for eligibility, **2005**

If you don't like golf, then you may as well move out for a week.

STEVE MORRIS, security official for the 2006 British Open at
Royal Liverpool GC, Wirral, on anticipated heavy traffic,
including eighty helicopter landings an hour, **2005**

The Masters

I'll be back every year, if I have to walk fifteen hundred miles to do it.

HERMAN KEISER, upon winning the Masters, **1946**

I'm a stupid. I just signed a wrong card. . . But I congratulate Bob Goalby, he gave me so much pressure that I lose my brain.

ROBERTO DE VICENZO, who signed for a four instead of a three for the seventeenth hole, losing the Masters by one shot, **1968**

When [Clifford] Roberts had first asked the show's sponsors . . . for fewer commercials, an agency man in New York had said, 'What does he think the Masters is, a moon shot?' The answer was no. Clifford Roberts thought the Masters was infinitely more important than that.

DAN JENKINS, *The Dogged Victims of Inexorable Fate*, **1970**

This is the only course I know where you choke when you come in the gate.

LIONEL HEBERT, **1970**

You can lick this course with your normal game – if you ever calm down enough to play your normal game.

FRANK BEARD, *Pro*, **1970**

Here's your headline for a picture of that: *Casper to Knees: Lord Says No.*

GEORGE ARCHER, as Billy Casper missed a putt at the eighteenth hole for an outright win, **1970**

On the fifteenth hole I had started thinking about the green jacket. They gave it to Charles Coody.

JOHNNY MILLER, finishing second, **1971**

The tournament brass will stop at nothing to keep Palmer happy. There is a story that he left the eleventh fairway one year to go into the woods and relieve himself. The next year a permanent restroom had been built on the spot.

DAVE HILL, *Teed Off,* **1977**

Green grass, green grandstands, green concession stalls, green paper cups, green folding chairs and visors for sale, green-and-white ropes, green-topped Georgia pines. . . If justice were poetic, Hubert Green would win it every year.

JOHN UPDIKE, *Thirteen Ways of Looking at the Masters,* **1980**

Reporter: Exactly what size is that jacket?
Stadler: I don't know, I'm not about to take it off and find out.

CRAIG STADLER, Masters champion, **1982**

My, even the fairways are fast!

BYRON NELSON, playing an exhibition before the Masters,
The New Yorker, **1982**

If you don't get an invitation, it's like being out of the world a whole week.

DOUG FORD, *San Francisco Examiner,* **1982**

The Masters is more like a vast Edwardian garden party than a golf tournament.

ALISTAIR COOKE, *TV Guide,* **1983**

If you didn't know better, six hours of the Masters on CBS could leave you with the feeling that Augusta National Golf Club is a holy land and the winner of the tournament will be passing through a corridor where no mere mortal will ever tread.

TOM GILMORE, *San Francisco Chronicle,* **1984**

I think Bobby Jones held up his hand from somewhere and said: 'That's enough, boy.'
NICK PRICE, after his course-record sixty-three during the third round of the Masters, **1986**

I don't visualize us having the Pizza Hut Masters.
HORD HARDIN, chairman of Augusta National, asked about possible corporate sponsorship, **1988**

You play a lot of rounds as a kid thinking you're at Augusta. And I never shot *that* good.
MIKE DONALD after a first-round sixty-four in the Masters, **1990**

A victory would have meant so much, you can't imagine. To win a major at this stage of my career would have been my wildest dream come true.
RAY FLOYD on losing the Masters to Nick Faldo, **1990**

I have a love-hate relationship with the Masters – I love it when I arrive and I hate it when I leave.
PAUL AZINGER, **1995**

Professional Golfers Association Championship

He may have gone to bed three hours ago. But he knows who he is playing. You can rest assured that he hasn't slept a wink.
WALTER HAGEN, on his match-play opponent, **1919**

I guess I was just plain scared to win that dude.
DON JANUARY, after losing in a play-off to Jerry Barber, **1961**

Another weekend with nothing to do.
ARNOLD PALMER, after missing the cut, *Golf Digest,* **1978**

The crowd was mumbling about Nicklaus, but I didn't need them to tell me that the Bear was coming.
HAL SUTTON, holding off Nicklaus to win, *Sports Illustrated,* **1983**

When I saw that four-inch putt for a par at eighteen. I have a good percentage at handling four-inch putts.
HAL SUTTON'S answer to the question, 'When did you think you had won the championship?' **1983**

United States Open Championship

Any player can win a US Open, but it takes a helluva player to win two.
WALTER HAGEN

I can't see why I broke so badly. Why, I am sure I could go out now and do better by kicking the ball around with my boot.
HARRY VARDON, on his seventy-eight in the final round, **1920**

Nobody wins the Open. It wins you.
DR CARY MIDDLECOFF

Palmer: Doesn't 280 always win the Open?
Jenkins: Yeah, when Hogan shoots it.
ARNOLD PALMER, and DAN JENKINS, sportswriter, at Cherry Hills, **1960**

I may buy the Alamo and give it back to Mexico.
LEE TREVINO, asked what he'd do with the winnings, **1968**

Well, I'm gonna buy this place. It doesn't have indoor plumbing.
LEE TREVINO, after going to San Antonio and seeing the Alamo,
1968

It was like unhitching a horse from a plough and winning the Kentucky Derby, or a guy stepping out of the audience, removing his coat and knocking out the heavyweight champion of the world.
JIM MURRAY, on unheralded Orville Moody winning
the US Open, *Los Angeles Times,* **1969**

What does it matter who Orville Moody is? At least he brought the title back to America.
DAVE MARR, on Moody succeeding Lee Trevino as the
US Open champion, **1969**

Another writer asked me what I thought the course needed and I said eighty acres of corn and a few cows. I borrowed that crack from Bob Rosburg.
DAVE HILL, on Hazeltine Golf Club, site of the 1970 US Open

One other important thing about this victory, it proved that my British Open victory was no fluke. It's always been my contention that the winners of major tournaments are the true champions, although at times some luck may play a part in the victory. Naturally, after I won the British Open, I entertained some suspicious thoughts about luck, but when I won the US Open, this was all dissolved.
TONY JACKLIN, on winning the 1970 US Open,
Great Moments in Golf

When I was walking down the fairway, I saw a bunch of USGA guys down on their hands and knees parting the rough trying to find my ball. I knew I was in trouble.

JIM COLBERT, on the US Open at Winged Foot Golf Club, **1974**.

It couldn't have been too bad a lie. I could still see your knees.

HUBERT GREEN, to Lanny Wadkins at Winged Foot, **1974**

The fringe around the greens isn't fringe at all but long grass . . . The scrambler is better off back home eating beer nuts and watching it on TV.

DAN GLEASON, on US Open courses,
The Great, The Grand and the Also-Ran, **1976**

All of a sudden I'm an expert on everything. Interviewers want your opinion of golf, foreign policy and even the price of peanuts.

HUBERT GREEN, upon winning the Open, **1977**

He played almost the entire final round without putting his spikes to a fairway. He spent so much time in sand that if you held his wedge to your ear, you could hear the ocean.

JOE GERGEN, on J. C. Snead, who finished second in the Open at Cherry Hills Country Club, *Newsday*, **1978**

I was so charged up I couldn't turn my engine off. I think this may have had something to do with the fact that I ran out of gas on the second nine today. I was operating just on vapour.

HALE IRWIN, after winning the Open at Inverness,
The New Yorker, **1979**

That's the way it is at the US Open golf tournament. Whoever's in the lead feels like the first guy onto the beach at Normandy on D-day.
GARY NUHN, *Dayton Daily News,* **1979**

There's really not much to do. We're just mowing the greens and letting the rough grow. When it gets so that only a couple of guys on our staff can break eighty it will be ready.
STEVE MCLENNAN, head pro, Pebble Beach, preparing the course for the Open, **1982**

Watson is doing to Nicklaus what Nicklaus was doing to me twenty years ago. I knew exactly what Nicklaus was thinking when Watson's chip went in.
ARNOLD PALMER, on Tom Watson's winning chip shot at the seventeenth hole at Pebble Beach to win the Open, **1982**

That took all the wind out of my sails and I just really never had a chance to get much going the rest of the year. It doesn't often happen with a shot by somebody else; you usually do it to yourself.
JACK NICKLAUS, on Watson's chip, *Golf Digest,* **1983**

When I saw Jack Nicklaus hit some shots out of it sideways yesterday, I was convinced it was tough.
LANNY WADKINS, on the rough at Oakmont Country Club, *San Francisco Chronicle,* **1983**

The US Open flag eliminates a lot of players. Some players just weren't meant to win the US Open. Quite often, a lot of them know it.
JACK NICKLAUS, *Golf Digest,* **1983**

18 ● Match Play

Do not allow yourself to be annoyed because your opponent insists on making elaborate study of all his putts.

HORACE G. HUTCHINSON, *Hints on the Game of Golf*, 1886

A secret disbelief in the enemy's play is very useful for match play.

SIR WALTER SIMPSON, *The Art of Golf*, 1887

A golf course exists primarily for match play, which is a sport, as distinguished from stroke play, which more resembles rifle shooting than a sport in that it lacks the joy of personal contact with an opponent.

FREDDIE TAIT, British professional, c. 1890s

A good player who is a great putter is a match for any golfer. A great hitter who cannot putt is a match for no one.

BEN SAYERS, Scottish professional, c. 1890s

This made him two up and three to play. What an average golfer would consider a commanding lead. But Archibald was no average golfer. A commanding lead for him would have been two up and one to play.
P. G. WODEHOUSE, *Archibald's Benefit,* **1919**

You know, Sam, man still is a primitive being. Let someone betray a weakness and he's ready for the kill.
FREDDIE MARTIN, West Virginia professional, advice to
Sam Snead, **1936**

I can beat any two players in this tournament by myself. If I need any help, I'll let you know.
BABE DIDRIKSON ZAHARIAS, to her partner Peggy Kirk Bell in a
four-ball event

We're five up now, but what's wrong with winning by eight or ten?
BEN HOGAN, at the Inverness Four-Ball tournament, to partner
Jimmy Demaret, **1941**

Reporter: What was the turning point, Jimmy?
Demaret: When I teed off at ten o'clock.
JIMMY DEMARET, on losing to Ben Hogan ten-and-eight at the
PGA Championship in Portland, **1946**

My father was thinking of coming out for this tournament. Then when he found out who I had drawn as my first opponent, he changed his mind. He decided it wasn't worth a trip to Colorado just to watch me play one round.
ROBERT T. JONES III, son of Bobby Jones, on being matched against
Jack Nicklaus in the National Amateur Championship, **1959**

If you keep shooting par at them, they all crack sooner or later.
BOBBY JONES

I have found, in my own matches, that if you just keep throwing consistent, unvarying bogeys and double bogeys at your opponents, they will crack up sooner or later from the pressure.

REX LARDNER, *Out of the Bunker and Into the Trees,* **1960**

I had held a notion that I could make a pretty fair appraisal of the worth of an opponent simply by speaking to him on the first tee and taking a good measuring look into his eyes.

BOBBY JONES, *Golf Is My Game,* **1960**

Over the years, I've studied habits of golfers. I know what to look for. Watch their eyes. Fear shows up when there is an enlargement of the pupils. Big pupils lead to big scores.

SAM SNEAD

No matter what happens – *never give up a hole.* . . In tossing in your cards after a bad beginning you also undermine your whole game, because to quit between tee and green is more habit-forming than drinking a highball before breakfast.

SAM SNEAD, *The Education of a Golfer,* **1962**

Everyone gets wounded in a game of golf. The trick is not to bleed.

PETER DOBEREINER, *Observer,* **1967**

Match play, you see, is much more of a joust. It calls for a doughty, resourceful competitor, the sort of fellow who is not ruffled by his opponent's fireworks and is able to set off a few of his own when it counts.

HERBERT WARREN WIND, *Golf Digest,* **1972**

I was paired with Tony Jacklin. 'I don't want to talk today,' he said. I said, 'That's OK. You listen. I'll talk.' I figure you are going to be out there four hours and if you keep your mouth closed for four hours you get bad breath.
LEE TREVINO, World Match Play Championship, **1972**

Stroke play is a better test of golf, but match play is a better test of character.
JOE CARR, Irish amateur

In match play you always have to expect the worst.
COLIN MONTGOMERIE, on holding off Mark O'Meara to win the World Match Play Championship, **1999**

Anybody can beat anybody. That's the problem with match play. Then again, that's the beauty of it.
TIGER WOODS, *Sports Illustrated*, **1999**

The better you play, the better it's making me look. So keep on going.
DARREN CLARKE, en route to beating Tiger Woods in the final of the Anderson Match Play Championship,
Sports Illustrated, **2000**

I think foursomes is a goofy game, frankly. It's a bloody British invention for old ladies at golf clubs. They love it . . . I think it's outdated, history, gone. The sooner we get rid of it the better.
PETER THOMSON, *The World of Professional Golf*, **2001**

19 ● Media

You could have shot off an elephant gun in my corner of the locker room and not winged a single sportswriter.
SAM SNEAD, recalling when he finished second as a rookie in the US Open in **1937**

Announcer: This is the big one, folks. . . Now he's sighting the putt. . . Now he's bending over and addressing the ball. . . Now he's glaring in my direction.
ROBERT DAY, cartoon in *The New Yorker,* **1950**

Sam Snead won the Masters yesterday on greens that were slicker than the top of his head.
DAN JENKINS, proposed lead, *Fort Worth Press,* **1952**

He's hit it fat . . . It will probably be short . . . It just hit the front edge of the green . . . It's got no chance . . . It's rolling but it will stop . . . It's rolling toward the cup . . . Well, I'll be damned!

JIMMY DEMARET, commenting on television on Lew Worsham's winning wedge shot at the World Championship, **1953**

So many of my golfing pals have been punching a typewriter between tournament dates that an awful lot of people were beginning to stare at me, wondering what was wrong. 'Do you think he's illiterate?' I heard one fellow whisper behind my back.

JIMMY DEMARET, *My Partner, Ben Hogan,* **1954**

If someone dropped an atom bomb on the sixth hole, the press would wait for a golfer to come in and tell them about it.

BEN HOGAN

Despite the abominable handling of the press luggage at Zurich airport, the Swiss Open managed to get off to a rather decent start yesterday.

LEONARD CRAWLEY, sportswriter, *Daily Telegraph*

Q: Have you noticed much difference between the various courses you've seen on television?
A: Not much. All of them seem to have 'one of the greatest finishing holes in golf'.

FRANK HANNIGAN, USGA official, *USGA Golf Journal,* **1964**

Cut your talk in half. You're not saying anything interesting anyhow.

FRANK CHIRKINIAN, CBS-TV producer, to his commentators at the Masters, **1966**

Next time I come back as a golf writer. No three putts. Never miss a cut. And somebody else pays.
ROBERTO DE VICENZO, **1967**

I just don't know about the guy. He looks like W. C. Fields in drag. But he happens to be the best in the business.
FRANK CHIRKINIAN, on commentator Henry Longhurst

They [the press] do an excellent job considering the fact that they're writing about something about which they know nothing.
FRANK BEARD, paraphrasing jockey Bill Hartack, *Pro,* **1970**

Even the announcers are choking.
TONY JACKLIN, on the CBS crew covering the Masters, **1970**

Fire away — and use real bullets.
TONY JACKLIN, to the media after a loss to Jack Nicklaus in the World Match Play Championship, **1970**

The first one is called 'How to Get the Most Distance Out of Your Shanks', and the other is 'How to Take the Correct Stance on Your Fourth Putt'.
LEE TREVINO, on possible titles for his books

If only I had taken up golf earlier and devoted my whole time to it instead of fooling about writing stories and things, I might have got my handicap down to under eighteen.
P. G. WODEHOUSE, *The Golf Omnibus,* **1973**

The professional golf watcher never catches the action. I could write a volume on Great Moments in Golf I Have Missed.
PETER DOBEREINER, *The Glorious World of Golf,* **1973**

Lie? I've got no f – ing lie. I don't even have a f – ing shot.
MILLER BARBER, when asked by Ken Venturi about his
lie on the CBS Golf Classic

As I said in the press tent, 'Man, I crawled on that shot like an
eight-wheel rig rollin' down Interstate 35. Just wore it out.
And the minute the ball started for the flagstick I knew the
war was over and it was time to call in the boats and piss on
the admiral.'
DAN JENKINS, *Dead Solid Perfect,* **1974**

Writers are very strict about touring pros having familiar
names. Editors make writers take laps and do push-ups when
Jack Fleck or Orville Moody wins a US Open.
DAN JENKINS, *Golf Digest,* **1975**

Chris, the boys are hitting the ball longer now because
they're getting more distance.
BYRON NELSON, to Chris Schenkel on ABC-TV

Lord Byron. ABC's golfing colourman who pioneered the
phrase, 'That's right, Chris.'
MARK MULVOY and ART SPANDER,
Golf: The Passion and the Challenge, **1977**

What the hell do I say about myself? I fantastic player? I win
fantastic play-off?
ANGEL GALLARDO, Barcelona golf writer who played
in and won the Spanish Open, **1977**

Maybe I said too much to the press but I don't regret anything I've said to any of them. Over the years people have said to me, you say too much, you open up the book, you should close it a bit, let them wonder and think . . . but I'm not like that.
TONY JACKLIN, *Tony Jacklin: The Price of Success*, **1979**

Nancy Lopez is planning to marry a sportscaster. I thought she had better taste.
DICK SCHAAP, *Sport*, **1979**

'I do not read papers,' Leon said. 'I look at the golf scores and then I wrap fish in them.'
DAN GLEASON, *Golf Digest*, **1981**

Looking back today, I can think of no surer way to find yourself a golf writer in your fifties than to think you were Ben Hogan in your twenties.
CHARLES PRICE, *Golfer-At-Large*, **1982**

ABC is star-oriented. They would rather watch Nicklaus walk than another player strike a golf shot.
FRANK CHIRKINIAN, CBS-TV golf producer,
Sports Illustrated, **1982**

Wright whispered, 'And it appears that, at last, the great man is going to strike his tiny spheroid; and will it find its way into that marvellous pit or will it stay, like a rebellious child, at the entrance and refuse to go in?'
KEVIN COOK, parodying golf announcer Ben Wright,
Playboy, **1982**

I don't go much for those in-depth interviews that want to know the colour of your curtains and how many times you make love to your wife.

TOM WATSON, *Daily Mail*, **1982**

The average golfer would rather play than watch. Those who don't play can't possibly appreciate the subtleties of the game. Trying to get their attention with golf is like selling Shakespeare in the neighbourhood saloon.

BOB TOSKI, *The Sporting News*, **1983**

I'm really going to do my homework. . . I'm going to be down there on the practice tee before the telecast, finding out if a guy's wife beat him up the night before. Important stuff like that. Stuff that people want to know.

LEE TREVINO, on his new job as TV golf commentator,
Golf Digest, **1983**

I don't mind that booth. That's pretty good money. I almost finish third every week I'm up there.

LEE TREVINO, *New York Times*, **1984**

I was afraid to move my lips in front of TV. The Commissioner probably would have fined me just for what I was thinking.

TOM WEISKOPF, on his thirteen in the 1980 Masters,
San Francisco Chronicle, **1984**

No one can misquote me, because they don't know what the hell I'm talking about.

GARY MCCORD, known as 'Space Cadet',
San Jose Mercury News, **1984**

The cameras affect my game. They make me nervous. I would rather make my money in front of nobody.
BETSY KING, *Golf Digest,* **1984**

There is one thing in this world that is dumber than playing golf. That is watching someone else play golf . . . What do you actually get to see? Thirty-seven guys in polyester slacks squinting at the sun. Doesn't that set your blood racing?
PETER ANDREWS, *Golf Digest,* **1984**

Watching the Masters on CBS is like attending a church service. Announcers speak in hushed, pious tones, as if to convince us that something of great meaning and historical importance is taking place. What we are actually seeing is grown men hitting little balls with sticks.
TOM GILMORE, *San Francisco Chronicle,* **1984**

Well, the Real Leader keeps sending us messages.
PAT SUMMERALL, when lightning struck,
'The Masters', CBS-TV, **1984**

I've been here since 1968, and I cry every time.
PAT SUMMERALL, as leader Ben Crenshaw came up the eighteenth fairway, CBS-TV, **1984**

The eighteenth . . . one of the great finishing holes in golf.
PAT SUMMERALL, *'Colonial National Invitation',* CBS-TV, **1984**

An empty cab drew up at Oak Tree last week and Jeff Sluman got out.
USA Today's comment about the anonymity of the new PGA champion in **1988**

I wish they would talk more about my golf and not my wardrobe. Print my score – not my measurements.
The slightly rotund CRAIG STADLER

It's Monday, guys. Don't start overloading me on Monday. There's still two days of hype left.
GREG NORMAN, Masters press conference, **1989**

This is probably not the best time to ask this question and I'm not sure you would answer it anyway so I won't ask it.
Irish golf writer to Irish golf pro RONAN RAFFERTY at the
Volvo Masters, **1989**

I would like to thank the press from the heart of my bottom.
NICK FALDO, after winning the Open at Muirfield, **1991**

I've read [*Golf in the Kingdom*] seven times. I've read it straight, I've read it stoned and I still don't get it.
TOMMY SMOTHERS, comedian, on the 1972 novel by
Michael Murphy, *Golfweek*, **1993**

Faldo to World Tour: Bugger Off
Mainichi Daily News headline, **1994**

Caterpillars were turning into butterflies in the time it took him to play some of his shots, and he even tossed up bits of grass to check the wind before he disappeared into the trees for a call of nature.
MARTIN JOHNSON, sportswriter, on slow play by one
particular player at the European Tour qualifying tournament,
Daily Telegraph, **2001**

If you are not going to ask me about my round, then I am going back to my hotel.
COLIN MONTGOMERIE, to the press at the Volvo Masters,
Golf Weekly, **2001**

You can do a lot of good work in a car, if you move the seat forward.
PETER ALLISS, commentator, when told Western Open
winner Mark Hensby used to sleep in his car,
ABC-TV, **2004**

Working with Faldo is shockingly enjoyable. We even drive to the course together. There are some quiet, awkward moments once in a while, but I'm four or five up in on-air heckles.
PAUL AZINGER, on his new relationship as a TV analyst with his
former on-course rival, *GolfWorld*, **2005**

I want to be factual, not personal. If a guy hits a great shot, I'll say it. If he hits a cow, I'll call it a cow.
NICK FALDO, on working as a TV analyst, *GolfWorld*, **2005**

This had better be riveting, because it's damned inconvenient.
NICK FALDO, on the telecast of a Monday play-off caused by
inclement weather at the Nissan Open, *GolfWorld*, **2005**

I thought the announcers were talking about the Pope's funeral, but it turned out to be the Masters.
MIKE LUPICA, *New York Daily News*, **2005**

I have come to understand and appreciate writers much more recently since I started working on a book last fall. Before that, I thought golf writers got up every morning, played a round of golf, had lunch, showed up for our last three holes and then went to dinner.
PHIL MICKELSON, *GolfWorld*, **2005**

20 ● Men's Tour

I've just discovered the great secret of golf. You can't play a really hot game unless you're so miserable that you don't worry over your shots . . . Look at the top-notchers. Have you ever seen a happy pro?
P. G. WODEHOUSE, *The Heart of a Goof*, 1923

Why shouldn't he? He's never done anything all his life but play golf.
MR TURNESA, upon hearing that his son, Joe,
was leading the US Open, 1926

There are two kinds of golf – golf and tournament golf. The latter is an ageing game.
BOBBY JONES, 1930

Golf championships are a good deal like omelettes. You cannot have an omelette without breaking eggs, and you cannot have a golf championship without wrecking hopes.
O. B. KEELER, biographer of Bobby Jones

Not really. After all, I put it there.
WALTER HAGEN, when a spectator mentioned the
bad luck of his lie

I think I missed the cut – if I teed off at all. I forget. In those
days, me and Clayton Heafner had a bad habit of being
withdrew.
GEORGE LOW, on the 1939 British Open

I guess I've travelled a hundred thousand miles a year on the
pro tour, but the only thing of interest I've ever seen is the
Washington Monument.
DON WHITT, c. **1950s**

Life on the Tournament Trail. The Road to Psychiatry.
JIMMY DEMARET, chapter heading in
My Partner, Ben Hogan, **1954**

The players themselves can be classified roughly into two
groups – the attractions and the entry fees.
JIMMY DEMARET, *My Partner, Ben Hogan,* **1954**

I have never felt so lonely as on a golf course in the midst of
a championship with thousands of people around, especially
when things began to go wrong and the crowds started
wandering away.
BOBBY JONES, *Golf Is My Game,* **1960**

Some of the things I didn't have to be taught as a rookie
travelling pro were to keep close count of my nickels and
dimes, stay away from whisky, and never concede a putt.
SAM SNEAD, *The Education of a Golfer,* **1962**

A golf professional is a fellow who never knows what town he's in till he calls downstairs to the desk clerk in the morning . . . but can read you the left-to-right break on every green in the town from memory.
JIM MURRAY, *The Sporting World of Jim Murray*, **1968**

Out here, you've got to realize that if you take an eight on a hole, ninety per cent of the other pros don't care and the other ten per cent wish it had been a nine.
MASON RUDOLPH, at the Tucson Open, **1969**

What golf needs is a fist-fight between Jack Nicklaus and Arnold Palmer on the eighteenth green of a nationally tele-vised tournament.
JEAN SHEPARD, humorist

What do I like about all this besides the money? This is my office, and I love my office.
CHI CHI RODRIGUEZ, waving at the fairways, *Playboy*, **1970**

The men's tour was quiet, after all. Terry Dill wouldn't be changing his grip for another week or so. Dick Lotz still had the same putter. Bert Yancey had postponed his annual interview until July.
DAN JENKINS, *Sports Illustrated*, **1971**

There's an old saying on tour, 'Set fire to the trees and cover the greens with broken glass, put the pros out there in gasoline-soaked pants and barefooted, and someone will break par.'
TOMMY BOLT, *The Hole Truth*, **1971**

I never knew what top golf was like until I turned pro-fessional – then it was too late.
STEVE MELNYK, former US Amateur champion, **1973**

The amateur who picks up his newspaper and remarks that he could shoot better golf than those guys on tour should pause and consider the prospects very carefully... It is not just a different game. It is not a game at all.
PETER DOBEREINER, *The Glorious World of Golf,* **1973**

In the past, I've usually played in about thirty-five tournaments a year, but I played so poorly last year that I didn't have the courage to leave home.
STEVE REID, *Golf Digest,* **1973**

About July, the steak in St Louis looks like the same one you had in Los Angeles. Don't talk about the potatoes and peas.
CHARLES COODY, **1973**

Before Arnold Palmer came along the only guys on the tour were a bunch of dull bastards.
HERB GRAFFIS, golf writer and editor

Every time a circus leaves town, there are people who'd like to leave with it. A lot of waitresses who've overheard the tour talk sigh and go back to eggs–over and the humdrum of soap operas.
DAN GLEASON, *The Great, The Grand and the Also-Ran,* **1976**

If backing a Broadway play is the worst investment in the world, sponsoring a pro golfer surely ranks a strong second.
MARK MULVOY and ART SPANDER,
Golf: The Passion and the Challenge, **1977**

If you travel first class, you think first class and you're more likely to play first class.
RAYMOND FLOYD, on why his tour expenses are
$60,000 a year, **1977**

It's a compromise of what your ego wants you to do, what experience tells you to do, and what your nerves let you do.
BRUCE CRAMPTON, on tournament golf

Only religious ceremonies proceed with more respect than the major golf tournaments in this country.
JIMMY CANNON, *Nobody Asked Me, But . . .*, **1978**

Resolve this thought in your mind. . . Arnold Palmer might be the greatest golfer in the world, but he probably doesn't know a carburettor from a tail pipe.
DAN JENKINS, *Golf Digest,* **1979**

To be in contention for three or four days is better than sticking a needle in the arm.
DAVID GRAHAM, *San Francisco Chronicle,* **1981**

Most of us would give up our wives, our firstborn and our favourite putters just to finish in the top ten in a major.
LEE TREVINO, *San Jose Mercury News,* **1981**

To be a successful tour golfer you have to hate everybody, your mom and dad, your wife, your children, your brothers and sisters, your friends – everybody. It takes total concentration and I mean total.
DAVE HILL, *Golf Digest,* **1982**

The only positive thing to come out of losing my exemption is that I found out who my friends are. I thought I had a million friends when I was playing well, but I've learned that I have damn few.
FRANK BEARD, *Golf Magazine,* **1981**

Sam Snead: If I putted like Jack Nicklaus, I'd have won a thousand tournaments.

Tommy Bolt: If Jack played in as many tournaments as you, he'd have won two thousand.

SAM SNEAD and TOMMY BOLT, *Golf Digest,* **1981**

If you call personality the battle of Hollywood stars, then, yes, we do lack personality. But the personality of golf is good golf. If you want to see a comedian, you ought to tune in to *Saturday Night Live.*

TOM WATSON, *The Sporting News,* **1982**

I can't believe the actions of some of our top pros. They should have side jobs modelling for Pampers.

FUZZY ZOELLER, *Golf Digest,* **1982**

Golf, especially championship golf, isn't supposed to be any fun, was never meant to be fair, and never will make any sense.

CHARLES PRICE, *Golfer-At-Large,* **1982**

My luck is so bad that if I bought a cemetery, people would stop dying.

ED FURGOL, *Golf Magazine,* **1982**

During the last hour and a half of play on this round, when the heat of the sun had diminished, we had one of those stretches when watching expert golfers in action seems like one of the high-ranking blessings of life.

HERBERT WARREN WIND, on the US Open at Oakmont, *The New Yorker,* **1983**

More money. Otherwise, no difference. Birdie the same. Par the same. Bogey the same. Out-of-bounds the same.

SEVE BALLESTEROS, on the difference between the Tour and the rest of the world, *Golf Magazine,* **1983**

Next the Golf Journeyman's Union will put in belly dancers, the tattooed lady and JoJo the dog-faced boy to make more money and degrade a sport that was once distinguished by class.

HERB GRAFFIS, golf writer, on the commercialization of the PGA tour, *Golf Digest,* **1983**

A bad week on the Tour is when the demons dance through your swing thoughts. In the real world a bad week is when you wake up to find you're a steelworker in Youngstown.

DON WADE, *Golf Digest,* **1983**

I'm so busy I can only play in one tournament at a time.

JACK NICKLAUS, *Golf Digest,* **1983**

I'd rather work in a 7-Eleven store than go back to playing the mini-tour.

KENNY KNOX, *Golf Digest,* **1983**

I couldn't believe it was that easy to win.

NICK PRICE after his first US Tour win, the 1983 World Series of Golf

You have to take this game through so many labyrinths of the mind, past all the traps — like, will my masculinity be threatened if I hit the ball well and still shoot seventy-two?

MAC O'GRADY, *Sports Illustrated,* **1984**

Sometimes you'd like to just stand there in the middle of the green and scream as loud as you can. But we're the perfect gentlemen.
RAYMOND FLOYD, *Golf Magazine,* **1984**

The trouble with this game is that they say the good breaks and bad breaks even up. What they don't tell you is that they don't even up right away. You might go two or three years and all you get is bad-break bad-break bad-break. That gets annoying in a hurry.
JOHNNY MILLER, *Golf Magazine,* **1984**

When you are on your own with no one to talk to and you can't get home, it's terrible. The worst week was the Masters.
IAN WOOSNAM, on tour life in the US, **1988**

When I started, the professional tour was like a travelling circus, a nomadic village. Players, officials and the press travelled and worked together, ate and drank together and even played golf together on practice days. Each was a specialist within the Big Top. But that has all gone, and now even the community spirit among players is breaking down.
PETER DOBEREINER, *The Golfer's Companion,* **1988**

When you only make three bogeys in ninety holes, break the record and lose, it doesn't make you very happy.
MARK O'MEARA after losing the play-off to Corey Pavin in the 1991 Bob Hope Chrysler Classic, after breaking the PGA Tour ninety-hole record

Well, I guess, hello, world.
TIGER WOODS, opening words of his 1996 announcement of his decision to turn professional,
Tiger: A Biography of Tiger Woods, **1997**

I feel like I live in dog years. It feels like I've been out here for a long time.

TIGER WOODS, during his fifth year on the PGA Tour, *GolfWorld*, **2000**

Tour pros would rather go through an IRS audit than play in a pro-am. Publicly they say they love meeting interesting people and how great the pro-ams are. In truth, they loathe them. They're out there for six hours, see countless bad shots and hear the same stale jokes.

TOM WEISKOPF, *GolfWorld*, **2002**

Playing golf in a club is very different from playing on a tour, where you have to be egotistical and selfish and look after only yourself. As a pro you are out amongst a lot of wolves, and you have to bite like them.

PETER THOMSON, *GolfWorld*, **2005**

We should change our motto from 'These guys are good' to 'These guys are slow'. When you're playing [as bad] as I am, you at least want to get it over fast.

NEAL LANCASTER, struggling US pro, *Raleigh (N.C.) News and Observer*, **2005**

Yeah, I travelled a lot last month. I flew Stockholm to Newark, Newark to Denver, Denver back to Newark, then Newark to Reno, Reno to San Francisco, San Francisco–Hong Kong, Hong Kong–Singapore, Singapore–Beijing, Beijing–Chicago, Chicago–Palm Beach, Palm Beach–Boston, then from Boston to here.

JESPER PARNEVIK, at the Bell Canadian Open in Vancouver, B.C., *Toronto Star*, **2005**

21 ● Modern Days/Olden Days

I noticed a lady in the clubhouse at the weekend. I urge the
Secretary to see that this does not happen again.
Entry in complaints register, Worcestershire Golf Club,
1881

The professional, as we are now chiefly acquainted with him,
is a feckless, reckless creature. In the golfing season in
Scotland he makes his money all the day, and spends it all the
night. His sole loves are golf and whisky.
HORACE G. HUTCHINSON, golf historian, **1900**

It was a nice slice of the century to be young in. The times
were good, the parties were frequent, the girls were pretty,
the drinks were long and the stock market was as strong as an
ox.
GENE SARAZEN, recalling the 1920s

For that kind of money, I'd wear a skirt.
JIMMY DEMARET, on the prize money of the 1930s, when
asked to wear a number on his back

Play is conducted at a snail's pace. Some golfers today remind me of kids walking to school and praying they'll be late . . . Golfers used to check the grass on the greens; today they study the roots under each blade.

JIMMY DEMARET, *My Partner, Ben Hogan,* **1954**

Nobody took notes in my day. I'm sure it's permissible. But they would have regarded it as unsporting and ungentle-manly. I used to think in terms of clubs. What club is it to there?

HENRY COTTON, in *The World of Golf,* **1971**

Q: When and how did golf begin?
A: Arnold Palmer invented it about eight years ago in a little town outside Pittsburgh.

FRANK HANNIGAN, USGA official, *USGA Golf Journal,* **1964**

All you got out there is a bunch of authors and haberdashers. All you got to do to write a book is win one tournament. All of a sudden you're telling everybody where the Vs ought to point. And them that don't win, they're haberdashers. They sell sweaters and slacks and call themselves pros.

GEORGE LOW, former touring professional, c. **1960s**

I've noticed some of them are off balance when they swing. They're top-heavy. They've got too much hair.

BEN HOGAN, on today's golfers, *Golf Digest,* **1970**

These kids have it mighty soft today. I recently heard one of my members say to his son: 'You're a golf bum. Are you going to be content to spend your life tramping around the golf course?' And the kid said, 'No, Pop, I've been meaning to speak to you about buying me my own golf cart.'

SAM SNEAD, *Golf Magazine,* **1970**

I just love to see you guys with long hair, because you can't see. I never saw a hippie playing golf.

BERT YANCEY, c. early **1970s**

Hickory golf was a game of manipulation and inspiration; steel golf is a game of precision and calculation.

PETER DOBEREINER, *The Glorious World of Golf,* **1973**

We always considered it quite a feat to get down our six-to-eight footers, but now if a fellow misses from forty feet he grimaces and agonizes like a cowboy struck in the heart by an Indian's arrow.

BEN HOGAN, *Sports Illustrated,* **1973**

Those young amateurs who join the tour remind me of young horses that have raced too much too soon. They're burned out before they get to the big races. Then they have to go back to the paddock and learn all over again.

CHI CHI RODRIGUEZ, *Golf Digest,* **1975**

Man, I've got to blow dry my hair or I've got to withdraw from the tournament. I don't play anywhere unless I can blow dry my hair.

BEN CRENSHAW, c. late **1970s**

Palmer and now Nicklaus have been trampled out of sight by these kids nobody has heard of, the colleges down South clone 'em, you can't keep their names straight from one tournament to the next.

JOHN UPDIKE, *Rabbit Is Rich,* **1981**

My God, the courses these kids play today are either half casual water or ground-under-repair . . . One of these days I'm going to write a book on drops. That ought to sell. The shot's become more popular than putting.
JIMMY DEMARET

We didn't have any money but we had some pork and beans and a siphon. The latter implement we called the Oklahoma credit card.
JIMMY DEMARET, on golf in the 1930s, *Golf Magazine,* **1983**

There are too many strange faces and computer minds out there these days. You don't even know the people you're playing with.
BILLY CASPER, cutting back his schedule, *Golf Digest,* **1983**

I come from a different era. I'm from the club era. I started out shining shoes, giving lessons, selling 10E shoes to some guy who wears 12C, and making him like it.
LEE TREVINO, *USA Today,* **1983**

There's so much money, all down the line, that some of 'em don't even drink coffee or a Coke. They say it might make them nervous. Now ain't that something.
SAM SNEAD, *Golf Magazine,* **1984**

There are no short hitters to tour anymore – just long and unbelievably long.
SAM SNEAD, as above

The only thing good about the old days is talking about them.
BILL MELHORN, *Golf Secrets Exposed,* **1984**

I can remember over the last few years times when I've played in a major championship like this, and I'd walk through a group of younger players and they never looked up. Today they looked up.

ARNOLD PALMER after shooting a sixty-eight in the 1989
US PGA Championship

I just want you to know it was a pleasure to watch you play in the Open.

JACK NICKLAUS to Nick Faldo, **1990**

Although golf was originally restricted to wealthy Protestants, today it's open to anyone who owns hideous clothing.

DAVE BARRY, American humorist

Slow play is a disease. It's the price you pay for modern golf. You could make the course less severe and turn it into a putting contest, but I'd rather have par mean something.

JEAN VAN DE VELDE, French pro, on six-hour rounds, **2000**

Annika Sorenstam is not going for her sixth consecutive win. She's going for her sixth win in tournaments she's entered. There's a big difference. We take records and do whatever we want with them these days.

MICKEY WRIGHT, *Palm Beach Post*, **2005**

If it was in America we would be paying a fortune to get on it. They should not be redesigning something which was laid out in the 1600s.

ALEX HAY, retired BBC golf commentator, on plans to change
the Musselburgh Links in Scotland to make room for
lighting stanchions at an adjacent racecourse,
Edinburgh Evening News, **2005**

I got no problem with the new breed. Practice, 18 holes, practice, gym, room service, couple of waters, bed. Whatever it takes. . . You know when I leave the locker room with maybe five or six beers for me and my caddie? The young guys look at me like I'm carrying a gun.

MARK CALCAVECCHIA, to columnist Bob Verdi,
GolfWorld, **2006**

22 ● Money

If you don't mind, Mr Crosby, I'd rather have cash.
SAM SNEAD, declining a $500 cheque for winning the
Bing Crosby Pro–Am, **1937**

Sam is the only man to make a million dollars and save two
million.
FRED CORCORAN, Sam Snead's former manager

However, 1940, when I won six of nine tournaments, including the Masters, was my big year. I was even able to hang onto
enough money so that I needed only a small loan for my car
fare home.
JIMMY DEMARET, *My Partner, Ben Hogan,* **1954**

I never wanted to be a millionaire; I just wanted to live like
one.
WALTER HAGEN, *The Walter Hagen Story,* **1957**

My yearly income averages about $10,000, but I spend $50,000 of my friends' money.
GEORGE LOW, former touring professional, *Golf Digest,* **1960**

Loaning you money is like sending lettuce by rabbit.
GEORGE LOW, to Al Besselink

The only pro golfer I would send my laundry to is Chen Ching-po.
DAVE MARR, on Arnold Palmer's laundry establishments

One pro said, 'Snead's so tight he'd spend his last dollar buying a pocketbook to put it in.'
SAM SNEAD, *The Education of a Golfer,* **1962**

Let's see, I think right now, I'm third in money-winning and first in money-spending.
TONY LEMA, to newsmen at the British Open, **1964**

Did I ever *win* that much before? I never *saw* that much before.
LEE TREVINO, on winning $6,000 for fourth place at the
US Open, **1967**

His idea of charity is that it begins – and ends – at home.
JIM MURRAY on Sam Snead,
The Sporting World of Jim Murray, **1968**

Some of the motels [in Palm Springs, California] are so incredibly lavish . . . that if the Queen of England ever came here she would go home and set fire to Windsor Castle.
JIM MURRAY, in *The Sporting World of Jim Murray,* **1968**

I'm on steak now. With $200,000 a year, ain't no sense in eating rice and beans anymore.
CHI CHI RODRIGUEZ, on his weight gain, **1970**

I've always argued that we ought to play right down the middle of Saigon if the price is right.
FRANK BEARD, *Pro,* **1970**

I'm in the process of looking for a cattle ranch. . . I keep hearing there's no money in it, but if that were true you couldn't buy a steak.
BEN HOGAN, *Golf Digest,* **1970**

Bet you have never heard of a tour player striking because they wouldn't give him weekends off, have you?
TOMMY BOLT, *The Hole Truth,* **1971**

Man: One thing is sure. Gene still has every one of those dollars.
Hagen: Hell, he still has the wheelbarrow.
WALTER HAGEN, on Gene Sarazen, **1972**

You know, someday somebody's gonna come out here and tee it up nude.
BOB WYNN, on endorsement money, **1975**

Every time you win a little prize of some kind, it stimulates you a little bit, if for no other reason than it's one time you didn't get your brains beat out at something.
DAVE MARR, **1975**

I just signed to do commercials for a mattress company and fulfilled my life's ambition. I'll get paid for lying down.
LEE TREVINO, **1976**

I'm working as hard as I can to get my life and my cash to run out at the same time. If I can just die after lunch Tuesday, everything will be fine.
DOUG SANDERS, *Golf Digest,* **1979**

The world's a funny place. When you have no money, no one will do anything for you. If you become successful and pile up enough money to buy anything you want, people deluge you with gifts you don't need and try to do all kinds of things for you.

LEE TREVINO, *The New Yorker,* **1980**

I owe everything to golf. Where else could a guy with an IQ like mine make this much money?

HUBERT GREEN, *Sports Illustrated,* **1981**

The guys out here are starting to look like race car drivers.

TOM WEISKOPF, on product logos on clothing and equipment, *Golf Digest,* **1981**

I dropped off the tour and went home and started working with my dad doing taxes. After two months of that, I decided golf looked pretty good.

JOHN FOUGHT, *'Bob Hope Desert Classic',* NBC-TV, **1983**

I'm not concerned about getting in the record books. A good obituary doesn't exactly excite me.

JOANNE CARNER, *Golf Digest,* **1983**

What's wrong with being a millionaire? We should all be one.

TERRY DIEHL, *Golf Digest,* **1983**

I'm going for broke. I was born broke, so I want to live like a millionaire and die poor. I don't want to live poor and die a millionaire.

CHI CHI RODRIGUEZ, at the Everett Open, **1984**

Things were a lot better when I had only one chequebook.

PATTY SHEEHAN, *Sports Illustrated,* **1984**

You can make a lot of money in this game. Just ask my ex-wives. Both of them are so rich that neither of their husbands work.
LEE TREVINO, *USA Today,* **1985**

I've taken one of those Trevino vacations – five or six weeks off. The tax man is after me.
PETER JACOBSEN, *'Honda Classic',* NBC-TV, **1985**

I wanted it badly, I've already spent two million.
CHI CHI RODRIGUEZ on eventually taking his career earnings in 1987 past $1 million

Everyone dreams of being a millionaire. If the taxman is not too harsh on me, I might have done it.
IAN WOOSNAM, after winning the Million Dollar Challenge, **1987**

Even my next door neighbour talks to me now.
CHRIS MOODY after winning £65,000 for capturing the 1988 European Masters

Winning used to be the important thing. The money was nice to have, but it was not the most important thing. Today the American player doesn't have that strong desire to win any more, he has the strong desire to win all this money.
RAY FLOYD, **1989**

Sure the purses are obscene. The average worker, let's say, makes $25,000 a year while a golfer makes $25,000 for finishing 10th. Our values have departed somewhat.
TOM WATSON, **1989**

You start playing for money instead of trophies and golf becomes a job.
DANIELLE AMMACCAPANE, on winning her first tournament on the LPGA Tour, **1991**

To walk into the locker room and have Arnold Palmer call you 'Moneybags' is kind of unbelievable. I feel like a male Cinderella. It's been a fairy tale.
RIVES MCBEE, former club pro, on his success on the Senior Tour, *Business Week*, **1991**

I feel like a million bucks – minus tax.
COREY PAVIN, after winning the Million Dollar Challenge, **1995**

Daddy, do you think when I turn pro you could live off $100,000 a year?
TIGER WOODS, at age ten in 1986,
The Makings of a Champion, **1997**

It makes me wonder where all the money went.
ANNIKA SORENSTAM, on topping the LPGA career money list with $6,957,044, **2001**

If I was the US [Ryder Cup] captain, I would put all the charity money in a pot. And every evening at dinner, the guys who played well and won points would get money for their charity, and the guys who didn't would get nothing. I guarantee you they'd play harder. [The] only way an American player equates playing hard is to get money back.
JOHNNY MILLER, *GolfWorld*, **2004**

I thought I could pay off the $80,000 I owe the Mirage by giving them $1,000 a month. Apparently, the Mirage doesn't like that idea as much as I like it. I don't know what will happen next, but I hope to find something to keep me going until the Champions Tour. I'm a couple of years away from that.

FULTON ALLEM, US Tour pro, age forty-seven, *GolfWorld,* 2005

Players have too many things to play in . . . [Too] much money. And they don't particularly like to travel. Point out you get $700,000 each if you win and they just shrug.

PETER ALLISS, TV commentator, on weak fields at the World Cup, *GolfWorld,* 2005

They just handed me a check for $792,000. To know that just five, six months ago I was thinking about hanging up the clubs, I get to hang up this nice, red [winner's] jacket. It's amazing where a little perseverance and grit and, maybe, a little ignorance can take you.

JASON GORE, on his first PGA Tour victory, *GolfWorld,* 2005

NASCAR golf, baby. Hey, all these checks on this thing, they don't bounce.

JOHN DALY, on the eight corporate logos on his shirts, *News & Observer (Raleigh, N.C.),* 2005

23 ● Nineteenth Hole

Moderation is essential in all things, madam, but never in my life have I failed to beat a teetotaller.
HARRY VARDON, when asked to join the temperance movement, c. **1915**

Hell, I don't even get up at that hour to close the window.
WALTER HAGEN, ignoring an early tee time

I always keep a supply of stimulants handy in case I see a snake, which I also keep handy.
W. C. FIELDS, putting whisky in his golf bag

I like to say I was born on the nineteenth hole – the only one I ever parred.
GEORGE LOW, touring professional

What the nineteenth hole proves beyond a shadow of a doubt is that the Scots invented the game solely in order to sell their national beverage in large quantities.
MILTON GROSS, in *Eighteen Holes in My Head,* **1959**

Jeez! I know I was drinking last night, but how did I get to Squaw Valley?

JIMMY DEMARET, seeing snow on the fairways at the
Bing Crosby Pro-Am, **1962**

I saw more than a few pros floating around bar rooms at night, trying to kiss the bartender good night because they couldn't tell him from their girlfriends.

SAM SNEAD, *The Education of a Golfer,* **1962**

Sam was born with a natural ability to keep his bar bills as low as his golf scores.

JIMMY DEMARET on Sam Snead,
My Partner, Ben Hogan, **1954**

If I try to leave the hotel tonight, put out a contract on me.

DAVE MARR, after starting a round with a hangover, **1968**

You know what I did here one year? I was so nervous I drank a fifth of rum before I played. I shot the happiest eighty-three of my life.

CHI CHI RODRIGUEZ, at the Masters, **1970**

At golf you've got to be mentally alert. You can't lean against a tree that isn't there.

DOUG SANDERS, on rumours of drugs on the tour, early **1970s**

Golfers don't fist fight. They cuss a lot. But they wouldn't punch anything or anybody. They might hurt their hands and have to change their grip.

DAN JENKINS, *Dead Solid Perfect,* **1974**

Reporter: Are you having a party if you win?
Trevino: If I win here Sunday, I won't know it till Thursday.
LEE TREVINO, at the Masters, **1978**

Baby, I counted fourteen beer bottles in there with your fingerprints on 'em. That must have been some party.
LEE TREVINO, to Dave Hill at the World Series of Golf

They're usually pretty red.
RAYMOND FLOYD, when asked the colour of his eyes,
Golf Digest, **1978**

I was in bed at 10 and up at 10.15. Who can sleep at a time like that?
FUZZY ZOELLER, the night before winning the Andy Williams
San Diego Open, **1979**

I have never led the tour in money winnings, but I have many times in alcohol consumption.
FUZZY ZOELLER, *San Francisco Chronicle,* **1979**

When Jack Nicklaus told me last night I had to play Seve Ballesteros, I took so many pills I'm glad they don't have drug tests for golfers.
FUZZY ZOELLER, at the Ryder Cup, *Sports Illustrated,* **1983**

I admit my personality is to have fun. . . I've been known to party day and night. Heck, in Las Vegas I paid a guy $50 an hour to sleep for me.
DOUG SANDERS, *San Jose Mercury News,* **1984**

I asked Jimmy Demaret what was his favourite drink and he said, 'The next one.'
PHIL HARRIS, commentator, *'Legends of Golf',* NBC-TV, **1984**

Weiskopf: Wouldn't it be great if you could come out here and just pick the tournaments you like to play, never practise, hang out at the bars and have a couple of drinks if you wanted, and just have fun?
Snead: Tom, that's what you've done your whole life.
TOM WEISKOPF and J. C. SNEAD, *San Francisco Chronicle,* **1984**

The way I hit the ball today, I need to go to the range. Instead, I think I'll go to the bar.
FUZZY ZOELLER, at the PGA Championship, *USA Today,* **1984**

There'll be beer and champagne and I'll have a bloody headache in the morning – and I don't care. Just so long as I am alive.
IAN WOOSNAM, on plans to celebrate victory at the
Cisco World Match Play Championship, *Guardian,* **2001**

I'm not a fan of whisky, so I can't celebrate by drinking Johnnie Walker.
SERGIO GARCIA, asked how he would celebrate if he won the
Johnnie Walker Classic (he didn't), *GolfWorld,* **2005**

I'm sure I kept a few pubs open tonight.
PADRAIG HARRINGTON, on his victory at the Honda Classic,
making him the first player from the Republic of Ireland to
win a PGA Tour event, *GolfWorld,* **2005**

We were married in Italy on May 5 . . . that's 05/05/05. Cinco de Mayo. Another excuse to drink margaritas, like I need one.
MARK CALCAVECCHIA, to columnist Bob Verdi, *GolfWorld,* **2006**

The reason I stopped is not because I was a bad drunk. On the contrary, I was a magnificent drunk. I was the Tiger Woods of drunks. But once you've beaten the game, you retire gracefully.

DAVID FEHERTY, reflecting on his first year of sobriety,
GolfWorld, **2006**

24 ● Philosophy and Advice

Tarn Arte Quam Marte: As much by skill as by strength.
Club motto, Royal Troon Golf Course, Troon, Ayrshire

Don't play too much golf. Two rounds a day are plenty.
HARRY VARDON

Keep on hitting it straight until the wee ball goes in the hole.
JAMES BRAID, British professional, c. 1910

What is Love compared with holing out before your opponent?
P. G. WODEHOUSE, *Archibald's Benefit,* 1919

It is nothing new or original to say that golf is played one
stroke at a time. But it took me many years to realize it.
BOBBY JONES, *Down the Fairway,* 1927

It seems paradoxical, but it is probably true that the way to
obtain a great reputation as a fighter is to forget that you have
an enemy − or at any rate an earthly one.
BERNARD DARWIN, writing about Bobby Jones

Me boy, never go to school on another man's club or ye'll not make a penny in this game.
WILLIE MACFARLANE, British professional, advice to the youngster Sam Snead

How well you play golf depends on how well you control that left hand of yours.
TOMMY ARMOUR

The average expert player – if he is lucky – hits six, eight or ten real shots in a round. The rest are good misses.
TOMMY ARMOUR

He enjoys that perfect peace, that peace beyond all understanding, which comes at its maximum only to the man who has given up golf.
P. G. WODEHOUSE

That little white ball won't move until you hit it, and there's nothing you can do after it has gone.
BABE DIDRIKSON ZAHARIAS

The Oldest Member: I always advise people never to give advice.
P. G. WODEHOUSE, *Tangled Hearts,* **1948**

Relax? How can anybody relax and play golf? You have to grip the club, don't you?
BEN HOGAN, *Time,* **1949**

I had gained an insurance stroke I hadn't deserved. Luck may be the residue of careful planning, as the wise men say, or it can be just plain luck.
GENE SARAZEN, *Thirty Years of Championship Golf,* **1950**

Nobody ever looked up and saw a good shot.
DON HEROLD, *Love That Golf,* **1952**

You're only here for a short visit. Don't hurry, don't worry.
And be sure to smell the flowers along the way.
WALTER HAGEN, *The Walter Hagen Story,* **1957**

Put your ass into the ball, Mr President.
SAM SNEAD, playing with Dwight D. Eisenhower

Lay off for three weeks and then quit for good.
SAM SNEAD, his advice to a pupil

Friends are a man's priceless treasures, and life rich in
friendship is full indeed.
BOBBY JONES, **1958**

The right way to play golf is to go up and hit the bloody
thing.
GEORGE DUNCAN, Scottish professional, **1959**

Always throw clubs ahead of you. That way you don't have to
waste energy going back to pick them up.
TOMMY BOLT, **1960**

It's all right to put all your eggs in one basket – if you've got
the right basket.
SAM SNEAD

If you sit and listen to the grass grow, sometimes your mind
opens to ideas you've been missing.
SAM SNEAD, on taking time off from golf,
The Education of a Golfer, **1962**

One thing that's always available on a golf course is advice. If you play like I do, you think everybody knows something you don't know. If I see a bird fly over, I think he's going to tell me something.
BUDDY HACKETT, *The Truth About Golf and Other Lies,* **1968**

A cardinal rule for the club breaker is never break your putter and driver in the same match or you are dead.
TOMMY BOLT, *How to Keep Your Temper on the Golf Course,* **1969**

The slow-play habit, let me say, is like the cigarette habit – it is so hard to break that a man is wisest not to begin it.
JACK NICKLAUS, *The Greatest Game of All,* **1969**

You have to know where you'll wind up before you start – otherwise you'll go broke.
BEN HOGAN, *Golf Digest,* **1970**

If you think you can, or if you think you can't – you're right.
DEANE BEMAN, his motto, *Golf Digest,* **1973**

Serenity is knowing that your worst shot is still going to be pretty good.
JOHNNY MILLER, *Sports Illustrated,* **1975**

Studying psychology isn't that relevant to the tour . . . What college really prepares you for is graduate school.
TOM WATSON, *Golf Digest,* **1977**

Don't let the bad shots get to you. Don't let yourself become angry. The true scramblers are thick-skinned. And they always beat the whiners.
PAUL RUNYAN, *Golf Digest,* **1977**

Golf is not a game you can rush. For every stroke you try to force out of her, she is going to extract two strokes in return.
DAVE HILL, *Teed Off,* 1977

Never do anything stupid.
BEN CRENSHAW, his philosophy, *Texas Monthly,* 1977

Have a blast while you last.
HOLLIS STACY, message on her T-shirt, *Golf Digest,* 1977

My goal is to play seventy-two holes someday without changing expression.
JACK RENNER, *Sports Illustrated,* 1979

Never give up. If we give up in this game, we'll give up on life. If you give up that first time, it's easier to give up the second, third, and fourth times.
TOM WATSON, *Golf Digest,* 1979

If the following foursome is pressing you, wave them through and then speed up.
DEANE BEMAN, PGA Tour Commissioner

The golfer who stands at the ball as rigid as a statue usually becomes a monumental failure.
DICK AULTMAN, *Golf Digest,* 1981

Golf is a friend. A friend is an antidote for despair.
BOB TOSKI, *Golf Digest,* 1981

He never backed off from anything, and I like that. No way would he ever have been penalized for slow play. He'd just step up and knock the hell out of the ball.
LEE TREVINO on Harry S. Truman, *They Call Me Super Mex,* 1982

There are two things that won't last long in this world, and that's dogs chasing cars and pros putting for pars.
LEE TREVINO, *PGA Tour News,* **1983**

If you try to break the ball to pieces, the sod may fly farther than your shots. You've got to be gentle. Sweet-talk that ball. Make it your friend and it will stay with you a lot longer.
SAM SNEAD, *Golf Digest,* **1983**

There are three types of bad shots in golf: those that cost you a half stroke, those that cost you a full stroke and those that cost you two strokes. Only stupidity costs you more than two strokes.
BOB TOSKI, *Golf Digest,* **1983**

I just wish all the people in the world could get together and stop this fussin' and fightin'. What a hell of a world it would be.
SAM SNEAD, *San Francisco Chronicle,* **1984**

I guess I've shrunk a little in this weather. There are a lot of guys six feet under who would love to be playing today.
GARY PLAYER, after a rainy round at the Open, **1987**

Out there you are either bleeding, haemorrhaging, or painting Mona Lisas.
MAC O'GRADY, during the US Open, **1987**

If you can bring the ship home with cargo and crew intact through the hurricane of the last day, that's an achievement. Right?
MAC O'GRADY, when asked how he rated his round, **1987**

The slums of Chicago are full of first-round leaders.
PETER JACOBSEN, **1990**

A champion is not a champion because he wins, but how he
conducts himself.
DOUG SANDERS, **1990**

Sometimes you play better when you're sick. Of course,
you've got to be a little sick to play this game.
BOBBY NICHOLS, *Business Week*, **1991**

Never criticize others. It only stirs resentment. Speak no ill of
anyone and all the good you know of everyone. Don't judge
a person too soon. God waits until the end.
HARVEY PENICK (1904–1995), professional and teacher

Jimmy Demaret and I had our own psychologist that we kept
in our locker. His name was Jack Daniels.
JACKIE BURKE JR, *Vegasgolfer*, **2000**

Golf giveth and golf taketh away, but it taketh away a hell of
a lot more than it giveth.
SIMON HOBDAY, Senior PGA pro

You go out and play your game. Sometimes it comes out as
68 and sometimes as 74. That's not fatalism, that's golf.
PETER OOSTERHUIS

25 ● Practice and Lessons

Y'know it's hard to teach the game. Man's like a narrow-mouthed whisky bottle. He can only take a word or two at a gulp. Ye have to take it slow.

ALEC (NIPPER) CAMPBELL, Scottish teaching pro,
The American Golfer, 1933

What a shame to waste those great shots on the practice tee . . . I'd be afraid to stand out there and work at my game like that. I'd be afraid of finding out what I was doing wrong.

WALTER HAGEN

Six years are needed to make a golfer – three years to learn the game, then another three to unlearn all you have learned in the first three years. You *might* be a golfer when you arrive at this stage, but more likely you're just starting.

WALTER HAGEN

If I miss one day's practice I know it; if I miss two days the spectators know it, and if I miss three days the world knows it.
BEN HOGAN, paraphrasing pianist Ignace Paderewski

If you can't outplay them, outwork them.
BEN HOGAN

My game is impossible to help. Ben Hogan said every time he gave me a lesson it added two shots to his game.
PHIL HARRIS, comedian

There are two things in life which Ben Hogan especially dislikes. One is losing a golf match. The other is teaching golf.
JIMMY DEMARET, *My Partner, Ben Hogan,* **1954**

Your first lesson is over. Ben Hogan can rest easy.
JIMMY DEMARET, to writer Milton Gross

You've just one problem. You stand too close to the ball – after you've hit it.
SAM SNEAD, to a pupil

Can anyone name the 'greatest' atomic energy scientist? Yet, designing, engineering and constructing an atomic bomb is simple compared to trying to teach a fellow how to stop shanking.
TOMMY ARMOUR, *Golfing,* **1952**

You have to build up the pupil's belief that you are delighted to see that the pupil isn't as hopelessly bad as he thinks he is.
BILLY BURKE, *Golfing,* **1952**

You make twenty mistakes going into your backswing and correct ten of them coming forward, but unfortunately you haven't quite balanced your budget.

HARRY OBITZ, teaching pro, to a student

There are three ways of learning golf: by study, which is the most wearisome; by imitation, which is the most fallacious; and by experience, which is the most bitter.

ROBERT BROWNING, in *A History of Golf*, **1955**

The nice thing about these [golf] books is that they usually cancel each other out. One book tells you to keep your eye on the ball; the next says not to bother. Personally, in the crowd I play with, a better idea is to keep your eye on your partner.

JIM MURRAY, *The Sporting World of Jim Murray*, **1968**

What did you expect from the US Open champion – ground balls?

LEE TREVINO, to an admiring spectator on the practice tee, **1969**

Golf Pro: An optimistic doctor who has a cure for dying.

JIM BISHOP, syndicated column, **1970**

They say 'practice makes perfect'. Of course, it doesn't. For the vast majority of golfers it merely consolidates imperfection.

HENRY LONGHURST

I don't need practice. I need a miracle.

BRUCE ASHWORTH, after an eighty-two at the US Open, **1973**

If you're not prepared, somewhere in the quiz there are going to be some questions you can't answer.
CHARLES COODY, on the need for practice, **1974**

Golf got complicated when I had to wear shoes and begin thinking about what I was doing.
SAM SNEAD

Watching Sam Snead practise hitting golf balls is like watching a fish practise swimming.
JOHN SCHLEE, *Golf Digest,* **1977**

Gary [Player] solicits far too much advice on the practice tee – I've seen him taking a lesson at the US Open from a hot dog vendor.
DAVE HILL, *Teed Off,* **1977**

The harder you work, the luckier you get.
GARY PLAYER

Not a week goes by without my learning something new about golf. That means, of course, that I was ignorant of eight things about golf two months ago. Extend that process back nearly twenty years and the result is an impressive accumulation of ignorance.
PETER DOBEREINER, *The World of Golf,* **1981**

Well, at $9.95 it did me some good.
BIG CAT WILLIAMS, when told by a reader that his instruction book didn't do him any good, **1981**

I am the most over-taught and under-learned golfer in the USA.
HERB GRAFFIS, golf writer and editor, *PGA Magazine,* **1983**

I just had a sixty-four. Boy, that's some shootin', isn't it? But Monday and Tuesday practice golf out here is like a boxer working on the punching bag. It doesn't hit back.

CHI CHI RODRIGUEZ, *New York Times,* **1984**

More instruction material on how to hit a middle iron is written in America during any six-month period than has been written about thoracic surgery since doctors stopped working out of the back rooms of barber shops.

PETER ANDREWS, *Golf Digest,* **1984**

I've stopped practising, I've stopped worrying, and I've got a new wife who travels with me. If I get any happier, I've got to be in heaven.

LEE TREVINO, **1984**

I've got to keep working on my game, fine-tune it over the next ten years. Golf is a funny business, it can bite your head off.

NICK FALDO, **1990**

I wasn't born with this ability. I had to work bloody hard to become the player I am today.

COLIN MONTGOMERIE

I open the driving range and I close it. I thought you ought to know that I work hard. I like practising. I enjoy it. If I did not enjoy it I would not do it. What is the point of going back to the hotel, having a drink and talking a load of bull?

VIJAY SINGH, to a newly hired caddie, *Independent,* **1992**

As I get older I must be becoming a better teacher. This must be true because more of my pupils have started hitting the ball out of my sight. Or could it be my eyes are fading?

HARVEY PENICK, *Little Red Book,* with Bud Shrake, **1993**

Golf instruction books can be immensely valuable to the novice. What you do is balance it on top of your head and then swing the club as hard as you can. Once you've mastered the art of taking a full vicious swing without dislodging the book, you can play golf.

PETER DOBEREINER, *Dobereiner on Golf*, **1996**

In this game you can work really hard and get worse. You can run, train, work out and you see results, but you work on your golf swing and you can go the opposite way.

JESPER PARNEVIK, *GolfWorld*, **2004**

26 ● Pressure

I am so tense at times like that, I can hear the bees farting.
MICK O'LOUGLIN, Irish pro, after a tough match, **1938**

One always feels that he is running from something without knowing what nor where it is.
BOBBY JONES, on tournament pressure

Everybody has two swings: the one he uses during the last three holes of a tournament and the one he uses the rest of the time.
TONEY PENNA, American professional

Golf, perhaps through its very slowness, can reach the most extraordinary heights of tenseness and drama.
HENRY LONGHURST, in *A Hard Case from Texas*, **1957**

Doctors and mind experts go around explaining that it's perfectly okay to explode on the course because it releases your built-up tensions. They don't tell you, though, how you can rave like a wild beast and break ninety.

SAM SNEAD, *The Education of a Golfer*, **1962**

It's that you lose *nerves*, not nerve. You can shoot lions in the dark and yet you can quiver like a leaf and fall flat over a two-foot putt.

JOHNNY FARRELL, American professional

Sometimes a particular hole will cause a choke – a choke hole. Like the eighteenth at Cypress. It's like walking into a certain room in a big dark house when you were a kid – you get this fear that hits you.

DAVE MARR

I was trying to get so far ahead I could choke and still win.

LEE TREVINO, at the US Open, which he won by four strokes over Jack Nicklaus, **1968**

If this was any other tournament but the Masters, I'd have shot sixty-six. But I was choking out there. That green coat plays castanets with your knees.

CHI CHI RODRIGUEZ, following a round of seventy, **1970**

Every day, every minute, the greens get a little more difficult to read, and the fairways grow narrower.

FRANK BEARD, on the Masters' pressure, **1970**

Q: Are you nervous?
Mann: No, I'm not, but my golf ball must be.

CAROL MANN, as her ball blew off the tee, *Golf Digest,* **1970**

Pressure is something every golfer feels at one time or another . . . Sometimes when I putted I looked like a monkey trying to wrestle a football.
SAM SNEAD, *Golf Digest,* **1970**

You don't know what pressure is until you play for five bucks with only two in your pocket.
LEE TREVINO, *Newsweek,* **1971**

When we come down to the final holes, some people find it very . . . hard . . . to breathe.
JACK NICKLAUS, **1975**

Anyone who hasn't been nervous, or who hasn't choked somewhere down the line, is an idiot.
DR CARY MIDDLECOFF, *Golf Digest,* **1977**

More so than the fans think, it's a game of who chokes the least.
DAVE HILL, *Teed Off,* **1977**

The person I fear most in the last two rounds is myself.
TOM WATSON, at the US Open, **1977**

A lot of guys who have never choked, have never been in the position to do so.
TOM WATSON, *Seattle Post-Intelligencer,* **1978**

It's awfully hard to smile when you're choking to death.
GARY PLAYER, on the last round of his fourth Masters' victory, *Minneapolis Tribune,* **1978**

Everyone has his own choking level, a level at which he fails to play his normal golf. As you get more experienced, your choking level rises.

JOHNNY MILLER, *Golf Digest,* **1979**

We all choke, and the man who says he doesn't choke is lying like hell. We all leak oil.

LEE TREVINO, *GolfWorld,* **1980**

Pressure is going out there on the golf course and thinking, 'If I don't do well, I'll have to rob another bank.'

RICK MEISSNER, former touring pro and convicted bank robber, *Esquire,* **1980**

You just hope you have enough chances to experience it, and get used to it.

JACK NICKLAUS, **1981**

I don't think I had enough sense to know what pressure was.

GENE SARAZEN, on playing Walter Hagen, *The New Yorker,* **1982**

Class, someone once said, is the ability to undergo pressure with grace. So what did I do? I just did what comes naturally. I vomited.

CHARLES PRICE, on leading the 1964 British Open, *Golfer-At-Large,* **1982**

Man, I couldn't even breathe. I couldn't smile because my lips were stuck to my teeth.

JOANNE CARNER, on the win which put her into the LPGA Hall of Fame, *San Francisco Chronicle,* **1982**

I used to think pressure was standing over a four-foot putt knowing I had to make it. I learned that real pressure was sixty-five people waiting for their food with only thirty minutes left on their lunch-hour break.

AMY ALCOTT, on waitressing in the off-season, *The Sporting News,* **1983**

I had a three-foot putt for $30,000. I made the putt, but my knuckles were white, and do you know how hard I have to squeeze the putter to get my knuckles white?

LEE TREVINO, *'Bob Hope Desert Classic'*, NBC-TV, **1983**

To what degree are you able to absorb the anxiety and pressure of this thing called the PGA Tour? . . . They have pills that can save you from absorbing radioactive isotopes. Perhaps they can develop a pill to protect us from the radioactivity of the tour.

MAC O'GRADY, *Sports Illustrated,* **1984**

Choker is the charmingly cruel American sporting term for a player who, when it comes to the crunch, crumbles . . . In Britain for some curious reason we call it losing one's bottle. Whatever it is called, it adds up to the same thing, a loss of nerve when faced with the final challenge, and it is a terrible tag to pick up and an even harder one to lose.

RENTON LAIDLAW, *Golfing Heroes,* **1987**

The job of non-playing captain for the Ryder Cup will give me more than enough worries. The days of a cinch win for America are over.

LEE TREVINO, **1987**

It gets to him, you know, all the pressure. The press, the telly and all the carry-on, it's a burden to bear. We thought he could bear it, but it turns out he's only human.
ALEX LYLE about son Sandy, **1989**

My first time on the first tee I was so pumped up, I hit a drive about 340 yards. I couldn't believe it. I didn't know I had that much power.
MARK LYE, US pro, on his first Masters, *GolfWorld*, **1991**

At the top of the back swing you feel – I do anyway – 'Please, please make sensible contact with the ball' and hopefully it will go somewhere straight.
COLIN MONTGOMERIE, on competing in the Ryder Cup

I like the feeling of trying my hardest under pressure. It's so intense sometimes, it's hard to breathe. It feels like a lion is tearing at my heart.
TIGER WOODS, *Tiger Woods: The Makings of a Champion*, **1997**

This was the first time in the majors I've really messed up. When I had chances in the past, other players did really well . . . But at my age [forty-two] you've got to think positively. There I go sounding like a bloody sports psychologist!
COLIN MONTGOMERIE, after flubbing an approach to the final green while in contention to win the US Open, leading to a double-bogey six and loss by one stroke, *scotsman.com*, **2006**

27 ● Putting

A man who can approach does not require to putt.
J. H. TAYLOR, British professional

Those who cannot drive suppose themselves to be good putters.
SIR WALTER SIMPSON, *The Art of Golf,* 1887

When a putter is waiting his turn to hole-out a putt of one or two feet in length, on which the match hangs at the last hole, it is of vital importance that he think of nothing. At this supreme moment he ought studiously to fill his mind with vacancy. He must not even allow himself the consolations of religion.
SIR WALTER G. SIMPSON, as above

This putting is wicked. It is sinful.
JAMES BRAID, at the British Open, 1900

Miss 'em quick!
MACDONALD SMITH, American tournament professional

Putting is not golf but croquet.
A. A. MILNE, *Not That It Matters,* **1919**

Talking turkey to a businessman, you must look squarely at him during the entire conversation. It's the same with putting. When you're talking turkey on the green, the face of your putter must look squarely at the hole.
GENE SARAZEN

Suffering – ! I've got a hen back home in Charlotte that can lay an *egg* further than that!
CLAYTON HEAFNER, upon missing a three-inch putt to give Jimmy Demaret the Oakland Open by one stroke

Drown, you sonofabitch. You'll never three-putt on me again!
KY LAFFOON, dousing his putter after three-putting two straight greens

It is a strange thing that we know just how to do a thing at golf, and yet we cannot do it.
BERNARD DARWIN, golf writer

Golf is really two games. One is the game in the air. The golfer can lick that part of the game.
CLAUDE HARMON

Reading a green is like reading the small type in a contract. If you don't read it with painstaking care, you are likely to be in trouble.
CLAUDE HARMON

Selecting a stroke is like selecting a wife. To each his own.
BEN HOGAN

I am still undecided as to which of these two is the hardest shot in golf for me – any unconceded putt, or the explosion shot off the first tee. Both have caused me more strokes than I care to write about.

RING LARDNER, American writer

Even when times were good, I realized that my earning power as a golf professional depended on too many ifs and putts.

GENE SARAZEN, *Thirty Years of Championship Golf*, **1950**

The yips are that ghastly time when, with the first movement of the putter, the golfer blacks out, loses sight of the ball and hasn't the remotest idea of what to do with the putter or, occasionally, that he is holding a putter at all.

TOMMY ARMOUR

I had a long putt for an eleven.

CLAYTON HEAFNER, on why he took a twelve

A noted psychiatrist's wife asked him why he never let her play golf with him. 'My dear,' he admonished her, 'there are three things a man must do alone: testify, die, and putt.'

BENNETT CERF, *The Laugh's on Me*, **1959**

If you couldn't putt you'd be selling hot dogs outside the ropes.

BILLY CASPER

Confidence builds with successive putts. The putter, then, is a club designed to hit the ball partway to the hole.

REX LARDNER, *Out of the Bunker and Into the Trees*, **1960**

The man who can putt is a match for anyone.

WILLIE PARK JR, Scottish professional

I putted like Joe Schmoe, and I'm not even sure Joe would appreciate that.
ARNOLD PALMER, at the Masters, **1960**

That's a bagful of indecisions.
JACKIE BURKE, on Arnold Palmer's eight putters

Arnie, you're gonna have to buy a bigger jet bag to carry all the putters.
FUZZY ZOELLER, as Palmer took six putters to the practice green

I'll tell you why putts go in. Because the old National Open champion in the sky puts 'em in.
BOB ROSBURG, **1962**

Hell, I'd putt sitting up in a coffin if I thought I could hole something.
GARDNER DICKINSON, on his putting styles, **1962**

Everyone wants to be known as a great striker of the ball, for some reason. Nobody wants to be called a lucky, one-putting s.o.b., and nobody thinks he is.
GARY PLAYER, **1962**

I call my putter 'Sweet Charity' because it covers such a multitude of sins from tee to green.
BILLY CASPER, **1963**

My putting was atrocious. I changed grips, stance, you name it. I tried everything but standing on my head.
ARNOLD PALMER, at the US Open, **1968**

Actually, I was always more of a breaker than a thrower – most of them putters. I broke so many of those, I probably became the world's foremost authority on how to putt without a putter.
TOMMY BOLT, *How to Keep Your Temper on the Golf Course,* **1969**

The devoted golfer is an anguished soul who has learned a lot about putting just as an avalanche victim has learned a lot about snow.
DAN JENKINS, *The Dogged Victims of Inexorable Fate,* **1970**

Prayer never seems to work for me on the golf course. I think this has something to do with my being a terrible putter.
REV. BILLY GRAHAM

Oh dear!
HENRY LONGHURST'S immortal comment about Doug Sanders' missed putt that cost him the 1970 British Open

The trouble with golf is you're only as good as your last putt.
DOUG SANDERS, after missing a short putt on the eighteenth to cost him the British Open Championship, **1970**

The way I putted, I must've been reading the greens in Spanish and putting them in English.
HOMERO BLANCAS, Mexican-American professional, after an opening round eighty-one at the Masters, **1970**

When the hole is back here, I'm down there. When the hole is down there, I'm up here.
CHI CHI RODRIGUEZ, as he faced a sixty-foot putt at the Masters, **1970**

But the bitter, inescapable truth remains. Once you've had 'em you've got 'em.
HENRY LONGHURST on the yips, *Golf Digest,* **1973**

That sure is a small ball you're trying to swing at. And it sure is a long way to that green. And when you get there that cup is not exactly as big as a corporation president's ego.
DAN JENKINS, *Dead Solid Perfect,* **1974**

Observer: Didn't you have any uphill putts?
Blancas: Sure. After each of my downhill putts.
HOMERO BLANCAS, after shooting a seventy-seven in the US Open at Winged Foot, **1974**

Good luck on this putt. They've got the original president of this club buried right there.
LEE TREVINO, as Dave Stockton faced a bumpy putt on the first green at the US Open, **1974**

Putting is Clutch City. . . Usually my putting touch deserts me under pressure. From five feet in to the hole you're in the throw-up zone.
DAVE HILL, *Teed Off,* **1977**

Putting from that distance [ninety feet] is a little like trying to touch a girl sitting on the far side of a couch. You can reach her, but you're not likely to accomplish much.
CHARLES PRICE, *Golf Magazine,* **1977**

When our putting is sour . . . then we are in honest, interminable, miserable trouble.
ARNOLD PALMER, C. **1970s**

I'm going to sleep with my putter tonight. My husband Don is going to have to sleep in the other bed.

JOANNE CARNER, after a hot putting round in the
Lady Keystone Open, **1980**

The divorce is from my old putter. I think it's final – at least we're due for a long separation. I've suffered with that old putter for two years now. It got so rude I couldn't stand it.

SHELLY HAMLIN, *Golf Digest,* **1980**

That putt was so good I could feel the baby applauding.

DONNA WHITE, seven months pregnant, after sinking
a long putt, *Sports Illustrated,* **1981**

My mother always putts up on the toes of her left foot and whistling. Everyone thinks she is so cool and casual. But I know it's her way to beat the yips.

AL GEIBERGER, *Golf Magazine,* **1982**

Putting isn't golf. Greens should be treated almost the same as water hazards: you land on them, then add two strokes to your score.

CHI CHI RODRIGUEZ, *Golf Magazine,* **1983**

I never really dreamed of making many putts. Maybe that's why I haven't made many.

CALVIN PEETE, *Sports Illustrated,* **1983**

I've never once seen the cup move towards the ball.

HENRY LONGHURST, on a putt left short,
'Nabisco Dinah Shore Invitational', NBC–TV, **1983**

I think all that rain shrunk the cups.

JULI INKSTER, after a poor putting day in the rain at the
San Jose Classic, **1983**

I saw Sir Edmund Hillary out there, and he had to walk around the greens.
TOM WEISKOPF, on the severely sloped greens at the
Tournament Players Club at Sawgrass, *USA Today*, **1983**

That probably was the shortest putt I've ever missed when I was trying.
HALE IRWIN, on a missed fifteen-inch putt at the Sea Pines
Heritage Classic, *Golf Digest*, **1983**

If God wanted you to putt cross-handed, he would have made your left arm longer.
LEE TREVINO on Tim Norris, *'Bob Hope Classic'*, NBC-TV, **1984**

I've gotten rid of the yips four times, but they hang in there. You know those two-foot downhill putts with a break? I'd rather see a rattlesnake.
SAM SNEAD, *San Francisco Chronicle*, **1984**

I don't have any big secret about putting. . . Just hit at it. It's either going to miss or go in.
BEN CRENSHAW, *San Francisco Chronicle*, **1984**

He's got a putt that's almost out-of-town.
LEE TREVINO, as Andy Bean faced an eighty-foot putt,
'Honda Classic', NBC-TV, **1984**

My caddie had the best answer to that – 'Just to let the other one know it can be replaced.'
LARRY NELSON, on why he carried two putters,
Golf Digest, **1984**

My only thoughts as I stood there were, 'Don't effing miss.'
EAMONN DARCY about his match-winning putt in the 1987
Ryder Cup

I miss the putt. I miss the putt. I miss the putt. I make.
SEVE BALLESTEROS, describing his four-putt at the Masters, **1988**

This putter won't be flying first-class on the way home.
NICK FALDO, after missing four short putts during the final round
of the PGA Championship at Oak Tree, **1988**

It's not the arrow. It's the Indian who is to blame.
JOSE MARIA OLAZABAL, on his putting at the French Open, **1989**

My suspicion is, the vast majority of plumb-bobbers don't have
any earthly idea what they're doing. But they've seen touring
pros doing it, so they think *they* should do it.
DAN JENKINS, *Fairways and Greens*, **1994**

My eyes go out of focus and my brain kind of goes out of a
little focus, too. So, I don't get hung up on trying to hit
anything on a perfect line. It's hard to explain. I kind of let
my eyes go into a blank stare.
LOREN ROBERTS, nicknamed 'Boss of the Moss', on his
technique, **1995**

Someone on The Weather Channel could best describe Tom
Watson's five putts at the 16th hole as 60 below, 6 above, 40
below, 4 above, 2 below.
DAVE ANDERSON, on Watson's struggles at the Masters,
New York Times, **1996**

I don't care what it looks like. We don't get paid for looking good. We get paid for getting the job done.
BERNHARD LANGER, on the long-handled putter, **1996**

Woods' putt resembled a train travelling from London to Bristol via Birmingham and Bournemouth.
JOHN HOPKINS, on a sixty-foot birdie putt at the Players Championship, *The Times*, **2001**

It was possibly the most calamitous loss of nerve ever seen in a major championship. Never was a shorter, easier putt for a major championship missed.
DAVID DAVIES, on Retief Goosen's 72nd hole miss at the US Open, *Guardian*, **2001**

In those days my ex-wife used to walk to the next tee when I had a four-footer because I never missed. Now that wouldn't happen, firstly because she's not there anymore and secondly because [I'm] all a bit sweaty over the short ones.
COLIN MONTGOMERIE, on how much better his putting used to be, *Independent,* **2005**

If I'm short on a putt, you can call me 'Alice' . . . Then, after I win, 'Your Majesty' is fine.
ALICE COOPER, to a playing partner at an outing, *GolfWorld*, **2005**

28 ● Real Golfers

They were real golfers, for real golf is a thing of the spirit, not of mere mechanical excellence of stroke.

P. G. WODEHOUSE, *A Woman Is Only a Woman,* **1919**

Real golfers, whatever the provocation, never strike a caddie with the driver. The sand wedge is far more effective.

HUXTABLE PIPPEY, San Francisco★

Real golfers don't miss putts: they are 'robbed'.

JOHN THOMAS TRIZUTO, Hayward

Real golfers don't step on their opponent's ball while looking for it in the rough.

JACK MALONEY, Vallejo

★The following quotations are taken from a Real Golfer contest held by Pat Sullivan for the *San Francisco Chronicle* in California

Real golfers always use a brand new ball on the sixteenth hole at Cypress Point.
MICHAEL GORDON, San Francisco

Real golfers never eat quiche; they eat hot dogs and club sandwiches.
JESS BRAGG, Carmel

Real golfers carry an eraser in case they get caught cheating.
LES COCHRAN, Guerneville

Real golfers don't use naked-lady tees.
STEVE LINDROTH, Truckee

Real golfers do not use their putters to get the ball out of the hole.
DEAN F. JAMES, PGA professional, Santa Rosa

Real golfers tape the Masters so they can go play themselves.
GEORGE W. ROOPE, Alameda

Real golfers never question their client's score.
D. G. MIX, Burlingame

Real golfers have two handicaps: one for braggin' and one for bettin'.
BOB IRONS, Red Bluff

Real golfers always say: 'It never rains on the golf course.'
JOHN KNAPP, San Francisco

Real golfers go to work to relax.
GEORGE DILLON, San Ramon

Real golfers don't go in the bushes.
BOB KUNSTEL, Carmichael

Real golfers don't look at their caddies when they hand them a club.
WESLEY R. RAINES, Antioch

Real golfers don't cry when they line up their fourth putt.
KAREN HURWITZ, Berkeley

Real golfers never complain about a hangover.
BOB LANE, Petaluma

Real golfers know how to count over five when they have a bad hole.
DUD SMITH, San Francisco

Real golfers don't say, 'Is that my friend in the trap or is the s.o.b. on the green?'
S. M. LEONARD, Belmont

Real golfers don't stop to smell the flowers.
WALTER E. BEARDEN, South San Francisco

Real golfers never pick up. This makes pro-ams a lot more fun to watch.
Golf Digest, **1983**

Real golfers never take lessons. They give lessons – usually at cocktail parties.
Golf Digest, **1983**

Real golfers never use metal woods. They own classic Tommy Armours, which accounts for the high incidence of poverty among real golfers.
Golf Digest, **1983**

Real golfers don't care what real golfers do.
LLOYD N. POPISH, Sunnyvale

29 ● Rules and Governing Bodies

There is only one way to play the game. You might as well praise a man for not robbing a bank.
BOBBY JONES, on the 1925 US Open when he penalized himself a stroke and lost the title by one shot

Players should pick up bomb and shell splinters from the fairways in order to save damage to the mowers.
War rule, Britain, c. **1940s**

If a ball comes to rest in dangerous proximity to a hippopotamus or crocodile, another ball may be dropped at a safe distance, no nearer the hole, without penalty.
Local rule, Nyanza Club, British East Africa, c. **1950s**

If a man is notified he has been appointed to serve on the rules committee for a certain tournament he should instantly remember that he must attend an important business meeting in Khartoum.
HERBERT WARREN WIND, *Sports Illustrated,* **1958**

Golf, in fact, is the only game in the world in which a precise knowledge of the rules can earn one a reputation for bad sportsmanship.
PATRICK CAMPBELL, *How to Become a Scratch Golfer,* **1963**

Next time? Next time, I bring my lawyer.
ROBERTO DE VICENZO, on his 1968 disqualification from the Masters, **1970**

The R&A, as Wordsworth said of the Thames, glideth at its own sweet will.
HERBERT WARREN WIND, chiding the Royal and Ancient Golf Club of St Andrews for taking so long to award the Open to Turnberry, *The New Yorker,* c. **1970**

Thou shalt not use profanity; thou shalt not covet thy neighbour's putter; thou shalt not steal thy neighbour's ball; thou shalt not bear false witness in the final tally.
Ground rules, clergyman's golf tournament, Grand Rapids, Michigan, *Golf Magazine,* **1974**

The entire handbook can be reduced to three rules. One: you do not touch your ball from the time you tee it up to the moment you pick it out of the hole. Two: don't bend over when you are in the rough. Three: when you are in the woods, keep clapping your hands.
CHARLES PRICE, *Esquire,* **1977**

Golf is the hardest game in the world to play and the easiest to cheat at.
DAVE HILL, *Teed Off,* **1977**

You mustn't blow your nose when your partner is addressing the ball – otherwise the book of rules is mostly nonsense.
HENRY LONGHURST, *The Best of Henry Longhurst,* **1978**

There is no surer nor [more] painful way to learn a rule than to be penalized once for breaking it.
TOM WATSON, author of a book on rules who was penalized two strokes, *New York Times,* **1980**

The only times you touch the ball with your hand are when you tee it up and when you pick it out of the cup. The hell with television towers and cables and burrowing animals and the thousand and one things that are referred to as 'not part of the golf course'. If you hit the ball off the fairway, you play it from there.
KEN VENTURI, *Golf Magazine,* **1981**

Is it against the rule to carry a bulldozer in your bag?
TOM WATSON, on the severe greens at the Tournament Players Club at Sawgrass, *Sports Ilustrated,* **1982**

I'd spend ninety-nine cents to make a buck.
GEORGE S. MAY, early golf promoter

He took the game away from the Scottish peasants and gave it to the American peasants.
BOB HARLOW, *GolfWorld* publisher, on George S. May, *Golf Magazine,* **1981**

Sir, would you mark yourself, please, while I try to get this one up?
DAVE MARR, to a noisy gallery marshall, **1968**

Perhaps, if A. W. Tillinghast had designed the Alamo, and the USGA had toughened it up, the Mexican siege would have failed.

DICK SCHAAP, *Massacre at Winged Foot,* **1974**

The tour used to be run very nicely with five or six men on the field staff. Now we have eleven or twelve, so one guy can carry coffee over to the other.

DAVE HILL, *Teed Off,* **1977**

The PGA has had a number of officers whose IQs weren't much higher than their golf scores.

CHARLES PRICE, *Golf Magazine,* **1981**

The USGA, whose sense of humour has always been on a par with that of the Internal Revenue Service.

CHARLES PRICE, *Golf Magazine,* **1981**

When I retire, I'm going to get a pair of grey slacks, a white shirt, a striped tie, a blue blazer, a case of dandruff and go stand on the first tee so I can be a USGA official.

LEE TREVINO, *San Francisco Chronicle,* **1981**

We have the best officials in all sports – you don't see them until you need them.

JERRY PATE, *Golf Magazine,* **1982**

Anybody who's played golf as long as I have and hit the ball as I do has got to be tough. You've got to be thick-skinned when you're looking at the green with a four-wood in your hand.

DEANE BEMAN, PGA Tour Commissioner, *Golf Digest,* **1983**

I know where all the holes are. Unlike the USGA, the R&A doesn't get some turkeys to go and change the holes around.
LANNY WADKINS, on why he wasn't practising at
St Andrews for the British Open, *Golf Digest,* **1984**

When you say something like, 'The Club is like our home and we invite whoever we want to our home. We have Japanese and Chinese but we don't have any blacks and we don't want any blacks,' that's letting me know they don't want me there.
CALVIN PEETE about the all-white Shoal Creek Golf Club, **1990**

Best rule in golf: That thing about the burrowing animal, whatever it means.
DAN JENKINS, *Fairways and Greens*, **1994**

Choosing not to play on a beautiful day simply because one of 54 holes was considered unplayable gives the impression that the players are wimps and that the game itself is so precious, so uptight, that it can't be conducted unless it conforms to a set of rules that are often absurd.
WALTER BINGHAM, writer, on the cancellation after
two rounds of the AT&T Pebble Beach National Pro-Am,
Sports Illustrated, **1996**

I've never met a player yet who was happy with a two-stroke penalty.
JOHN PARAMOR, European Tour official, after a call went
against Sergio Garcia, **2001**

The rule has been made by a lot of idiots, and I think they've lost their heads. . . The LPGA should stop protecting the weaker US players.
LAURA DAVIES, upset that some of her winnings don't count
as official LPGA earnings, *GolfWorld*, **2004**

If Franklin Roosevelt can run the country out of a wheel-chair, we should be able to use a golf cart.
CHI CHI RODRIGUEZ, on the Champions Tour's decision to ban carts, *Savannah Morning News*, **2005**

I can't for the life of me see why we shouldn't have testing. Who knows what's out there? If no one's doing anything, what's the problem? If we're clean, then let's find out that we're clean.
CRAIG PARRY, supporting Australasian Tour officials' call for drug testing, *The Age*, **2005**

I played until I was 40 with no rules officials on the course, and we managed just fine. When they emerged, I thought that our game [did] not need policemen. Now, of course, very few players know the rules. They don't have to, not with a walking rule book right behind them.
PETER THOMSON, *GolfWorld*, **2005**

If the man himself says it is not an issue, it would be a bit impolite to now try and stuff an award down his throat.
PETER LINDSAY, secretary of the St Andrews community council, after Jack Nicklaus said he wasn't offended at not being named an honorary freeman, *The Scotsman*, **2005**

We want evolution at the R&A, not revolution.
PETER DAWSON, secretary of the Royal & Ancient Golf Club of St Andrews, on the possibility of a woman some day playing in the British Open, *GolfWorld*, **2005**

30 ● Scoring

Bob, you can't always be playing well when it counts. You'll never win golf tournaments until you learn to score well when you're playing badly.

JIM BARNES, teaching professional, advice to a young
Bobby Jones, c. **1915**

The income tax has made more liars out of the American people than golf has.

WILL ROGERS, humorist

Magellan went around the world in 1521, which is not too many strokes when you consider the distance.

JOE LAURIE JR, American vaudevillian

Some lies are believable and some are not. The technique of lying and the timing of lies are at least as important as mastering the drive.

REX LARDNER, *Out of the Bunker and Into the Trees,* **1960**

A pastime that has since created more lying Americans than any other save fishing.
CHARLES PRICE on golf, *The World of Golf,* **1962**

How strange are the lapses of human memory – and none more strange than those suffered by people who play, attempt to play, or watch the game of golf.
HENRY LONGHURST, golf writer, **1965**

One of the troubles with a very high handicap is that the owner is either looked upon as a poor golfer or a possible cheat.
GEORGE PLIMPTON, *The Bogey Man,* **1968**

You play the game by the rules and that in itself is an infallible mark of a gentleman of quality. Nobody ever cheats anybody else at golf. The one who is cheated is the one who cheats.
TOMMY ARMOUR, *A Round of Golf with Tommy Armour,* **1969**

One good thing about shooting the way I've been shooting. You get to play early while the greens are still smooth.
ARNOLD PALMER, at the Masters, **1970**

I'm playing like Tarzan – and scoring like Jane.
CHI CHI RODRIGUEZ, at the Masters, **1970**

'Shot a sixty-nine,' he says, 'but I played badly.' Only Jack Nicklaus can play badly at Augusta and shoot a sixty-nine.
DICK SCHAAP, *The Masters,* **1970**

Well, in plain old English, I'm driving it bad, chipping bad, putting bad, and not scoring at all. Other than that, and the fact I got up this morning, I guess everything's okay.
BOB WYNN, **1975**

Golf is a game in which you yell Fore, shoot six, and write down five.
PAUL HARVEY, news commentator, *Golf Digest,* **1979**

The knack for scoring can go at any moment. It can go while you're walking from the second green to the third tee. But it's like worrying about an atom bomb hitting you. You can't worry about it.
HOWARD TWITTY, US tour pro, **1980**

January: Man, how many do you want to win by, Sam?
Snead: You never know, them folks up ahead might be cheatin'.
DON JANUARY and SAM SNEAD, winning the Legends of Golf
by twelve shots, *Sports Illustrated,* **1982**

Golf appeals to the idiot in us and the child. What child does not grasp the pleasure-principle of miniature golf? Just how childlike golf players become is proven by their frequent inability to count past five.
JOHN UPDIKE, *US Amateur Championship programme,* **1982**

The last time I birdied the first hole, I tried to lay up for the next seventeen.
CHARLES PRICE, *Golfer-At-Large,* **1982**

I don't think that was me that shot that eighty-four. It must have been somebody else. Actually, I was trying to get my handicap squared away.
FUZZY ZOELLER, at the Greater Greensboro Open, **1982**

It was ten years ago, and I've been down a lot of fairways since, and quite a bit of rough, too.
JOHNNY MILLER, on his sixty-three at the US Open,
Golf Magazine, **1983**

After that, I got myself together and bogeyed the last three.
BEN CRENSHAW, on knocking three balls in the water for an eleven at the fourteenth hole, Sea Pines Heritage Classic, **1983**

Golf is based on honesty. Where else would someone admit to a seven on an easy par three?
JIMMY DEMARET

People who say golf is fun are probably the same people who rationalize the game by saying they play it for their health. What could be fun about a game in the entire history of which nobody has ever shot the score he thought he should have?
CHARLES PRICE, *Golf Digest,* **1983**

I'm a nineteen and I think he's about a nineteen, but he cheats more than I do.
DOLORES HOPE, on her husband Bob's handicap,
Golf Digest, **1983**

It's hard to keep score like I do with someone looking over your shoulder.
BOB HOPE, '*Nabisco Dinah Shore Invitational*', NBC-TV, **1983**

It's good to be the first one in the clubhouse with a low score. You can't bogey from the scoreboard.
LEE TREVINO, '*Isuzu-Andy Williams San Diego Open*',
NBC-TV, **1984**

Must have been when I went from nappies to shorts.
NICK FALDO, when asked at the PGA Championship if he could recall the last time he shot an eighty, **1990**

I don't know my slope. I will never know my slope. I don't even *want* to know my slope. I don't even want to know what a slope *is*.
DAN JENKINS, *Fairways and Greens*, **1994**

I'm shell-shocked. No, I'm sorry. I'm flabbergasted.
NICK FALDO, on his eighty-one at the Masters, **1997**

Sometimes I wish there was no tomorrow.
NICK FALDO, on his eighty-three in the Players Championship, **1999**

If you want to be a great player you must be able to get up and down. I've watched Tom Watson hit seven greens and shoot seventy in the British Open. I think that's the art of playing golf well.
HAL SUTTON, **2000**

Tiger Woods.
STUART APPLEBY, Austrian-born US tour pro, when asked what he had to shoot in order to win a tournament, *Sports Illustrated*, **2000**

No matter where you go in the golfing world, there's always a wall with Jack Nicklaus on it.
THOMAS BJORN, after his sixty-three at the PGA Championship tied the Baltusrol GC course record, *GolfWorld*, **2005**

It's easy at times to win golf tournaments and shoot 59, and sometimes it's hard to post an 85.

DAVID DUVAL, after a seventy-four, *GolfWorld*, **2005**

It's like trying to eat an elephant. I can do it, but only bite by bite.

COLIN MONTGOMERIE, on efforts to improve his position in the World Ranking, *europeantour.com*, **2005**

Today it was like, 'Wow.' It's like, 'I can't believe I'm doing this bad.' I want some chocolate.

MICHELLE WIE, after shooting a wind-blown seventy-nine in the first round of the PGA Tour's Sony Open, *Associated Press*, **2006**

I hit it seven times.

BEN CURTIS, on how he made a triple-bogey seven at the Buick Invitational, *San Diego Union-Tribune*, **2006**

31 ● Seniors

A game in which you claim the privileges of age, and retain the playthings of childhood.
SAMUEL JOHNSON, on golf

To that man, age brought only golf instead of wisdom.
GEORGE BERNARD SHAW

Golf, like measles, should be caught young, for, if postponed to riper years, the results may be serious.
P. G. WODEHOUSE, *A Mixed Threesome*, **1920**

Any game where a man sixty can beat a man thirty ain't no game.
BURT SHOTTEN, major-league baseball manager

I can't stand the thought of shooting another eighty.
WALTER HAGEN, when asked why he was retiring, **1940s**

My handicap? Arthritis.
BOBBY JONES, aged forty-five, **1947**

It isn't golf, it's the travelling. I want to die an old man, not a young man.

BEN HOGAN, cutting back on his schedule, **1949**

Golf is like driving a car; as you get older you get more careful.

SAM SNEAD

Look at 'em! They roll 'em in from the middle of the fairway – no idea of how tough the game is. They'll learn, but the trouble is, there'll be a new crop of 'em along about this time next year. Just ain't no way of keeping ahead of 'em.

SAM SNEAD, on the youngsters on the tour, **1960s**

Getting my first Social Security cheque.

GENE SARAZEN, on his greatest thrill

I'm thirty-four, but a Puerto Rican thirty-four is like an American fifty.

CHI CHI RODRIGUEZ, **1970**

The fairways get longer and the holes get smaller.

BOBBY LOCKE, aged fifty-seven, *Golf Digest,* **1972**

People tell me just to put the putter down and putt, but that's like telling a guy to go stand still by a rattlesnake – easier said than done.

SAM SNEAD, aged sixty-two, *San Francisco Chronicle,* **1974**

A caddie watched him miss a short putt that second day at the Hope. 'Hole used to be scared of him. He'd look at it and the hole got scared. Now he's scared of the hole. The hole knows it too.'

DAN GLEASON, on Arnold Palmer, at age forty-five,
The Great, The Grand and the Also-Ran, **1976**

When you're my age, you can't remember a practice round the next day, anyway.
GENE SARAZEN, aged seventy-four, *Golf Digest*, **1976**

Sam Snead, trying to shoot his age the day after his sixty-fourth birthday, instead shot Cliff Roberts' age and missed the cut by two shots.
BEV NORWOOD, writing on Snead's eighty-three in the
Memorial Tournament, **1976**

Only old people follow me around now. Our eyesight isn't what it used to be. They can't see me and I can't see them.
JULIUS BOROS, aged fifty-seven, when asked if big crowds
bothered him, *Golf Digest*, **1977**

If I'm breathing heavy while walking on a green, I'm going uphill. If I trip, I'm going downhill.
DAVID (SPEC) GOLDMAN, Dallas senior golfer, on how he
reads greens, *Golf Digest*, **1979**

My God, it looks like a wax museum!
GEORGE LOW, former touring pro, at his first seniors' event, **1980**

Who does he think he is, Jack Nicklaus again?
ANDY BEAN, after Nicklaus won the PGA Championship at
age forty, **1980**

I retired from competition at twenty-eight, the same age as Jones. The difference was that Jones retired because he beat everybody. I retired because I couldn't beat anybody.
CHARLES PRICE, *Golf Digest*, **1982**

At twenty-five, I thought a course that wasn't seven thousand yards long was a joke. At fifty, I thought there ought to be a law against them.
CHARLES PRICE, *Golfer-At-Large,* **1982**

If anybody yelled 'sick call', the line would run all the way from the locker room to the first tee.
DOUG FORD, on the Senior Tour, *Golf Magazine,* **1982**

I have so many aches and pains that when I go outside my shadow refuses to come along.
WALTER BURKEMO, aged sixty-four, *Golf Magazine,* **1982**

What other sport holds out hope of improvement to a man or woman over fifty? For a duffer like the above-signed, the room for improvement is so vast that three lifetimes could be spent roaming the fairways carving away at it, convinced that perfection lies just over the next rise.
JOHN UPDIKE, *US Amateur Championship programme,* **1982**

When I was inducted into the World Golf Hall of Fame in September of 1981, I passed another milestone. Now I know that some day I can officially become a has-been.
LEE TREVINO, *They Call Me Super Mex,* **1982**

I can't tell if a putt is uphill or downhill, and all short putts look straight.
SAM SNEAD, aged seventy, *The Sporting News,* **1983**

The older you get, the longer you used to be.
CHI CHI RODRIGUEZ, *PGA Tour News,* **1983**

The Senior Tour is like a class reunion. It's the same as it was thirty years ago. We tell the same dirty jokes – only they're funnier now.
BOB TOSKI, *Golf Digest,* **1983**

Like a lot of fellows around here, I have a furniture problem. My chest has fallen into my drawers.
BILLY CASPER, on the Senior Tour, *The Sporting News,* **1983**

I really haven't given it much thought. After all, I won't become eligible for another forty-two months, five days, eight and a half hours.
BUTCH BAIRD, asked if he'd join the Senior Tour,
Golf Digest, **1983**

I'm like a '67 Cadillac. I've changed the engine twice, rolled back the odometer and replaced the transmission. But now all the tyres are goin' flat. It's time to put it in the junkyard.
LEE TREVINO, aged forty-three, *Washington Post,* **1983**

I don't have some long-range goal that I've always wanted to do after I grew up. What am I supposed to say? Yeah, I'm forty-three, and when I'm through with golf I'd like to be an astronaut?
LEE TREVINO, *Golf Digest,* **1983**

It kept me from taking an honest job. My theory is never work for a living if you don't have to.
DON JANUARY, on the Senior Tour, *San Francisco Examiner,* **1984**

I never thought I'd live to shoot my age. I thought somebody would shoot me first.
DALE MOREY, shooting a sixty-five on his sixty-fifth birthday,
Golf Digest, **1984**

My trouble is I can't turn. When you can't turn, you look at your driver after you hit it 'cause you think you left the head-cover on.

SAM SNEAD, aged seventy-one, *Golf Digest,* **1984**

This makes seven halls of fame I'm in. The one in West Virginia you have to either die or retire to get in, but the boys there said, 'It don't look like he's gonna do either, so we better take down the bars and let him in.'

SAM SNEAD, *San Francisco Chronicle,* **1984**

I had forgotten just how sweet the click of a ball sounds.

ARNOLD PALMER, aged fifty-four, on his new hearing aid,
San Francisco Examiner, **1984**

He's the king of kings. . . There's a strength about the man that people want to be around. Anybody who resents Arnold getting more attention than the rest of us doesn't deserve to use his head for more than a hat rack.

DOUG SANDERS, on Arnold Palmer's popularity on the Senior
Tour, *Sports Illustrated,* **1984**

I didn't realize how long some of these seniors have been around. Yesterday I saw a guy signing his scorecard with a feather.

BOB HOPE, *Confessions of a Hooker,* **1985**

I'm 52. If I can last out here [on the Senior Tour] until I'm 65, I'll be able to retire without ever having held a real job.

JOHN BRODIE, former San Francisco 49ers quarterback and
TV golf analyst, *San Francisco Chronicle,* **1987**

Why should I want to be out there with all those young guns? No sense playing the flat bellies when you can play the round bellies.

LEE TREVINO on becoming a 'Senior', **1989**

This is it, these are my boys. I can go in the locker room and bum a cigarette. You go inside on the other tour and all they are doing is drinking orange juice and eating bananas.

LEE TREVINO, **1989**

All you have to do is not fall out of the cart and you make $10,000.

GARY PLAYER, on life and earning a living on the
Senior Tour, *GolfWorld*, **2000**

All I know is that my kids' education is paid for and I don't have to wash and iron my own clothes anymore.

PETE OAKLEY, asked how winning the Senior British Open
(and $289,152) changed his life, *GolfWorld*, **2004**

Saying you have a bad back on the Champions Tour is like saying you're growing less hair on your head and more in your ears.

JIM MORIARTY, writer, *GolfWorld*, **2005**

32 ● The Swing

There is one essential only in the golf swing: the ball must be hit.

SIR WALTER SIMPSON, *The Art of Golf,* **1887**

Golfers find it a very trying matter to turn at the waist, more particularly if they have a lot of waist to turn.

HARRY VARDON

Golf is an awkward set of bodily contortions designed to produce a graceful result.

TOMMY ARMOUR

Nobody ever swung the golf club too slowly.

BOBBY JONES

You know how it is. If you have a broken heart, it's bound to give you a twinge now and then, and if this happens when you are starting your down swing, you neglect to let the club head lead.

P.G. WODEHOUSE, *There's Always Golf,* **1937**

He took a swing like a man with a wasp under his shirt and his pants on fire, trying to impale a butterfly on the end of a scythe.

PAUL GALLICO, *Golf Is a Nice Friendly Game,* **1942**

Take it easily and lazily, because the golf ball isn't going to run away from you while you're swinging.

SAM SNEAD, *How to Play Golf,* **1946**

Yes, you're probably right about the left hand, but the fact is that I take the cheques with my right hand.

BOBBY LOCKE, on his weak left-hand grip, **1947**

I once played with Henry Ford II and told him, 'You can buy a country, but you can't buy a golf swing. It's not on a shelf.'

GENE SARAZEN

Don't change the arc of your swing unless you are fairly sure you blundered in some way earlier.

REX LARDNER, *Out of the Bunker and Into the Trees,* **1960**

The best place to refine your swing is, of course, right out on the practice range . . . You will have an opportunity to make the same mistakes over and over again so that you no longer have to think about them, and they become part of your game.

STEPHEN BAKER, *How to Play Golf in the Low 120s,* **1962**

Hope: What do you think of my swing?
Palmer: I've seen better swings in a condemned playground.

BOB HOPE and ARNOLD PALMER,
'Chrysler Presents a Bob Hope Special', NBC-TV, **1963**

Always fade the ball. You can't talk to a hook.

DAVE MARR, **1968**

I tried for years to slow my swing. Then all of a sudden it came – like whistling.
TONY JACKLIN, after winning the Open at Royal Lytham, **1969**

Too many golfers grip the club at address like they were trying to choke a prairie coyote to death.
CURT WILSON, Las Vegas trick-shot artist, *Golf Digest,* **1970**

Hook: The addiction of fifty per cent of all golfers.
Slice: The weakness of the other half.
JIM BISHOP, syndicated column, **1970**

To get an elementary grasp of the game of golf, a human must learn, by endless practice, a continuous and subtle series of highly unnatural movements, involving about sixty-four muscles, that result in a seemingly 'natural' swing, taking all of two seconds to begin and end.
ALISTAIR COOKE

How do I address the ball? I say, 'Hello there, ball. Are you going to go in the hole or not?'
FLIP WILSON, *'The Flip Wilson Show'*, NBC-TV, **1972**

Everybody has two swings – a beautiful practice swing and the choked-up one with which they hit the ball. So it wouldn't do either of us a damned bit of good to look at your practice swing.
ED FURGOL, *Golf Magazine,* **1974**

Here we are, making thousands of dollars a year, and we're trying to change our swings.
JOHNNY MILLER on the practice tee, *Golf Digest,* **1974**

The golf swing is like sex in this respect. You can't be thinking about the mechanics of the act while you're performing.
DAVE HILL, *Teed Off,* **1977**

'We know a lot about the swing,' one college golf coach said to me, 'but not much about how to help golfers learn it.'
W. TIMOTHY GALLWEY, *The Inner Game of Golf,* **1979**

I remember being upset once and telling my dad I wasn't following through right, and he replied, 'Nancy, it doesn't make any difference to a ball what you do after you hit it.'
NANCY LOPEZ, *The Education of a Woman Golfer,* **1979**

The only thing that you should force in a golf swing is the club back into the bag.
BYRON NELSON

We are getting too mechanical about the golf swing. . . Golf was never meant to be an exact science – it's an art form. Einstein was a great scientist but a lousy golfer.
BOB TOSKI, *Golf Digest,* **1981**

Just hit the ball and go chase it. You will probably make your best effort on each shot.
JOHNNY MILLER, *Golf Magazine,* **1982**

If a great swing put you high on the money list, there'd be some of us who would be broke!
RAYMOND FLOYD, *Golf Magazine,* **1982**

Golferswhotalkfastswingfast.
BOB TOSKI, *Golf Digest,* **1982**

No one who ever had lessons would have a swing like mine.
LEE TREVINO, '*The Tonight Show*', NBC-TV, **1983**

I still swing the way I used to, but when I look up the ball is going in a different direction.
LEE TREVINO, *Golf Digest,* **1984**

You show me a player who swings out of his shoes and I'll show you a player who isn't going to win enough to keep himself in a decent pair of shoes for very long.
SAM SNEAD, *Golf Digest,* **1984**

If that ball hit the 17 Mile Drive, it'll be a 23-mile drive.
VERN LUNDQUIST, on a slice at Pebble Beach,
'*Bing Crosby National Pro-Am*', CBS-TV, **1984**

My golf swing is a bit like ironing a shirt. You get one side smoothed out, turn it over and there is a big wrinkle on the other side. Then you iron that one out, turn it over and there is yet another wrinkle.
TOM WATSON, **1987**

That's the worst swing I've ever heard.
PAT BROWNE, American national blind golf champion, about one of his playing partners, **1988**

I am a perfectionist. I knew I had a lot of work to do before I could rely on my swing absolutely.
NICK FALDO, on his two-year effort to make swing changes in the mid-1980s, *PGA European Tour Yearbook*, **1988**

The only difference between an amateur and a pro is that we call a shot that goes left-to-right a fade and an amateur calls it a slice.
PETER JACOBSEN, **1990**

It's like a colour movie. First I see the ball where I want it to finish. Then the scene quickly changes and I see the ball going there. Then there is a sort of fade-out and the next scene shows me making the kind of swing that will turn the previous images into reality.

JACK NICKLAUS, **1992**

Of course a woman's chest interferes with making a swing. How could it not? The trick is to swing the arms over the bosom, not under. To do that, we have to bend over at the hips a little more to give our arms room to swing. It's not natural. For the record, having breasts is not an advantage.

'BIG MAMA' JOANNE CARNER, *Golf Digest*, **2003**

Draw the club straight back. Never mind about what the books din into you about turns and pivots. Just draw it straight back as far as is comfortable and let nature take its course.

PETER THOMSON, five-time British Open winner,
GolfWorld, **2005**

33 ● Tournaments

Look at that little pissy-assed medal of yours. I got real dough.
JOCK HUTCHISON, to amateur Chick Evans at the US Open, **1916**

I've seen more people on the back of a motorcycle.
GEORGE LOW, to Bing Crosby, on the crowds at his fledgling
tournament, c. **1940s**

Hell, I didn't even know he was in the field. I thought he was
there peddling headcovers or something.
SAM SNEAD, on Toney Penna, who defeated him in the
North-South Open, **1948**

I hope I don't upset Jack's game. No one has ever watched
me play but cows.
HANS SCHWEIZER, Swiss golfer, on being paired with Jack
Nicklaus at the World Team Amateur Championship, **1960**

Now on the pot, Johnny Tee.
ANNOUNCER, on first tee of the Los Angeles Open,
introducing Johnny Pott, c. **1960s**

The record book has me down for a seventy-nine on the
final day. That looks pretty woeful, but considering what
happened the night before it was a pretty good round of golf.
TONY LEMA, on the 1959 San Diego Open, *Golfer's Gold,* **1964**

Reporter: What happened, Marty?
Fleckman: I got back on my game. That's all.
MARTY FLECKMAN, on shooting an eighty after leading after
three rounds of the US Open, **1967**

When they say they have a 'Sudden Death Play-Off', it's not
always just a figure of speech. You need penicillin in your bag
more than a one-iron. It's known to some of the pros as 'The
VapoRub Open'.
JIM MURRAY, on the Bing Crosby National Pro-Am,
The Sporting World of Jim Murray, **1968**

My wife's got a broken wrist, we've got a ten-week-old baby,
and our dog's pregnant. I came out here to rest.
LEE TREVINO, at the Byron Nelson Classic, **1969**

These greens are so bad the Dallas Cowboys wouldn't play on
'em. They ought to plough 'em up and plant 'em with potatoes.
LEE TREVINO, at the World Cup in Buenos Aires, **1970**

My putter had a heart attack the last nine holes and just died
on me.
LANNY WADKINS, after leading for three rounds and slipping to
fourth in the Byron Nelson Classic, **1973**

I'd played in the Open before, of course. Several times. And I'd been in all of the other majors now and then. But I'd never been any closer to the lead than the parking lot.
DAN JENKINS, *Dead Solid Perfect,* **1974**

The greens are the biggest joke since Watergate.
LEE TREVINO, on the Victorian Open played at Royal Lemborne, Melbourne, Australia, **1974**

The fourteenth hole was the turning point. When I four-putted for the second time, I knew I was in trouble.
BILL ERFURTH, Chicago club pro, on shooting an eighty-eight at the US Open at Winged Foot, **1974**

The pin placements weren't too tough, but whoever set them missed ten greens.
LEONARD THOMPSON, at the Greater Greensboro Open, **1975**

Trying to catch Nicklaus from that far back is like trying to climb Mount Everest in street shoes.
TOM KITE, eight shots behind after two rounds of the Sea Pines Heritage Classic, **1975**

The only way I could have beaten him was if he fell into a lake and couldn't swim.
GEORGE BAYER, on losing to Don January by eight shots in the PGA Senior Championship, **1980**

It wasn't much fun being an amateur. I got tired of polishing the silverware.
PATTY SHEEHAN, *San Jose Mercury News,* **1980**

It was a very long day. I don't know how long we've been out here, but I know it's time to shave again.
FUZZY ZOELLER, on playing thirty-six holes on the final day of the rain-delayed Colonial National Invitation tournament, **1981**

Some girl in sprayed-on jeans followed him around all day, which just proves that even Nathaniel can be distracted.
KATHRYN CROSBY, as her son Nathaniel shot an eighty in qualifying for the US Amateur, **1981**

Everybody in my family is talented. My father, my mother, my brother, my sister Mary. She shot J. R. Gosh, I had to win the Amateur.
NATHANIEL CROSBY, on winning the US Amateur, **1981**

I hadn't won in so long, I wanted to be sure this one soaked in.
JERRY PATE, after he jumped in the lake upon winning the Danny Thomas-Memphis Classic, **1982**

The ball jumped out of the hole and hit me on the foot. Technically, it was only a seven-putt green.
JERRY PATE, after taking nine shots from the fringe at Firestone's second hole at the World Series of Golf, **1982**

I shot a Red Grange today – seventy-seven. Somebody should have shot me. I looked like I needed a white cane.
TOM WATSON, at the US Open, **1982**

It looked like a civil rights march out there. People were afraid we were going to steal their hubcaps.
CHI CHI RODRIGUEZ, on being paired with Homero Blancas and Rod Curl at the Anderson-Pacific Golf Classic, **1983**

Hell, he's been one back, or one or two ahead, all his life.
JAY HAAS, leading the Los Angeles Open, asked if he was
worried about Jack Nicklaus, one shot back, **1984**

This is a nice tournament. Of course, you have to caddie for
Bob Hope before you get an invitation.
JOEY BISHOP, comic, *'Bob Hope Classic'*, NBC-TV, **1984**

I realize that's why we play golf, to hit the ball into the hole.
But it's such a strange feeling when you hit a shot and it
actually goes in.
HOLLIS STACY, after holing a 123-yard seven-iron at the
US Women's Open, **1984**

They ought to give away the car for hitting the green at all.
MARK MCCUMBER, on the car given away for an ace at the
windblown seventh hole at the Honda Classic, **1984**

From April to August, I went to so many golf tournaments I
felt like an alligator on a shirt pocket.
DAN JENKINS, *Life Its Ownself*, **1984**

I got a room once for $36 a night. At Pebble Beach, that was
my major accomplishment.
GARY MCCORD, on the Bing Crosby National Pro-Am, **1984**

What do I think of the pin placements? I think every green
should have a pin placement.
GARY MCCORD, at the Hawaiian Open, **1985**

Losing the Ryder Cup did not bother me as much as the
behaviour of the galleries. All that cheering when we missed
shots. I've never known anything like it before and especially
not from a British crowd. You expect so much from them.
PETER JACOBSEN, following the matches at The Belfry, **1985**

I meant to tell Lee Trevino not to be too despondent. This cup is going to change hands quite often in the future. He will not be the last losing American captain.
TONY JACKLIN, at The Belfry, **1985**

I never thought I would live to see golf played the way it was today.
TONY JACKLIN about his European Ryder Cup team's win on American soil for the first time, **1987**

We shall brush aside all doubts, handle all adversity and sweep to victory. If I go any further, I will break into song.
NICK FALDO, predicting Europe's Ryder Cup win, **1995**

The Ryder Cup brings out the best in me and I'm glad it does.
COLIN MONTGOMERIE, **1999**

We are playing for our souls.
BEN CRENSHAW, Ryder Cup captain, *Ryder Cup Magazine*, **1999**

I felt embarrassed for golf. It went beyond the decency you associate with proper golf. I love the Ryder Cup and I don't want to see it degenerate into a mob demonstration every time we play.
SIR MICHAEL BONALLACK, following the Ryder Cup matches at The Country Club, won by the US, **1999**

We just live for this. We can't wait to play in this event. You probably try harder and believe in yourself more than in some other tournaments.
SERGIO GARCIA, on the Ryder Cup matches, *GolfWorld*, **2004**

34 ● Tour Players: Men

George Archer, American 1939–2005

His personal life will never hurt his nerves. George's idea of a big night out is a hamburger at McDonald's and a science fiction movie.
DAVE HILL, *Teed Off,* **1977**

Tommy Armour, American, 1895–1968

Tommy Armour has a mouth like a steel trap, a nose like a ski jump, hands like the fins of a shark, and eyes which indicate he would enjoy seeing you get a compound fracture of the leg. He is as temperamental as a soprano with a frog in her throat.
CLARENCE BUDINGTON KELLAND, in *The American Golfer,* **1935**

Ian Baker-Finch, Australian, born 1960

To this day, I would love to be able to go out and play in a tournament and perform well, just to show people, even one time, that I can still play and that I'm not a 90s shooter.
IAN BAKER-FINCH, 1991 British Open champion, contemplating a return to competition after a five-year hiatus, *GolfWorld*, **2005**

Seve Ballesteros, Spanish, born 1957

He goes after a golf course like a lion at a zebra. He doesn't reason with it; he tries to throw it out of the window or hold its head under water till it stops wriggling.
JIM MURRAY, *Los Angeles Times*, **1976**

I'd like to see the fairways more narrow. Then everybody would have to play from the rough, not just me.
SEVE BALLESTEROS at the British Open, *Golf Digest*, **1979**

Seve drives the ball into territory Daniel Boone couldn't find.
FUZZY ZOELLER, **1981**

Seve's never in trouble. We see him in the trees quite a lot, but that looks normal to him.
BEN CRENSHAW, *Sports Illustrated*, **1983**

Trying to catch Seve is like a Chevy pickup trying to catch a Ferrari.
TOM KITE at the Masters, *The Sporting News*, **1983**

Sometimes I think the only way the Spanish people will recognize me is if I win the Grand Slam and then drop dead on the eighteenth green.
SEVE BALLESTEROS, on his lack of recognition in his home country, *GolfWorld,* **1984**

Seve has the charisma to dominate you. When he walks on to the course, he looks as though he owns the place. And when he holes a good putt he makes you think he's unstoppable.
RODGER DAVIS, Australian pro, after a win over Ballesteros in the World Match Play Championship, **1986**

When Seve gets his Porsche going, not even San Pedro in heaven could stop him.
JOSE MARIA OLAZABAL, on partnering with Ballesteros in a Ryder Cup match, which they won six and five, **1989**

I don't know how he can keep going. If I played like that I'd have to go away and sort it out and if I couldn't sort it out, I'd pack up.
IAN WOOSNAM, *Daily Mail,* **2001**

The Spaniard has become, through a combination of injury and mind-boggling technical inefficiency with the longer clubs, a snarling shadow of the smiling youth he once was. Majesty for mediocrity is a tough swap.
JOHN HUGGAN, writer, *GolfWorld,* **2005**

Miller Barber, American, born 1931

Miller has always been a bit of a hypochondriac... His golf bag looks like something Marcus Welby might carry... Before he heads for the first tee, 'X' is armed and ready to face the wilderness.
BEN CRENSHAW, *Golf Magazine,* **1981**

When Barber swings, it looks as if his golf club gets caught in a clothesline.
BEN CRENSHAW, *The Sporting News,* **1984**

His swing reminds me a lot of a machine I once saw at a country fair making saltwater taffy. It goes in four directions and none of them seem right.
BUCK ADAMS, director of golf, Country Club of North Carolina, *GolfWorld,* **1984**

Andy Bean, American, born 1953

He's a superstar from the neck down.
DAVID OGRIN, *Golf Digest,* **1984**

Frank Beard, American, born 1939

He looks like a bad doctor from Elko, Nevada, whose chemistry set blew up and he's golfing for penance.
DON RICKLES, comedian

Tommy Bolt, American, born 1918

Tommy Bolt's putter has spent more time in the air than Lindbergh.
JIMMY DEMARET

Turning off his temper is rather like capping Mount Vesuvius – interesting but impractical.
JIM MURRAY, *Los Angeles Times*

I must say he's my type of man. He just doesn't give one hoot for anybody.
ERIC BROWN, in *Out of the Bag,* **1964**

Julius Boros, American, 1920–1994

Julius Boros is all hands and wrists like a man dusting the furniture.
TONY LEMA on his swing, *Golfer's Gold*, **1964**

Gay Brewer, American, born 1932

Gay Brewer? I always thought he was a little fag wine maker from Modesto.
PHIL HARRIS to Chris Schenkel,
'Bing Crosby National Pro-Am', ABC-TV, **1974**

He swings the club in a figure eight. If you didn't know better you'd swear he was trying to kill snakes.
DAVE HILL, *Teed Off*, **1977**

Rex Caldwell, American, born 1950

I have a reputation now of being an excellent putter. The other guys figure I must be putting good to win so much money, because the rest of my game is so bad.
REX CALDWELL, *Golf Digest*, **1978**

'Rex has been a rabbit so long that his nose twitches when he gets around a salad bar,' says one pro.
BARRY MCDERMOTT, *Sports Illustrated*, **1983**

I'm not your stereotyped golf pro. I say dirt when it's dirt.
REX CALDWELL, *Sports Illustrated*, **1983**

Michael Campbell, New Zealander, born 1969

I'm good, but I'm not that good.
MICHAEL CAMPBELL, apologizing for the rain at a parade in
New Zealand to celebrate his US Open victory,
GolfWorld, **2005**

Joe Carr, Irish, 1922–2004

That Irishman is so popular in the United States that he
could stand for President. What's more, he'd probably be
elected!
GENE SARAZEN

Billy Casper, American, born 1931

Billy Casper, currently one of the best putters from four
hundred yards in to the hole that the tour has ever seen.
TONY LEMA, *Golfer's Gold,* **1964**

I feel sorry for Casper. He can't putt a lick. He missed three
thirty-footers out there today.
GARY PLAYER, at the US Open, **1964**

Billy could putt in a ploughed field.
JOHN SCHLEE, *Golf Magazine,* **1968**

Allergic to everything but money and religion.
MARK MULVOY and ART SPANDER,
Golf: The Passion and the Challenge, **1977**

Bobby Clampett, American, born 1960

He is a tall, slender young man who, from a distance, looks a bit like Harpo Marx in double knits.
JIM MORIARTY, *Sport,* **1982**

I told Bobby, 'I don't like your golf swing and I never have.' He had more moves than an erector set.
JIMMY BALLARD, teaching professional, *Golf Digest,* **1984**

Darren Clarke, British, born 1968

I saw a Darren Clarke today I hadn't seen before. I knew he was capable, but he did to Tiger Woods what Tiger Woods has been doing to other people. He kicked his butt and looked him in the eye as he was doing it.
BUTCH HARMON, after Clarke beat Woods to win the
Anderson Consulting Match Play Championship, **2000**

He knows the outside of a cigar, the inside of a Ferrari and the bottom of a glass of Guinness.
JOHN HOPKINS, *The Times,* **2003**

Bobby Cole, South African, born 1948

Cole is the second shortest South African on the pro tour. . .
He is one inch taller than Gary Player and a million dollars poorer.
DICK SCHAAP, *Massacre at Winged Foot,* **1974**

Charles Coody, American, born 1937

Charlie Coody is unbelievable. He'll give you his entire round right down to the number of tees he broke. When I see him, I say, 'I hope you shot sixty-four, Charlie, so it'll take you only an hour to tell me about it.'
FRANK BEARD, *Golf Digest,* **1975**

Henry Cotton, British, 1907–1987

You couldn't tell whether Cotton was in the right or left side of the fairway because his ball was so close to the middle.
BOB TOSKI, *Golf Digest,* **1983**

Bruce Crampton, Australian, born 1935

Bruce Crampton, an Australian who'd had a terrible time getting people to like him, even on those rare occasions when he tried.
DAN GLEASON, *The Great, The Grand and the Also-Ran,* **1976**

Ben Crenshaw, American, born 1952

He hits it in the woods so often he should get an orange hunting jacket.
TOM WEISKOPF, **1979**

I sometimes wonder if he shouldn't stop reading so much about golf history and start making some.
DAVE MARR, *Golf Digest,* **1981**

Ben is the best damn second-and-third-place finisher in the majors the world will ever know.
KEVIN COOK, *Playboy,* **1982**

I don't remember Ben ever missing a putt from the time he was twelve until he was twenty.
TOM KITE, after Crenshaw won the Masters, his first major,
Sports Illustrated, **1984**

John Daly, American, born 1966

It's great to see. He's like every fifteen- and sixteen-year-old kid. He just rears back and hits it as far as he can, and if he can find it, he's okay.
CRAIG STADLER, on Daly's stunning victory at the PGA
Championship, **1991**

Jimmy Demaret, American, 1910–1983

Best Wind Player: This one easily goes to Jimmy Demaret. He could come in first in this category just using his mouth.
CHARLES PRICE, *Golf Magazine,* **1975**

People say it was amazing that Jimmy could win three Masters almost without practising. I think it's amazing he could win them almost without sleeping.
SAM SNEAD, *Golf Digest,* **1983**

That's what caused both of my divorces, spending too much time with Jimmy.
LEE TREVINO, *'Legends of Golf',* NBC-TV, **1984**

Jim Dent, American, born 1939

Jim Dent is the longest hitter around today. He not only has a graphite shaft, he has graphite arms, too.
GEORGE BAYER, *Golf Magazine,* **1974**

Roberto de Vicenzo, Argentinian, born 1923

Play good, Roberto, I'm betting on you to be low Mexican.
JIMMY DEMARET

What player on the tour would you *least* want to figure your income tax?
DAVE MARR, referring to de Vicenzo's Masters' scorecard incident, **1968**

Leo Diegel, American, 1899–1951

Leo Diegel, a perfectionist who unfortunately had the nerves of a schoolgirl.
CHARLES PRICE, *The World of Golf,* **1962**

They keep trying to give me a championship, but I won't take it.
LEO DIEGEL

Lee Elder, American, born 1934

I like Lee. He's a cheerful, easygoing guy. He could sleep through the most important appointment of his life.
DAVE HILL, *Teed Off,* **1977**

Ernie Els, South African, born 1969

Ernie is very good at plodding along and taking chances when they come up. . . No one grinds it out like him.
THOMAS BJORN, *GolfWorld,* **2004**

Nick Faldo, British, born 1957

He has the long, graceful swing to my short, flat one. He's more elegant. I'm a bit of a plodder.
SANDY LYLE, *Ryder Cup Magazine*, **1987**

Another thing is his course management is different. I would have loved to have smashed a driver down that first hole but no. Three wood, keep it on the left-hand side, draw it in here, hold it up here, fade it in here. I think sometimes Faldo is trying to do too much with the ball instead of actually standing up and hitting it.
COLIN MONTGOMERIE, *Golf Digest*, **1997**

He may come off as more affable . . . these days, but when he's out playing, he doesn't say a thing. Playing with Nick Faldo is like playing with yourself – only slower.
MARK CALCAVECCHIA, *Palm Beach Post*, **2005**

Raymond Floyd, American, born 1942

Raymond has done it all. If he were playing Sunday in Miami and there was a party that night in Dallas, he'd charter a plane.
LANNY WADKINS, *Golf Digest*, **1982**

Ivan Gantz, American, 1903–1990

Worst temperament? . . . My choice has to be Ivan Gantz, who has long since abandoned the tour. He used to get so disgusted at himself that he threw clubs on the *practice tee*!
CHARLES PRICE, *Golf Magazine*, **1975**

Sergio Garcia, Spanish, born 1980

He wakes up early and then it's full speed. At least he took care of the kids some, and then he was chasing the nannies the rest of the time.

JESPER PARNEVIK, on his house guest, *GolfWorld*, **2001**

Al Geiberger, American, born 1937

There are certain things you don't believe in: the Easter Bunny, campaign promises, the Abominable Snowman, a husband with lipstick on his collar, and a guy who tells you he shot fifty-nine on his own ball – and his wife didn't keep score.

JIM MURRAY, on Geiberger's fifty-nine in the Danny Thomas Memphis Classic, *Los Angeles Times,* **1977**

Retief Goosen, South African, born 1969

Obviously, I'd like to keep moving up and see if I can move into the 'Big Four' category, but then they'll probably change it to the 'Big Three.'

RETIEF GOOSEN, on his perceived status as the fifth best player in golf – behind Tiger Woods, Phil Mickelson, Vijay Singh and Ernie Els, *GolfWorld*, **2005**

David Graham, Australian, born 1946

Expressionlessly erect, alone in the throng beneath the afternoon sun, the picture of Graham recalled a line from Carl Sandburg: Having only the savvy God gave him, lacking a gat, lacking brass knucks.

EDWIN POPE, US sports columnist, on Graham's demeanour in winning the 1981 US Open at Merion, *US Open Official Magazine,* **1984**

Hubert Green, American, born 1946

His swing looks like a drunk trying to find a keyhole in the dark.

JIM MURRAY, *Los Angeles Times*

I don't try to analyze my swing. I looked at it once on film and almost got sick.

HUBERT GREEN, *Golf Digest,* **1977**

Aw, that's just Hubert over there fixing his golf swing.

FUZZY ZOELLER, hearing a chain saw, *Golf Digest,* **1983**

Walter Hagen, American, 1892–1969

Walter is not a religious man. I know he believes in God, but if I ever wanted to go looking for him I wouldn't start with a church. I have an idea he's broken eleven of the Ten Commandments.

FRED CORCORAN, executive director of the PGA, to Monsignor Robert Barry, **1940**

Hagen could relax sitting on a hot stove. His touch was sensitive as a jeweller's scale. If he estimated a club's weight and the scales didn't check with Walter's guess, the scales were wrong.

TOMMY ARMOUR

One thing about Walter, he wouldn't spend your money any faster than he spends his own.

BOB HARLOW, Hagen's manager

Golf has never had a showman like him. All the professionals who have a chance to go after the big money today should say a silent thanks to Walter each time they stretch a cheque between their fingers.

GENE SARAZEN, *Thirty Years of Championship Golf,* **1950**

He was not the pushy type and never sought an invitation. With the then Prince of Wales tagging Walter's footsteps, somehow he didn't have to.

GRANTLAND RICE, *The Tumult and the Shouting,* **1954**

He carried it off big. He was gorgeous. One got the impression that he had invented the game.

CHARLES PRICE, *The World of Golf,* **1962**

Hagen spent money like a King Louis with a bottomless treasury. In the credit-card age, he might have broken American Express. As it was, he got by.

AL BARKOW, *Golf's Golden Grind,* **1974**

The best putters have almost invariably been slow movers. Walter Hagen took five minutes to reach for and lift a salt shaker, forty-five minutes to shave. He just *never* rushed into anything.

GEORGE LOW, *The Master of Putting,* **1983**

Clayton Heafner, American, 1914–1960

Clayton Heafner. He's mad *all* the time.

JIMMY DEMARET, asked which player on the tour had the most even disposition

Clayton had a bad temper. The only time he could putt was when he was mad enough to *hate* the ball into the hole.

DR CARY MIDDLECOFF, ESPN-TV, **1982**

Lionel Hebert, American, 1928–2000

Here comes old Lionel Hebert. He'll either give you a lesson or take one.
SAM SNEAD

Dave Hill, American, born 1937

I had knee surgery late in 1973 and one of my smart-assed fellow pros said, 'How's that going to help his head?'
DAVE HILL, *Teed Off,* **1977**

I'm crazy, but I have an advantage over most people. I know it.
DAVE HILL, *Teed Off,* **1977**

Ben Hogan, American, 1912–1997

It takes him three hours to go nine holes in practice... He'll even memorize the grain of the grass. He'll putt till hell won't have it.
CLYDE STARR, caddie, *Time,* **1949**

I'm only scared of three things – lightning, a side-hill putt, and Ben Hogan.
SAM SNEAD

Hogan came as near to dehumanizing golf as anyone has ever done.
PAT WARD-THOMAS, golf writer

The answer to Hogan is, I fancy, that if Hogan means to win, you lose.
HENRY LONGHURST, *Round in Sixty-eight,* **1953**

If he had needed a sixty-four on the last round, you were quite certain he could have played a sixty-four. Hogan gave the distinct impression he was capable of getting whatever score was needed to win.
BERNARD DARWIN, golf writer, after Ben Hogan shot a closing sixty-eight to win the British Open, **1953**

I am happy to have lived long enough to see Ben Hogan play golf.
BERNARD DARWIN, aged seventy-six at the British Open, **1953**

I've always been friendly with Ben until the past two years or so, I guess, but we haven't had much to do with each other. But, then, Hogan doesn't have much to do with anybody.
LLOYD MANGRUM, **1953**

Ben wants to know the place so well that he could give a biologist a thorough life history of the four rabbits who hole up off the fourteenth fairway.
JIMMY DEMARET, *My Partner, Ben Hogan,* **1954**

Ben Hogan is what is known as a 'hard case'. You could see him sitting at a poker table saying, 'Your thousand – and another five.' He might have four aces, or a pair of twos.
HENRY LONGHURST, in *A Hard Case from Texas,* **1957**

'Those steel-grey eyes of his,' one friend once remarked with a slight shudder. 'He looks at you like a landlord asking for next month's rent.'
WILL GRIMSLEY, *Sport,* **1961**

All I know is that Nicklaus watches Hogan practise and I never heard of Hogan watching Nicklaus practise.
TOMMY BOLT, *Golf Digest,* **1978**

Hale Irwin, American, born 1945

Maybe I'll come out tomorrow on a pogo stick. Maybe they'll notice me then.
HALE IRWIN, on his lack of image, **1974**

Hale Irwin isn't the sort of golfer who celebrates victories by buying champagne for the house. His idea of a party is drinking a sugar-free cola and contemplating prudent ways of investing his latest pay cheque.
FRED GUZMAN, *San Jose Mercury News,* **1984**

Bobby Jones, American, 1902–1971

They wound up the Mechanical Man of Golf yesterday and sent him clicking round the East Lake course.
KERR PETRIE, on the Southern Open
New York Herald Tribune, **1927**

One might as well attempt to describe the smoothness of the wind as to paint a clear picture of his complete swing.
GRANTLAND RICE, sportswriter

The steady-going and unimaginative will often beat the more eager champion and they will get very near the top, but there, I think, they will stop. The prose labourer must yield to the poet, and Bobby as a golfer had a strain of poetry in him.
BERNARD DARWIN, British golf writer

He had supernatural strength of mind.
BEN HOGAN

From the time Jones was fourteen to the time he was twenty-eight, no man ever beat him twice in championship match play...To deprecate Jones's record would be a little like saying the Civil War wasn't on the level.
CHARLES PRICE, *The World of Golf,* **1962**

Gary Koch, American, born 1952

If that kid ever forgets how to putt, he might as well give up.
PETER COOPER, veteran professional, on Koch at age sixteen, **1968**

Lawson Little, American, 1910–1968

There were a number of reasons Little's career as a professional was relatively lacklustre...After winning a tournament, for one thing, he was often too busy celebrating to win the next one.
CHARLES PRICE, *Golfer-At-Large,* **1982**

Gene Littler, American, born 1930

Doesn't take a Rolls-Royce long to warm up, does it?
TOMMY AARON, watching Littler on the practice tee, **1970**

He gave me a typical Littler conversation. Three yeps, two nopes and two nods.
TED SCHROEDER, father of pro John Schroeder, **1974**

There's no such guy as Littler. He mails in his scores.
BOB DRUM, sportswriter, on Littler's image, *Golf Digest,* **1975**

Bobby Locke, South African, 1917–1987

He was not like Jack Nicklaus, who careens along the fairways, then takes aeons over the shot. Locke has just two speeds for everything – leisurely and slow.
KEN BOWDEN, *Golf Digest,* **1972**

That son of a bitch Locke was able to hole a putt over sixty feet of peanut brittle.
LLOYD MANGRUM, *Golf Magazine,* **1982**

George Low, American, 1912–1995

He is, all at once, America's guest, underground comedian, consultant, inventor of the overlapping grip for a beer can, and, more importantly, a man who has conquered the two hardest things in life – how to putt better than anyone else, and how to live lavishly without an income.
DAN JENKINS, *The Dogged Victims of Inexorable Fate,* **1970**

He was born retired.
JIMMY DEMARET

Mark Lye, American, born 1952

Are you guys as surprised as I am?
MARK LYE, leading the Masters, to the press, **1984**

A lanky figure moving down the fairways with the wide, clumping strides one usually associates with farm boys.
HERBERT WARREN WIND, on Lye at the Masters,
The New Yorker, **1984**

Johnny McDermott, American, 1891–1971

For practice McDermott used to hit balls to a newspaper spread out on a field, and the story goes that he sometimes got mad if the ball failed to stop on the right paragraph.
CHARLES PRICE, *The World of Golf,* **1962**

Dave Marr, American, 1933–1997

Some days I felt like Superman and other days I found I was made of Jell-O.
DAVE MARR, *Golf Digest,* **1980**

Billy Maxwell, American, born 1929

Billy Maxwell leaps at the ball like a panhandler diving for a ten-spot.
TONY LEMA, *Golfer's Gold,* **1964**

Phil Mickelson, American, born 1970

He could play with a banana and a hockey stick.
DAVID FEHERTY, on Mickelson's sixty-two at Spyglass Hill,
USA Network, **2005**

Yeah, but is that the true Phil? Is that the true person? Do you see the true side of Phil? I don't know. I cannot speak for Phil. But you see the true me. I don't hide things.
VIJAY SINGH, asked to compare his image with that of
Mickelson's, *'Real Sports'*, HBO, **2005**

Cary Middlecoff, American, 1921–1998

Cary, a splendid champion, was forever a slow player...A joke on the tour used to be that Cary gave up dentistry because no patient could hold his mouth open that long.
DAN JENKINS, *The Dogged Victims of Inexorable Fate,* **1970**

Middlecoff the dentist . . . he doesn't hit his irons, he drills them...Every time he wins another tournament, he raises his dental rates.We only hope he fills cavities faster than he plays golf.
MARK MULVOY and ART SPANDER,
Golf:The Passion and the Challenge, **1977**

Johnny Miller, American, born 1947

Schenkel: Johnny Miller has a smooth touch.
Harris: Yeah. As smooth as a man lifting a breast out of an evening gown.
CHRIS SCHENKEL and PHIL HARRIS,
'*Bing Crosby National Pro-Am*', ABC-TV, **1974**

Young John is the tour's Mr Clean. He doesn't smoke, drink, cuss, or wink at strange girls. He plays pool – but only in Billy Casper's recreation room.
DAVE HILL, *Teed Off,* **1977**

As comfortable in the desert as a cactus.
NICK SEITZ, *Superstars of Golf,* **1978**

I had a stretch there for a few years where I played some golf that bordered on the Twilight Zone... I can remember that I was literally getting upset that I had to putt.
JOHNNY MILLER, on his play in the mid-1970s,
Golf Magazine, **1982**

Colin Montgomerie, British, born 1963

It's a lovely feeling to have whacked Monty. He's a good friend but he's the last man you want breathing down your neck in a tight situation. When he gets the bit between his teeth, he's hard to beat.
FRANK NOBILO, on winning the TPC of Europe, **1996**

Monty is the greatest harumpher since Colonel Hathi in *The Jungle Book*.
JOHN HUGGAN, columnist, *GolfWorld*, **1998**

Sometimes the guy has no filter between his heart, his brain and his mouth, but his opinions aren't detrimental to the game.
JOHNNY MILLER

Orville Moody, American, born 1933

Nor did his cross-handed putting method particularly recommend him, since no man had ever putted cross-handed and won more than a kick in the ass with a cold boot.
DAN JENKINS, *The Dogged Victims of Inexorable Fate*, **1970**

If you had to pick one man you would *not* want putting for your life, he would be it.
BRUCE DEVLIN, 'Seiko-Tucson Match Play Championship',
ESPN-TV, **1984**

Byron Nelson, American, born 1912

I wouldn't bet *anyone* against Byron Nelson. The only time Nelson left the fairway was to pee in the bushes.
JACKIE BURKE, *Golf Magazine*, **1981**

Larry Nelson, American, born 1947

Most weeks he couldn't putt the ball into a two-car garage.
DAN LAUCK, *Golf Magazine,* **1984**

Jack Nicklaus, American, born 1940

Jack is playing an entirely different game – a game I'm not even familiar with.
BOBBY JONES, at the Masters presentation ceremony, **1965**

He gives the ball a blow like the kick of a mule.
BERNARD DARWIN, golf writer

A lot of us [golf fans] never personally liked him. He was the bully on the block who owned the bat and the ball, had the first car, got the first girl; and when he sliced off tackle for twelve yards it always took three of us to drag him down. He was too much.
WILLIAM PRICE FOX, *Golf Digest,* **1973**

I said to the writers, 'There's Nicklaus, for example, only five strokes back. I wouldn't feel safe from Jack if he was in a wheelchair.'
DAN JENKINS, *Dead Solid Perfect,* **1974**

Nicklaus may be the only pro in the world who can frighten other pros with his practice shots.
DICK SCHAAP, *Massacre at Winged Foot,* **1974**

You worry about Jack when you see him signing up for the tournament.
JOHN JACOBS, at the Bing Crosby National Pro-Am, **1975**

I did my best, but chasing Nicklaus is like chasing a walking record book.
TOM WEISKOPF, finishing second at the Masters,
Golf Digest, **1975**

Most of the time he plays with the timidity of a middle-aged spinster walking home through a town full of drunken sailors, always choosing the safe side of the street.
PETER DOBEREINER, *Observer,* **1975**

He wouldn't three-putt a supermarket parking lot.
DAVE HILL, *Teed Off,* **1977**

When Nicklaus says he has a given number of yards left to the green . . . believe him. When it comes to shot-making, he knows everything down to the wind-chill factor.
MARK MULVOY and ART SPANDER,
Golf: The Passion and the Challenge, **1977**

If Nicklaus says an ant can pull a bale of hay, hitch it up. Jack doesn't say anything he doesn't mean and he doesn't know what it is to lie.
LEE TREVINO, *Golf Digest,* **1978**

He's a real live wire. His idea of fun is to sit home on a Saturday night with a glass of hot cocoa singing Ohio State fight songs.
DON RICKLES, comic

I wouldn't care if I got beat by twenty shots. I'd still like to see how God does it.
ED FIORI, on being paired with Nicklaus, *Golf Digest,* **1979**

I enjoyed playing in the last group of the day behind Nicklaus. Only trouble was [Tournament Director] Jack Tuthill kept taking the pins off the greens once Nicklaus played through.
LOU GRAHAM, *Golf Digest,* **1979**

Jack Nicklaus has become a legend in his spare time.
CHI CHI RODRIGUEZ, *Golf Digest,* **1979**

To win the things he's won, build golf courses around the world, be a daddy to all those kids, and be a hell of an investor, too, it's phenomenal. Hey, stick a broom in his rear end and he could probably sweep the USA.
JACKIE BURKE, *Golf Magazine,* **1981**

The difference between Jack and me is that when I got to the top of the mountain in 1974 and 1975, I said, 'Hey, it's time to stop and check out the view.' Whenever Jack reaches the top of a mountain, he starts looking for another.
JOHNNY MILLER, *PGA Tour News,* **1983**

I never thought his short game was very good. Of course, he hit so many damn greens, it didn't make any difference.
TOM WATSON, *Golf Digest,* **1983**

Greg Norman, Australian, born 1955

Greg Norman reminds me of the movies. Every time you think he's going to get the girl and ride off into the sunset, his horse breaks a leg.
RICK REILLY, on Norman's disappointments in major championships, *Sports Illustrated*

I have to be honest. I look at his swing and it's got faults. Under the severest pressure will it hold up? It's way too loose.
NICK FALDO

Greg's the big shark and I'm a little fish. But I'm a bigger fish now than I was yesterday.
STEVE ELKINGTON, Australian pro, after winning the
Players Championship, **1991**

He is a very exciting player but unfortunately some of his worst days have been the most highly viewed in the history of sport.
MARK MCCORMACK, *Golf Digest,* **1998**

The world never really saw what he was capable of. I reckon if he'd won the Masters in 1981 he might have won a bunch of majors.
FRANK NOBILO, *GolfWorld,* **2001**

Moe Norman, Canadian, 1930–2004

The Canadian Moe Norman can not only get the ball up and down from the ball washer, he could, if motivated, play it out of the cup and back *into* the ball washer.
PETER DOBEREINER, *Golf Digest,* **1983**

Christy O'Connor, Irish, born 1928

Christy is one of the most natural players I have ever seen.
GARY PLAYER

To watch Christy is to watch a craftsman at work.
HENRY COTTON

Mac O'Grady, American, born 1951

Anytime you talk to him, you'll hear three words you never heard before.
MIKE NICOLETTE, *Sports Illustrated*, **1984**

Jose Maria Olazabal, Spanish, born 1966

It looks like the only way I'll ever beat this guy is if he's taken ill.
COLIN MONTGOMERIE, after losing the Lancome Trophy to Olazabal, who previously had beaten Montgomerie for the British and European Amateur titles, **1990**

Be patient. You know exactly how to play this course. You are the greatest golfer in the world.
SEVE BALLESTEROS, note left for Olazabal before final round of the Masters, which he won, **1994**

Ollie commands universal respect. The same cannot be said of 'Nasty Nick' or the man long known as 'Boozy Woosie'.
JOHN HUGGAN, columnist, on prospective Ryder Cup captains, *GolfWorld*, **2005**

Arnold Palmer, American, born 1929

If ever I had an 8-foot putt and everything I owned depended upon it, I'd want Arnold Palmer to take it for me.
BOBBY JONES, paying Palmer a great compliment

I'll guarantee you he'll get it in the hole if he has to stare it in.
BOB ROSBURG, on Palmer's winning putt in the Masters, **1960**

Palmer usually walks to the first tee quite unlike any other pro on the circuit. He doesn't walk onto it so much as climb into it, almost as though it were a prize ring; and then he looks around at the gallery as though he is trying to count the house.
CHARLES PRICE, *The World of Golf,* **1962**

If Arnold asked all of those people to go jump into the river for him, they would march straight to the river and jump.
GARY PLAYER, on Arnie's Army

Palmer not only makes a golf tournament seem as dangerous as an Indianapolis 500, but he crashes as often as he finishes first.
MARK H. MCCORMACK, *Arnie: The Evolution of a Legend,* **1967**

His epitaph might well be: 'Here lies Arnold Palmer. He always went for the green.'
HENRY LONGHURST, in
Arnold Palmer – A Very Considerable Man, **1967**

He first came to golf as a muscular young man who could not keep his shirttail in, who smoked a lot, perspired a lot and who hit the ball with all of the finesse of a dock worker lifting a crate of auto parts.
DAN JENKINS, *The Dogged Victims of Inexorable Fate,* **1970**

He's the reason we're playing for all this money today. Arnie made it all possible. I'll tell you what I think of the man. If he should walk in the door right now and say, 'Shine my shoes,' I'd take off my shirt, get down on my hands and knees, and shine his shoes.
KEN STILL, *Golf Magazine,* **1970**

Golf was a comparatively sexless enterprise before Palmer came a-wooing. His caveman approach took the audience by storm. He was Cagney pushing a grapefruit in Mae Clarke's face, Gable kicking down the door to Scarlett O'Hara's bedroom.
JIM MURRAY, *Los Angeles Times,* **1974**

Under a new USGA rule, anyone using the word *charisma* in writing about Palmer is henceforth subject to a two-stroke penalty and loss of down.
HERBERT WARREN WIND, *Golf Digest,* **1975**

I don't think I can ever be another Arnold Palmer. No one could. He can hitch up his pants or yank on a glove and people will start oohing and aahing. When I hitch up mine, nobody notices.
JACK NICKLAUS

It was more fun watching Palmer lose than watching the rest of them win.
DAN GLEASON, *The Great, The Grand and the Also-Ran,* **1976**

Arnold Palmer had everything except a brake pedal.
PETER DOBEREINER, *Golf Digest,* **1982**

He was aggressive. He might be leading by one or two shots but he wouldn't be cautious. He'd go for the flag from the middle of an alligator's back.
LEE TREVINO, *They Call Me Super Mex,* **1982**

I could never call him Arnie. I called him Mr Palmer. He has an aura. Everybody who calls out his name, he gives them something – a look or a smile. He's a special man.
DAVID DUVAL, *GolfWorld,* **1995**

He's done everything for the Open here. But for Palmer in 1960 who knows where we'd be? Probably down in a shed on the beach.
NICK FALDO, during Palmer's last Open, **1995**

I'm like the old soldier. I'm never going to quit, I'm just going to fade away.
ARNOLD PALMER, asked about his retirement plans,
San Francisco Chronicle, **2005**

Jesper Parnevik, Swedish, born 1965

He thinks his clothes are more important than his clubs.
TIGER WOODS, in jest, after Parnevik forgot to ship his
clubs to the Masters because he was preoccupied with
packing his eclectic wardrobe, *GolfWorld*, **2005**

Jerry Pate, American, born 1953

I'm surprised he didn't drown, because he can't keep his mouth shut.
JACK NICKLAUS, after Pate dived into a pond after winning the Memphis Open, **1981**

Jerry had everything – from the neck down. With my brains and his swing, we were unbeatable.
LEE TREVINO, on his Ryder Cup partner, *Golf Digest,* **1982**

What I can't figure out is, if I'm so dumb, how am I making so much money? Me and Terry Bradshaw ... he's so dumb he wins four Super Bowls, and I'm so dumb I'm making a million dollars a year.
JERRY PATE, *Inside Sports,* **1982**

Billy Joe Patton, American, born 1922

He was always 'up'. If he wasn't talking, you knew he was ill.
JACK NICKLAUS, *The Greatest Game of All,* **1969**

Bareheaded, bespectacled, grinning, with a faster swing than
a kitchen blender.
DAN JENKINS, *The Dogged Victims of Inexorable Fate,* **1970**

Corey Pavin, American, born 1959

Corey is a little on the slight side. When he goes through a
turnstile, nothing happens.
JIM MORIARTY, *Golf Digest,* **1984**

Calvin Peete, American, born 1943

He has a crooked left arm – until he reaches out for the pay
cheque.
LEE TREVINO on Peete's elbow injury,
San Francisco Examiner, **1983**

Gary Player, South African, born 1935

He was very mystical, a health fanatic who was big on the
power of positive thinking. . . Were he to land in hell, his
critics said, he would probably immediately start talking
about what a wonderful place it is.
DAN GLEASON, *The Great, The Grand and the Also-Ran,* **1976**

He runs and lifts weights and eats health foods. That's all well
and good, but I get tired of hearing him brag about it. So
what if he has the most perfect bowel movements on the
tour?
DAVE HILL, *Teed Off,* **1977**

I believe that if a man takes care of himself, then, all things being equal, he should be as competent a golfer at fifty as he was at thirty.

GARY PLAYER, after winning the Masters, **1978**

Gary Player is all right if you like to see a grown man dressed up like Black Bart all the time.

DON RICKLES, comic

Playing against him, you begin hoping he'll be on grass rather than in sand. From grass you expect him to pitch the ball close. From a bunker you're afraid he'll hole it out!

JACK NICKLAUS, *Golf Magazine,* **1982**

Here he comes . . . the Queen Mother of golf. All he needs is a couple of corgis.

PETER ALLISS, on Player's arrival at Royal Lytham's eighteenth green during the Open, **2001**

Nick Price, South African, born 1957

I was born in South Africa, raised in Rhodesia. I have a British passport and I live in the US. Pick one.

NICK PRICE, asked his nationality during a press conference, **1988**

Ted Ray, British, 1877–1943

As for Ray, he was usually as dour as an elephant with a sore foot.

GRANTLAND RICE, in *The Tumult and the Shouting,* **1954**

Phil Rodgers, American, born 1938

In my next life, I'd like to be an otter. They only do two things – eat abalone and play.
PHIL RODGERS, *Golf Digest*, **1983**

Chi Chi Rodriguez, Puerto Rican, born 1935

You should have seen how little I was as a kid. I was so small that I got my start in golf as a ball marker.
CHI CHI RODRIGUEZ, **1971**

I'm going for the flag today. I'm gonna be a firecracker out there. I'm gonna be so hot they're gonna be playing on brown fairways tomorrow.
CHI CHI RODRIGUEZ, at the US Open, **1974**

He hits the ball so straight. It's from hitting it in those Puerto Rican alleys.
DAVE STOCKTON, at the Everett Open, **1984**

Justin Rose, British, born 1980

He was treated like a horse. Put him in every race no matter how good he was.
DAVID LEADBETTER, after Rose missed twenty-one consecutive cuts after turning pro, **2000**

Paul Runyan, American, 1908–2002

Watch Paul's unhurried swing. It's as lazy as a Spanish siesta, as delicately fashioned as a flower petal.
HORTON SMITH

Doug Sanders, American, born 1933

Doug Sanders braces himself with a wide stance that looks like a sailor leaning into a northeast gale.
TONY LEMA, *Golfer's Gold,* **1964**

Doug Sanders has said he likes to have sex and a hot tub bath every morning and he's loose and ready to go. Of course, if Sanders had scored half as often with women as he claims he has, he'd be dead.
DAVE HILL, *Teed Off,* **1977**

Emmett Kelly picks out his clothes. Smart outfits. Doug looks like he took a bad trip through a paint factory.
DON RICKLES, comedian

He had the flashiest clothes and the flashiest women. . . I spent a night in his place in Dallas once. All he had in it was booze and about a hundred and fifty pairs of golf shoes.
LEE TREVINO, *They Call Me Super Mex,* **1982**

Because of his world-famous colour-coordinated outfits . . . Doug has been described as looking like the aftermath of a direct hit on a pizza factory.
DAVE MARR, *Golf Digest,* **1983**

He is a dashing Southerner with a fetching smile and a ready eye for the ladies. Put him on the North Pole and he'll have every Eskimo around at a party within twenty-four hours.
DAN HRUBY, *San Jose Mercury News,* **1984**

Gene Sarazen, American, 1902–1999

Heck, if it wasn't for golf, Sarazen would be back on a banana boat between Naples and Sicily.
JIMMY DEMARET

John Schroeder, American, born 1945

Hey, Schroeder, you're gonna be the first guy ever penalized for slow play in a driving contest.
A pro, quoted in *Golf Digest,* **1974**

Charlie Sifford, American, born 1923

The first time I played here, back in 1959, I'll never forget it. People looked at me as if I had a tail.
CHARLIE SIFFORD, on being an early black golfer at the
US Open at Winged Foot, **1974**

Sifford was a very talented player whose trademark cigar seemed to be eternally short, perhaps because he got so many doors slammed in his face.
DAN GLEASON, *The Great, The Grand and the Also-Ran,* **1976**

Dan Sikes, American, born 1930

Before entering professional golf, Dan was a lawyer, which may possibly explain why he doesn't feel right unless he's complaining about something.
JACK NICKLAUS, *The Greatest Game of All,* **1969**

Scott Simpson, American, born 1955

There will be days when others beat him, but there will not
be many when Simpson beats himself.

JACK NICKLAUS about the US Open champion, **1987**

Vijay Singh, Fijian, born 1963

It's Tiger Woods without the charisma.

PAUL AZINGER, on Singh's nine-victory season, *GolfWorld*, **2004**

Macdonald Smith, American, 1890–1949

He has the cleanest twenty-one-jewel stroke in golf. He
treats the grass of a golf course as though it were an altar
cloth.

TOMMY ARMOUR, *The American Golfer*, **1935**

J. C. Snead, American, born 1941

When J.C. was a kid, he was so ugly, they had to tie a pork
chop around his neck to get the dog to play with him.

LEE TREVINO, *Golf Digest*, **1978**

Sam Snead, American, 1912–2002

At the start, Sam Snead was a simple lad who couldn't tell the
time in a clock factory.

HERB GRAFFIS, golf writer and editor

The only difference in Snead is that he's gettin' humpbacked
from pickin' balls out of the can.

JIMMY DEMARET, on Snead's comeback, **1949**

Where I lived, near Bald Knob, the roads got littler and littler until they just ran up a tree. Big cities were something I'd just heard rumours about.
SAM SNEAD, *The Education of a Golfer*, **1962**

Sam Snead's got more money buried underground than I ever made on top. . . He's got gophers in his backyard that subscribe to *Fortune* magazine. He's packed more coffee cans than Brazil.
ARNOLD PALMER, '*Chrysler Presents a Bob Hope Special*',
NBC-TV, **1963**

Any guy who would pass up a chance to see Sam Snead play golf would pull the shades driving past the Taj Mahal.
JIM MURRAY, *The Sporting World of Jim Murray*, **1968**

It's called colour. Some people have it and some don't. As for Slammin' Sam Snead, he has enough colour to outfit a couple of rainbow factories.
REX LARDNER, *The Great Golfers*, **1970**

Craig Stadler, American, born 1953

Some guys hope to shoot their age. Craig Stadler hopes to shoot his waist.
JIM MURRAY, *Los Angeles Times*, **1980**

How can I not like Craig? He's the best thing that ever happened to me. He makes me look good.
TOM WEISKOPF, on Stadler's temper, *Sports Illustrated*, **1982**

The man they call 'Superslob' yesterday took command of the Open and inspired every beer paunch in the land to sag with pride.
Newspaper story, after Stadler took a three-stroke lead at
Royal Birkdale, *Daily Mail*, **1983**

He . . . created a new definition of the split second, this being the time between his making contact with the ball and his setting off in search of it.

DAVID DAVIES, on Stadler's wild third round at the Open, **1988**

Curtis Strange, American, born 1955

There are two things I promise you'll never hear me say: 'I'm in the best shape of my life' and 'I'm playing better than I ever have'.

CURTIS STRANGE, upon turning fifty, *GolfWorld*, **2005**

Hal Sutton, American, born 1958

If God were a teenager and descended to give us the Word, He'd probably look like Hal Sutton.

NATHANIEL CROSBY, *Golf Magazine*, **1983**

Peter Thomson, Australian, born 1929

Peter is splendidly balanced. The way he plays golf is the way he is. Of course, there are many, many people who find his complete balance irritating.

MICHAEL WOLVERIDGE, Thomson's course-design partner, *GolfWorld*, **2005**

Jerry Travers, American, 1887–1951

Travers was the greatest competitor I have ever known. I could always tell just from looking at a golfer whether he was winning or losing, but I *never* knew how Travers stood.

ALEX SMITH, Scottish professional

Lee Trevino, American, born 1939

If he didn't have an Adam's apple he'd have no shape at all.
GARY PLAYER, *Sports Illustrated,* **1972**

He's the only man I've ever known to talk on his backswing.
CHARLEY MCCLENDON, LSU football coach,
Sports Illustrated, **1972**

He knows how to live. The breweries will have to go on
overtime while he is in the money, and everybody had better
lock up their daughters.
PETER DOBEREINER, *GolfWorld,* **1973**

I can't wait to wake up in the morning to hear what I have to
say!
LEE TREVINO

I can't keep my mouth shut for four hours around a golf
course. If I did, I'd get bad breath.
LEE TREVINO, *Golf Digest,* **1974**

Lee's got more lines than the Illinois Railroad.
FUZZY ZOELLER, *San Francisco Chronicle,* **1979**

I'm very lucky. If it wasn't for golf I don't know what I'd be
doing. If my IQ had been two points lower, I'd have been a
plant somewhere.
LEE TREVINO, *They Call Me Super Mex,* **1982**

When Lee Trevino says, 'Sir,' he's either talking to the King of
Morocco or he's one unhappy guy. He called me 'Sir' once.
I'm not the King of Morocco.
MARINO PARACENZO, writer, *Golf Digest,* **1989**

Harry Vardon, British, 1870–1937

At that time, Vardon was the most atrocious putter I have ever seen. He didn't three-putt, he *four-putted*.
GENE SARAZEN, on Vardon in the early 1920s

The groove in his swing was so obvious you could almost see it. I was so impressed that during the last round, when my swing started to leave me, I started imitating his. And it worked, too. Fact is, I almost caught him with his own swing.
WALTER HAGEN, on the 1913 US Open

A grand player up to the green, and a very bad player when he got there. But then, Vardon gave himself less putting to do than any other man.
BERNARD DARWIN, British golf writer

He would not play any course twice in the same day, you know. Why not? Because he was so accurate, that in his second round his shots finished in the divot holes he had made in the morning, and that took the fun out of the game for him.
HENRY COTTON, *Country Life,* **1948**

He held on to the club as though it were a garden rake, addressed it as though he were about to pick up a piano, and swung at it as though he were trying to get out of the way of something.
CHARLES PRICE, *Golfer-At-Large,* **1982**

Camililo Villegas, Columbian, born 1982

It's hard to fly under the radar in yellow pants, especially when you hit the ball more than 300 yards and all the young women in the gallery are screaming your name.
TIM ROSAFORTE, writer, *GolfWorld,* **2006**

Lanny Wadkins, American, born 1949

He's the most tenacious player I've ever seen. You put a pin in the middle of a lake and Lanny will attack it.
JOHN MAHAFFEY, *Golf Digest,* **1983**

Lanny is a self-confessed optimist, the kind who, if he falls in a sewer, checks his pockets for fish.
MICKEY HERSKOWITZ, *Golf Digest,* **1983**

Lanny is back home in Maine painting his house. As fast as he does everything: what's he going to do on the second day?
DAN JENKINS, *'PGA Highlights'*, ESPN-TV, **1985**

Tom Watson, American, born 1949

Watson walks about his golf-course business like a young trial lawyer going from one courtroom to the next.
AL BARKOW, *Golf's Golden Grind,* **1974**

Watson scares me. If he's lying six in the middle of the fairway, there's some kind of way he might make a five.
LEE TREVINO, *San Francisco Chronicle,* **1979**

Tom Watson is a hell of a golfer, but he sure could use a choreographer. Watching him shoot sixty-six is like watching the President sign a bill.
JAY CRONLEY, *Playboy,* **1981**

Watson's close friends enjoy describing him as 'the worst walker and worst dresser in golf'.
HERBERT WARREN WIND, *The New Yorker*, **1981**

Any self-respecting tournament wants to be won by Tom Watson.
JIM MURRAY, *Golf Magazine*, **1983**

When you drive into the left rough, hack your second out into a greenside bunker, come out within six feet of the hole and sink the slippery putt – when you do that, you've made a Watson par.
ANDY BEAN, *Golf Digest*, **1984**

Tom Weiskopf, American, born 1942

Tom Weiskopf is getting ready to issue his first quote of the year, and I don't want to miss it.
DAN JENKINS, *Sports Illustrated*, **1971**

His swing was made in heaven, part velvet, part silk, like a royal robe, so sweet you could pour it over ice cream.
JIM MURRAY, *Los Angeles Times*

He knows more ways of choking than Dracula.
COLMAN MCCARTHY, *The Pleasures of the Game*, **1977**

I'm not an intellectual person. I don't get headaches from concentration. I get them from double bogeys.
TOM WEISKOPF, *Golf Digest*, **1978**

Lee Westwood, British, born 1973

Fortunately, I haven't been pushed into the 'best player never to win a major' category yet. I suppose it's because I'm only 26 years old and I suppose it's because I haven't come close to winning one yet.

LEE WESTWOOD, **1999**

Tiger Woods, American, born 1975

If he can handle all the attention, all the pressure from you folks, Tiger can be as good or better than anybody who ever played the game.

JACK NICKLAUS, Masters Tournament press conference, **1996**

Tiger will do more than any other man in history to change the course of humanity . . . I don't know yet exactly what form this will take, but he is the Chosen One. He'll have the power to impact nations. Not people. *Nations.* The world is just getting a taste of his power.

EARL WOODS, *Sports Illustrated*, **1996**

I'll be satisfied if he's just a great person. I don't give a shit about the golf.

EARL WOODS, *GQ*, **1997**

He was the best fifteen-year-old player I had ever seen. He was the best at sixteen and seventeen and so on. He's the best twenty-one-year-old player anyone has ever seen. I'm excited to see how good he's going to be when he's twenty-two. If he keeps getting better, oh boy. I'm not sure golf has seen anything like him before. Maybe Bobby Jones.

BYRON NELSON, *Sports Illustrated*, **1997**

He's God's gift to the game, that's all.
CHARLIE SIFFORD, pioneer African-American pro,
NBC News, **1997**

He still leads the world in police escorts going from tee to
green and walking to the clubhouse every day.
JOHN FEINSTEIN, commentator, National Public Radio, **1998**

You do get the feeling sometimes that the rest of us are all
out here playing for second place.
FRED COUPLES, after Woods' sixth victory of the year, **1999**

He has the ability to do things no one else can do and yet has
a short game where, if he makes mistakes, he can correct it.
That's what's so phenomenal about him.
JACK NICKLAUS, host of the Memorial Tournament,
won by Woods, **1999**

I didn't win any golf tournaments by 15 shots. When he gets
ahead, I think he's superior to me. I never spread-eagled the
field.
JACK NICKLAUS, *GolfWorld*, **2000**

Tiger Woods makes people think winning is easy.
ERNIE ELS, *Sports Illustrated*, **2000**

Cut him open and I'll tell you what you'll find – a bunch of
wires and levers, and a big-assed heart.
ROCCO MEDIATE, *GolfWorld*, **2000**

He's a freak of nature, worlds apart from us in every way.
MICHAEL CAMPBELL

Does he get preferential treatment? No question. If Tiger wants hot and cold running beer in his house, anybody would arrange it to get him to play in their tournament.
BUDDY MARTIN, media director of the International,
Sports Illustrated, **2000**

Some day I'll tell my grandkids I played in the same tournament with Tiger Woods. We are witnessing a phenomenon the game may never, ever see again.
TOM WATSON, *GolfWorld*, **2000**

If it [golf] is your life-long passion, you can't imagine not being a part of it. I might be like Arnie, play until I'm seventy.
TIGER WOODS, *New York Times*, **2000**

He'll be just like me at seventy-one, still playing the game as hard as he can, still kidding himself that there is something left in the tank.
ARNOLD PALMER, **2000**

When I look at Tiger Woods, I think of Arthur Ashe. I don't know what he's going to do with his life after golf, if he's made that decision. But he certainly has the ability to impact the world.
DAVID FAY, USGA executive director, *GolfWorld*, **2000**

He's raised the bar to a level only he can reach.
TOM WATSON, **2000**

Woods is the most amazing performer I've ever seen, and I've seen Ali, Gretzky, Jordan, Montana, and Nicklaus. What Woods is doing is so hard it's like climbing Everest in flip-flops, performing heart transplants in oven mitts.
RICK REILLY, columnist, *Sports Illustrated*, **2000**

My reservoir of words to describe it is bone dry. What do you say? He's remarkable, he's unbelievable, he's incredible. None of those words are appropriate. . . I'm waiting for the football season to begin because I don't have anything else to say.

JIM NANTZ, sports announcer, after Woods' eighth of nine victories for the year, CBS-TV, **2000**

Tiger is a great guy, probably the most professional sportsman in the world, but the intensity of his life is just ridiculous. That was really brought home to me when he explained why he loved scuba diving so much. He said it was because the fish didn't recognize him.

LEE WESTWOOD, *Mail on Sunday*

I want to become a champion like him, so I can make Afghanistan famous.

MOHAMMED HASHEM, nineteen, who took up golf after the re-opening of Kabul GC in 2004, *Washington Post*, **2005**

Woods: You can play the wuss tees if you want. Otherwise you can stand back here like a man and weep.
Clinton: So I sucked it up. One hole I made a birdie on and he didn't. And he beat me by 25 strokes.

BILL CLINTON, former US president, on their round at Shady Canyon GL, Irvine, Calif., on the occasion of the opening of the Tiger Woods Learning Center, Anaheim, Calif., *GolfWorld*, **2006**

Is there any other parent of any athlete in any other sport that you even recognize?

JIMMY ROBERTS, sports commentator, reflecting on the death of Earl Woods, seventy-four, NBC-TV, **2006**

Ian Woosnam, British, born 1958

Perhaps if I dyed my hair peroxide blond and called myself the 'Great White Tadpole' that would help.
IAN WOOSNAM about the lack of media attention he was receiving despite his successes, **1987**

If he ever grows up, he'll hit the ball 2,000 yards.
SANDY LYLE, after losing the final of the World Match Play Championship, *Daily Mail*, **1987**

Fuzzy Zoeller, American, born 1951

When I catch my driver and Fuzzy catches his one-iron, I can get within thirty yards of him.
HALE IRWIN, *Sports Illustrated*, **1981**

When your name is Zoeller, and so many things are done in alphabetical order, you expect to be last.
FUZZY ZOELLER

Maybe Fuzzy Zoeller plays golf the way everybody should. Hit it, go find it, hit it again. Grin, have a smoke, take a sip, make a joke and every so often win a major championship.
DAN JENKINS, *Sports Illustrated*, **1984**

35 ● Tour Players: Women

Amy Alcott, American, born 1956

It's easy to be liked if you're 100th on the money list. You may have to worry about making ends meet but everyone will love you.
AMY ALCOTT, on her image among fellow players,
Golf Digest, **1984**

Pat Bradley, American, born 1951

I swear, I'm the queen of the lip-out and the rim-out. The ball comes out, and looks at me and grins as if to say, 'Too bad. You missed again.'
PAT BRADLEY, *Golf Digest,* **1979**

JoAnne Carner, American, born 1939

The ground shakes when she hits it.
SANDRA PALMER, who nicknamed Carner 'Big Mama',
Sports Illustrated, **1982**

Her weight is a state secret.
JOHN P. MAY, *Golf Digest*, **1982**

We have so many small players out here on tour, that's why I look like Big Mama.
JOANNE CARNER, '*LPGA Kemper Open*', NBC–TV, **1983**

The only thing I never learned from Billy Martin was how to knock a guy out in a bar.
JOANNE CARNER, who says the Yankees manager taught her how to win

Beth Daniel, American, born 1956

Chasing Beth is like swimming upstream against the current.
BONNIE LAUER, at the Birmingham Classic, **1982**

Laura Davies, British, born 1963

She's just a great player and she's going to get better. She has the game to dominate the tour in the future. Once she gains experience we're all going to be in trouble.
NANCY LOPEZ, **1988**

I hit it as far as most of them. On my day I fancy my chances against any of them.
LAURA DAVIES, regarding male pros

At the moment I can't beat the girls, so I'm certainly not going to have a crack at the men.
LAURA DAVIES, asked if she planned to attempt to qualify for the British Open, *The Age*, **2005**

Sally Little, American, born 1951

I kept seeing her ass all day, bending over to pick her ball out of the hole.
HOLLIS STACY, on Little's closing sixty-four in the Nabisco Dinah Shore Invitational, *Sports Illustrated*, **1982**

Nancy Lopez, American, born 1957

They've got the wrong person playing Wonder Woman on television.
JUDY RANKIN, *Golf Digest*, **1978**

We're all trying to steal Nancy's birth-control pills, but so far we've been unsuccessful.
JOANNE CARNER, *Golf Digest*, **1980**

She just goes to prove that golf is not a hard game to learn. Her old man could fix a fender in the morning and teach her how to play golf in the afternoon.
HERB GRAFFIS, *Golf Digest*, **1981**

My swing is no uglier than Arnold Palmer's, and it's the same ugly swing every time.
NANCY LOPEZ, *Golf Digest*, **1984**

Cathy Reynolds-Derouaux, American, born 1957

Her looks cause as much stir as her golf.
PETER ALLISS, *Who's Who in International Golf*, **1984**

Patty Sheehan, American, born 1956

I need five weeks off. Everybody keeps telling me how great I am. I can't be a jerk even if I want to, and it's driving me nuts.
PATTY SHEEHAN, *Sports Illustrated*, **1984**

It's nice to have the opportunity to play for so much money, but it's nicer to win it.
PATTY SHEEHAN, *Golf Magazine*, **1985**

Annika Sorenstam, Swedish, born 1970

I . . . love the times when I can put on a ski helmet. Then nobody recognizes me. I'm just me.
ANNIKA SORENSTAM, *Callaway Golf Magazine*, **2005**

Muffin Spencer-Devlin, American, born 1953

Oh, no. I've been at it much too long and have too much experience. I'd say I'm a Space Captain.
MUFFIN SPENCER–DEVLIN, asked if she was a Space Cadet,
San Francisco Examiner, **1982**

When I was born, they had to use forceps and there were indentations in my forehead. My grandmother said, 'Why, she looks just like a little muffin!'
MUFFIN SPENCER–DEVLIN, on how she got the name Muffin,
Safeco Classic, **1984**

Now I've got to call my editor and ask for more space. . . Where would we have been for three days without her?
LYNN MUCKEN, *Seattle Times* golf writer, after listening to Spencer-Devlin's tales at the Safeco Classic, **1984**

Sandra Spuzich, American, born 1937

Maybe she's starting a new trend in golf – no practice. The only exercise Spooz gets before a round is swinging that weighted doughnut on her driver.

JOANNE CARNER, *Golf Digest*, **1983**

Hollis Stacy, American, born 1954

Shirttail hanging out, hair blowing in the wind, dragging on a cigarette. That's sex appeal.

ARNOLD PALMER, **1981**

Jan Stephenson, Australian, born 1951

I may not be the prettiest girl in the world, but I'd like to see Bo Derek rate a '10' after playing 18 holes in 100-degree heat.

JAN STEPHENSON, on hearing a writer rated her a '6',
San Jose Mercury News, **1981**

Maybe people will stop thinking of me only as a sex symbol and realize I can really play golf.

JAN STEPHENSON, **1983**

Glenna Collett Vare, American, 1903–1989

No one else quite so adequately expressed how far women's golf had come since those far-off days when women swung at the ball as though they were beating off purse-snatchers with an umbrella.

CHARLES PRICE, *The World of Golf*, **1962**

Joyce Wethered, British, 1901–1997

Good *swing?* My god, mon! She could hit a ball 240 yards on the fly while standing barefoot on a cake of ice.
WILLIE WILSON, Scottish professional

I played an exhibition with her at East Lake in the '30s after she had turned professional. She not only didn't miss a shot, she didn't even *half* miss one.
BOBBY JONES

Michelle Wie, American, born 1989

At least the pre-teens have their priorities straight: first they'll go out and hit balls; then they'll go out and hit puberty.
KEVIN COOK, writer, on Wie, then twelve,
Sports Illustrated, **2002**

You watch her swing and say, 'That's normal.' Then you realize that she's only thirteen . . . that's unbelievable.
VIJAY SINGH, **2003**

That golf swing of hers, it's the best golf swing I've ever seen in my life.
BOBBY VERWEY, veteran caddie, **2004**

My son now thinks that since he's 10, 'Well in five years I can be on tour.' That's the influence she has and that's why it's good for the game. Just like Tiger Woods. . . Her influence will be just as great, especially for little girls.
DAVIS LOVE III, *GolfWorld*, **2004**

I didn't even know how to shave at 15.
PAUL AZINGER, on Wie turning pro a week before her sixteenth birthday, *GolfWorld*, **2005**

My opinion is that anyone who doesn't think she should get an invite is crackers. She's great for the tour, and anyone who . . . doesn't like it is very short-sighted. She's exciting, and we need excitement.
LAURA DAVIES, on Wie getting a sponsor's exemption into the LPGA Championship, *Baltimore Sun*, **2005**

She belongs here. Anyone who doesn't believe that has rocks in their head.
LAURA DAVIES, after Wie's runner-up finish in the LPGA Championship, **2005**

Fanny [Sunesson] caddied for her a few times and says it's really easy. If it used to be a 6-iron for me, she gives [Michelle] a 7.
NICK FALDO, **2005**

She says she wants to play the men's tour. Why? It's a little insulting. I feel she should play out here and beat Annika first before she even tries to play the men.
NANCY LOPEZ, *Guardian*, **2005**

She's going to make a [men's] cut eventually. She's never going to win, period. Maybe once she makes a cut, she'll forget about it. . . I think she should try to win some LPGA tournaments first and go from there.
MARK CALCAVECCHIA, to Doug Ferguson, *Associated Press*, **2006**

Mickey Wright, American, born 1935

We had some great head-to-head matches. Nine times out of ten, she won.
KATHY WHITWORTH, *Golf Magazine,* **1983**

Babe Didrikson Zaharias, American, 1914–1956

If ah didn't have these ah'd hit it twenty yards further.
BABE DIDRIKSON ZAHARIAS, on her breasts

There's only one thing wrong about Babe and me. I hit the ball like a girl and she hits like a man.
BOB HOPE, c. **1940s**

36 ● Winning and Losing

If you hear a man complaining of having 'lost all interest' in a match which he has lately played, you will be pretty safe in inferring that he lost it. The winner very seldom experiences this feeling.

HORACE G. HUTCHINSON, *Hints on the Game of Golf,* **1886**

Given an equality of strength and skill, the victory in golf will be to him who is captain of his soul. Give me a clear eye, a healthy liver, a strong will, a collected mind, and a conscience void of offence both toward God and toward man, and I will back the pigmy against the giant.

ARNOLD HAULTAIN, *Atlantic Monthly,* **1908**

The one stroke marks the difference between fame and oblivion.

SAMUEL L. PARRISH, USGA treasurer, *The American Golfer,* **1929**

The life of a professional athlete is precarious at best. Win and they carry you to the clubhouse on their shoulders; lose and you pay the caddies in the dark.

GENE SARAZEN, *Thirty Years of Championship Golf,* **1950**

In order to win you must play your best golf when you need it most, and play your sloppy stuff when you can afford it. I shall not attempt to explain how you achieve this happy timing.

BOBBY JONES, *Golf Is My Game,* **1960**

I wouldn't hurt a chicken crossing the road, but if I got a man in trouble on the golf course I'd kick the hell out of him. I don't care if he's my best friend.

SAM SNEAD, *Golf Digest,* **1972**

Before the last round I called my wife and told her I had a seventeen-stroke lead over last place.

ROD FUNSETH, leading the Glen Campbell-Los Angeles Open, **1973**

I really don't like play-offs. I feel sorry for the other guy if I win and feel worse if I lose.

CHI CHI RODRIGUEZ, *Golf Digest,* **1974**

Youngster: Well, if you don't win, how come you're a pro?
Shaw: You've got a good point.

TOM SHAW, at the US Open, **1974**

I prefer to think of it as fourth.
HALE IRWIN, finishing last in the World Series of Golf,
Golf Digest, **1974**

People don't seem to realize how often you have to come in second in order to finish first. . . . I've never met a winner who hadn't learned how to be a loser.
JACK NICKLAUS, who has finished second over fifty-five times,
Golf Magazine, **1976**

The best thing that ever happened to me was coming second in the 1971 Masters. I couldn't have coped if I'd won.
JOHNNY MILLER, **1976**

I can't describe how I feel. It's the greatest thing in the world to win a professional golf tournament – especially if you're a professional golfer.
DAVE EICHELBERGER, upon winning the Milwaukee Open,
Golf Digest, **1977**

The difference between shooting a sixty-three and a seventy-three might even be just between your ears. It's such a fine line that it's almost scary.
JOHNNY MILLER, *San Francisco Chronicle,* **1979**

Most golfers prepare for disaster. A good golfer prepares for success.
BOB TOSKI, *Golf Digest,* **1981**

The arc of your swing doesn't have a thing to do with the size of your heart.
CAROL MANN, *Newsweek,* **1981**

If you aspire to be a champion, it's up to you to find a way to get the ball in the cup on the crucial holes on the last day.
TOM WATSON, *The New Yorker,* **1981**

Ah well. If we hit it perfect every day, everybody else would quit.
LEE TREVINO to Tom Watson, *Esquire,* **1982**

Show me someone who gets angry once in a while, and I'll show you a guy with a killer instinct. Show me a guy walking down the fairway smiling and I'll show you a loser.
LEE TREVINO, '*Bob Hope Classic*', NBC–TV, **1983**

Winning is the greatest feeling. It's like walking barefoot in the mud.
LYNN ADAMS, upon winning the Orlando Classic,
Golf Digest, **1983**

Victory is everything. You can spend the money, but you can never spend the memories.
KEN VENTURI, '*Colonial National Invitation*', CBS–TV, **1983**

If you want to whip somebody on the golf course, just get him mad.
DAVE WILLIAMS, University of Houston golf coach,
Golf Magazine, **1984**

If you ever feel sorry for somebody on a golf course, you better go home. If you don't kill them, they'll kill you.
SEVE BALLESTEROS, *Seve: The Young Champion,* **1984**

Most people thrive on winning. I don't. Hell, if I finish second, I consider it a victory. If I finish third, I feel great.
FUZZY ZOELLER, *US Open Official Magazine,* **1985**

If anybody calls me a choker they had better be 7ft 5in tall or else they will choke on my fist.
BOBBY WADKINS after throwing away a three-shot lead
in the Atlanta Golf Classic, **1987**

I know now how Lawrence of Arabia must have felt after spending most of his time under the ropes and in the sand.
CRAIG PARRY, after struggling in the final round and winning
the New South Wales Open, **1987**

Everybody should feel like this once in their life. If I felt any better it probably would be illegal.
TONY JOHNSTONE, after winning the British PGA
Championship, **1992**

I feel incredibly relieved. The hounds would have been at me if I had lost.
NICK FALDO, on winning the Irish Open in a play-off after
blowing a four-stroke lead, **1992**

We must always talk about winning. Never losing. We must never give up. That is too easy. When I play with Jose Maria Olazabal there are no 'sorrys' between us if either of us hits a bad shot. We just make sure we get the next one right.
SEVE BALLESTEROS, *Daily Mail*, **1993**

If golf was would-haves, could-haves and should-haves, I would have won everything by now.
AMY ALCOTT, after losing the LPGA Classic, **1994**

All men are created equal. I'm just one stroke better than the rest.
GENE SARAZEN, after winning the 1922 US Open,
GolfWorld, **1995**

No one deserves a victory more than I do. I didn't come here to be second.

COLIN MONTGOMERIE, at the German Open, **1995**

I tell him, 'Tiger, you play like shit, but Mom still loves you.'

KULTIDA WOODS, after her son's final-round collapse in
his third tournament as a professional,
Tiger: A Biography of Tiger Woods, **1997**

You figure winning a major will make you feel on top of the world for a long time, and then you realize it doesn't.

DAVID DUVAL, winner, 2001 British Open, *Sports Illustrated*, **2003**

Don't let the bastards get you down over this.

NICK FALDO, revealing his private comment to Greg Norman
after overtaking him to win the 1996 Masters, *Life Swings*, **2004**

I know what they're saying. They're saying I'm no good because I haven't won again, which is ridiculous.

BEN CURTIS, 2003 British Open champion,
GolfWorld, **2005**

Sometimes you're a hero, sometimes you're a villain, sometimes you're a comic. Sometimes you spill blood on the stage.

MIKE REID, US tour pro, on the ups and downs of competition,
Salt Lake City Tribune, **2005**

37 ● Women

Three things are as unfathomable as they are fascinating to the masculine mind: metaphysics, golf, and the feminine heart.

ARNOLD HAULTAIN, *The Mystery of Golf,* **1908**

Call every woman 'Sugar' and you can't go wrong.

WALTER HAGEN

During the last three holes of the 1919 US Open, which The Haig won for the second time, he smiled at a pretty girl on the sixteenth tee, struck up a conversation with her on the seventeenth fairway, and made a date with her as he walked off the eighteenth green. After The Haig, nobody would take golf *too* seriously.

CHARLES PRICE

Golf humanizes women, humbles their haughty natures, tends, in short, to knock out of their systems a certain modicum of the superciliousness, that swank, which makes wooing a tough proposition for the diffident male.

P. G. WODEHOUSE

Love has had a lot of press-agenting from the oldest times; but there are higher, nobler things than love. A woman is only a woman, but a hefty drive is a slosh.

P. G. WODEHOUSE, *A Woman Is Only a Woman,* **1919**

His handicap was down to twelve. But these things are not all. A golfer needs a loving wife, to whom he can describe the day's play through the long evenings.

P. G. WODEHOUSE

Joe Bean says one thing about caddying for these dames, it keeps you out of the hot sun. . . And another time he said that it was not fair to charge these dames regular ladies' dues in the club as they hardly ever used the course.

RING LARDNER, *A Caddy's Diary,* **1922**

If your wife interferes with your golf, get a new wife. If your business interferes with your golf, get a new business.

DON OLD, *Love That Golf,* **1952**

He married the first girl who would shag balls for him.

GEORGE LOW, on Arnold Palmer, **1955**

Golf and sex are about the only things you can enjoy without being good at it.

JIMMY DEMARET

Golf is a diabolical contrivance, but it is not so devilish as the woman scorned for a driving range.
MILTON GROSS, *Eighteen Holes in My Head,* **1959**

There are plenty of golfers in this country who take almost an eternity to select the club, and in the United States a number of first-class performers take just as long to make a selection as they do to choose a wife – and sometimes they make the wrong choice in each case.
DAI REES, *Dai Rees on Golf,* **1959**

Aware of their long life expectancy, they play slowly, hunt for a ball for twenty minutes and permutate their scores the way they figure out who has to pay for what after lunch at Schrafft's.
REX LARDNER, on women golfers,
Out of the Bunker and Into the Trees, **1960**

I've always had a wife – golf. No man should have more than one.
FREDDIE MCLEOD, American pro, on why he never married

I'll buy me another wife.
PETER THOMSON, Australian pro, asked what he'd do
with his money

Oh, man, Mary Rose worked me so hard at home that I had to come back out on the tour to get my health back.
JOHNNY POTT, on his wife

I wouldn't advise any professional golfer to marry before the age of thirty. Marriage means a division of interests, and golf, particularly tournament golf, demands all your time.
HENRY COTTON, **1962**

Jack, you spent more time in the recovery room than your
wife did.
DR WILLIAM COPELAND, to Jack Nicklaus on the
birth of his first child, **1963**

When I come back in the next life, I want to come back as a
golf pro's wife. She wakes up every morning at the crack of
ten, and is faced by her first major decision of the day:
whether to have breakfast in bed or in the hotel coffee shop.
DAN SIKES, American touring professional

When we were really kids out there, it was great. But the
longer you stay out, the more ding-a-lings you find. Really.
There are just too many places, like Palm Springs, that are
dingy. They bell me out.
SUSAN MARR, wife of touring pro Dave Marr, **1968**

I wasn't taking much of a risk – I knew she was a beauty queen.
DAVE STOCKTON, on the blind date with his future wife,
Golf Digest, **1970**

This guy has fifteen kids. *Bleeped* himself right out of a seat in
the car.
BEN HOGAN, on a restaurant manager, *Golf Digest,* **1970**

I have to win this tournament. My wife bought $50,000
worth of furniture last week. And you should see the house
she built around it.
LEE TREVINO, at the US Open, **1974**

'A bad wife'll strap a terminal hook on you,' Donny said
once. 'You can just start walking left every time you swing
the club.'
DAN JENKINS, *Dead Solid Perfect,* **1974**

Golf may have driven more people crazy than women.
DAN JENKINS, as above

Hawaii has so many girls on the island. You've got to weigh that. And let's not sell Jacksonville short. Jacksonville, as a matter of fact, is the only place where the girls find out where you're staying and call *you*.
JOHN JACOBS, on the best tour stops, **1975**

Maybe I'll regret not playing in the United States. But what's the use of having children if you don't live with them?
TONY JACKLIN, declining the American tour,
Golf Digest, **1975**

He looks for 'em in the gallery, and man, he spots one, we gotta lose three strokes.
DOUG SANDERS' CADDIE, on women at tournaments

Shorts and a tight sweater have caused more guys to bogey a hole than a bad slice.
JIM MURRAY, *The Sporting World of Jim Murray,* **1968**

Question: Is golf better than booze and broads?
Demaret: I don't know about you, young fellow, but I've been playing golf man and boy for thirty-four years – to get money for booze and broads.
JIMMY DEMARET

She said, 'Oh, I'm so excited! I've never been on a par five in two before. If I sink this putt, it'll be my first eagle! I'll kill myself!' Her husband said, 'It's a gimmie.'
BUDDY HACKETT, *The Truth About Golf and Other Lies,* **1968**

He overheard one guy say: 'I just got a new set of clubs for my wife.' And the other replied: 'Now that's what I call a real good trade.'
JOE CHASE, Plantation Golf Club professional,
Golf Magazine, **1970**

If he had a job as an accountant, I wouldn't go down to watch him work.
LESLIE THOMPSON, on why she doesn't follow her husband
Leonard on tour, **1975**

To me getting laid is no major accomplishment. While I am getting laid, probably four hundred million other people around the world are getting laid, too. Big deal. I've never found sex that exciting, not nearly as exciting as golf.
DAVE HILL, *Teed Off,* **1977**

I was playing once with the King of Samoa. I asked him what his handicap was. 'Six wives,' he said.
JACK REDMOND, American trick-shot artist, *Golf Digest,* **1977**

I've always had three rules for playing well on the tour: no push-ups, no swimming and no sex after Wednesday.
SAM SNEAD, *Golf Digest,* **1977**

Nuthin' on the planet smart as a woman. . . There's no foolin' round they don't know about! Let me tell ya, baby! No corporation, no government, no anything can check and collect like they can! No way!
LEE TREVINO, *Golf Digest,* **1978**

My wife doesn't care what I do when I'm away, as long as I don't have a good time.
LEE TREVINO

He's a newlywed, and he might be thinking, 'Honey, I just hit our new freezer into the lake at twelve.'
DAVE MARR, commentator, ABC-TV, **1978**

You women want equality, but you'll never get it because women are inferior to men in all sorts of ways – physically, intellectually, and morally. There are exceptions, but on the whole women are inferior to men.
SEVE BALLESTEROS, *El Pais* (Madrid), **1980**

Son, the only way to forget a woman is with another one.
LEE TREVINO, quoting his grandfather,
They Call Me Super Mex, **1982**

At a press conference someone asked me if I brought my wife. 'Naw,' I said. 'You don't bring a ham sandwich to a banquet!'
LEE TREVINO, at a party-filled San Antonio tournament,
They Call Me Super Mex, **1982**

I'm asked all the time what my secret is. 'The only secrets I have,' I say, 'are the ones I keep from my wife.'
BOB TOSKI, teaching professional, *Golf Digest,* **1982**

My enthusiasm for the game has dwindled in that I've found something more interesting than golf – a wife.
BRUCE LIETZKE, **1982**

You take twenty senior events and fifteen regular tour events and what you've got is a divorce.
MILLER BARBER, *Sports Illustrated,* **1982**

I'm not winning, but I think my ex-wife is the twelfth leading money winner on tour.
REX CALDWELL, *Golf Digest,* **1983**

My wife's idea of camping out is staying at the Marriott or Howard Johnson's.
JOHNNY MILLER, *Golf Digest,* **1983**

I've been cooking his eggs for thirty years, and he still thinks he has to be in the kitchen telling me how to do it.
WINNIE PALMER, on husband Arnold, *Golf Magazine,* **1983**

It's the first job he's had since I married him.
JEANNE WEISKOPF, on husband Tom's job as a
course designer, *Golf Digest,* **1983**

It was a complete surprise to me, but, on the other hand, it didn't surprise me at all. That'll happen when you haven't been home in eighteen years.
LEE TREVINO on his divorce, *Washington Post,* **1983**

Same name, that way I won't forget it. And I don't have to change the towels. I got a $1.4 million home with my initials all over it, so I might as well live with someone whose name begins with a C.
LEE TREVINO, on his second wife, also named Claudia,
San Jose Mercury News, **1983**

She's loud like me. She laughs like me – and the more people who are around her, the more she puts on her act.
LEE TREVINO about his eighteen-month-old daughter
Olivia Leigh, **1990**

Ken may dress like a nerd, look like a nerd, but he isn't a nerd.
MRS KEN GREEN, **1990**

The fact that I didn't win an eighth Order of Merit title was probably what saved my marriage.
COLIN MONTGOMERIE, **2000**

Fine. I'm gay. Now let's go play golf.
ROSIE JONES, LPGA pro, tag-line to her first-person story, *New York Times*, **2004**

38 ● Women's Tour

You trying to ask me do I wear girdles and bras and the rest of that junk? What do you think I am? A sissy?

BABE DIDRIKSON ZAHARIAS, c. **1940s**

Look at him! When I married him, he was a Greek God. Now he's a big fat Greek.

BABE DIDRIKSON ZAHARIAS, on her husband George

Just ask yourself how good Nicklaus would be if he had to do his nails and put up hair every night before a tournament? Could he shoot sixty-eight if he was trying to make up his mind which dress to wear to the party that night?

JIM MURRAY, *The Sporting World of Jim Murray,* **1968**

Before that tournament started I wrote six things in lipstick on the mirror. . . They were six things I wanted to do with my game. By the time the week was over I hadn't done any of them – and I'd added three more!

JOANNE CARNER, at the US Women's Open, *Golf Digest,* **1971**

Where I came from, a so-called lady golfer was always something to be hollered at, like an overheating '53 Buick blocking traffic, or a sullen waitress who couldn't remember to put cheese on the burger and leave off the onions. . . That's how it was growing up back in Texas.
DAN JENKINS, *Sports Illustrated,* **1971**

The Ladies Professional Golfers Association did build a fairly busy tournament circuit, and has in recent years grown to where the women play for over a million dollars in . . . can we call it purse money?
AL BARKOW, *Golf's Golden Grind,* **1974**

When you first start on the tour, you do a lot of sightseeing. But after you've seen the Alamo five times, what do you do?
JAN FERRARIS, *Wall Street Journal,* **1975**

It's still a financial struggle. The sixtieth woman player in 1974 made exactly $5071.25, and probably used the twenty-five cents to do her own laundry.
DAN GLEASON, *The Great, The Grand and the Also-Ran,* **1976**

If it weren't for golf, I'd be waiting on this table instead of sitting at it.
JUDY RANKIN, *Golf Digest,* **1977**

After a tournament, I'll usually pile into a car with a bunch of girls, and we'll go out and drink beer at some sleazy bar. You know, once in a while I'll get lucky.
MCLEAN STEVENSON, on his backing of the LPGA,
Golf Magazine, **1977**

What we need is less leg and more length. . . We have too many players thinking about diets and getting their hair curled.
DEBBIE MASSEY, *Golf Digest,* **1979**

After seeing Amy Alcott in the Women's US Open on TV, I was impressed with how she kissed her caddie when she won. My next move is to fire my caddie and find me one I can kiss.

LOU GRAHAM, *San Jose Mercury News,* **1980**

Look like a woman, but play like a man.

JAN STEPHENSON, *Golf Magazine,* **1981**

I have a pilot's licence myself, and I don't fly into those big airports. I fly into those little ones, where I can just get on the radio and say, 'Here I come so get out of the way.'

JERILYN BRITZ, *Golf Digest,* **1981**

Now I don't dare throw a club.

JOANNE CARNER, on winning the Bob Jones Award for sportsmanship, **1981**

The pleasure derived from hitting the ball dead centre on the club is comparable only to one or two other pleasures that come to mind at the moment.

DINAH SHORE, *Golf Magazine,* **1981**

Dinah's a great gal... One year she let me play in the tournament on Thursday and I was leading after five holes. Then my wig fell off and they discovered I wasn't Sandra Palmer.

BOB HOPE, *Golf Digest,* **1981**

The LPGA needs a player that looks like Farrah Fawcett and plays like Jack Nicklaus. Instead, they've got players who look like Jack Nicklaus and play like Farrah Fawcett.

ANON, quoted in *Golf Digest,* **1981**

Is our organization so unaware of the real glamour and attraction staring it in the face that it must resort to such trash?
JANE BLALOCK, on the pin-up feature in the LPGA's
Fairway magazine, **1981**

I didn't join the Tour to be in a chorus line.
KATHY WHITWORTH, on the *Fairway* flap, *Golf Magazine,* **1981**

When my mother saw the slides, she asked, 'How did they get your face on Betty Grable's body?'
MUFFIN SPENCER-DEVLIN, on her pin-up picture in the
LPGA magazine, *The Sporting News,* **1982**

I keep telling them that they need a little cellulite – a Miss Piggy of the LPGA.
JOANNE CARNER, on posing for the pin-up section of the
LPGA's *Fairway* magazine, *Orlando Sentinel,* **1982**

He quit playing when I started outdriving him.
JOANNE CARNER, on her husband Don, *Sports Illustrated,* **1982**

I visualize hitting the ball as far as JoAnne Carner, putting like Amy Alcott, looking like Jan Stephenson and having Carol Mann's husband.
DINAH SHORE, *Des Moines Register,* **1982**

Larry doesn't do the logical thing. He doesn't do things like a man. He fights like a woman. He won't fight fair.
JAN STEPHENSON, on her estranged husband Larry Kolb,
Golf Digest, **1982**

Jan is no more responsible for her actions than Patty Hearst was when she was calling her parents 'Pigs' and shooting up banks with machine guns.
LARRY KOLB on Stephenson, *Sports Illustrated*, **1982**

The subjects guaranteed to get the most ink in women's golf are pornography, marriage and divorce, and homosexuality.
RAY VOLPE, LPGA Commissioner, *Oui*, **1982**

I've quit worrying about poor shots. I just tell myself, 'Relax, Bozo. If you can't have fun, you shouldn't be out here.'
PATTY SHEEHAN, **1982**

Women Who Seek Equality With Men Lack Ambition.
PATTY SHEEHAN, bumper sticker on her car,
The Sporting News, **1983**

Instead of my yardage book, I was reaching for my flight guide.
JOANNE CARNER, upon shooting an eighty-one,
Sports Illustrated, **1983**

I did something by climbing over 113 golfers. The only trouble is there were 114 ahead of me.
JOANNE CARNER about her climb from 115th after the first round of the 1983 US Women's Open

I went into a dry-cleaning store and the guy asked me what I did for a living. I told him I was a professional golfer and he said, 'Oh, only Nancy Lopez makes any money.'
HOLLIS STACY, *San Francisco Chronicle*, **1983**

I've had sex in a lot of places. I wouldn't want to have it in the bunker, because of the sand. I'd kind of like to have it on the green; it would be nice and soft.
JAN STEPHENSON, *Playboy,* **1983**

I'll take the two-stroke penalty, but I'll be damned if I'll play it where it lays.
ELAINE JOHNSON, Canadian amateur golfer, as her ball landed in her bra, *Sports Illustrated,* **1983**

It's a hard way to make an easy living.
JOYCE KAZMIERSKI, winless on the LPGA tour for fourteen years, *Golf Digest,* **1983**

I was concentrating so hard on that putt I forgot what was going on.
CATHY MANT, missing a birdie putt, **1984**

What club? A putter.
AYAKO OKAMOTO, when asked what club she used to birdie a hole, **1984**

I was a cheerleader in seventh grade and hated it. . . I wanted to be out there on the field playing and competing, not on the sidelines bouncing around.
JULI INKSTER, *Seattle Post-Intelligencer,* **1984**

I'm getting serious about my career because I'm going to be a mother. My dog is pregnant.
MUFFIN SPENCER-DEVLIN, at the Safeco Classic, **1984**

I do all the endorsements because I'm the one they want. Pat Bradley is a great player, but what can you say about Pat Bradley but what she shot? All she does is practise and play.
JAN STEPHENSON, at the Virginia Bank Classic, **1984**

Them two [Pat Bradley and Jan Stephenson] don't get along. It's like the Celtics playing the Lakers. Whenever they're matched, they both shoot well because they hate each other.
JERRY WOODARD, Bradley's caddie, *Sports Illustrated*, **1985**

I had really planned on winning. Really planned on it. But I didn't handle my jar of negative thoughts very well. I couldn't keep the cap on.
ROSIE JONES after losing the LPGA title to Beth Daniel, **1990**

When we complain about conditions, we're just bitches. But when the men do it, people think, 'Well, it really must be hard.'
BETSY KING, at the US Women's Open at Colonial CC,
Fort Worth, Texas, **1991**

There are a few players on the LPGA Tour who might be mistaken for someone at the hot dog stand – players I've threatened to buy a [clothes] iron for. If you had an ironing contest between the PGA Tour and the LPGA Tour, right now the men would win.
JUDY RANKIN, TV analyst and former tour player,
Golf Digest, **2004**

Probably the toughest job in sports is to deal with 200 women.
ANNIKA SORENSTAM, on the difficulty of being commissioner of the LPGA Tour, *GolfWorld*, **2005**

39 ● Woods and Irons

I call my sand wedge my half-Nelson, because I can always strangle the opposition with it.
BYRON NELSON, *Collier's*, 1945

There's ninety ways to get out of the rough after a long drive, but no way at all to pick up those yards you've lost by hitting them soft.
SAM SNEAD, advice to Johnny Weismuller, 1947

I hit a hook that went so far out of bounds I almost killed a horse in some stables a cab ride from the first fairway. I was so nervous I didn't have the strength to push the tee in the ground.
MIKE SOUCHAK, on beginning his career at the
Los Angeles Open

The only fun in the game is watching the ball fly through the air.
JACKIE BURKE

What other people may find in poetry or art museums, I find in the flight of a good drive.
ARNOLD PALMER, *My Game and Yours,* **1965**

Anytime a golfer hits a ball perfectly straight with a big club it is, in my view, a fluke.
JACK NICKLAUS

The chip shot from a bunker is like the lapidary's stroke of a diamond.
HENRY COTTON

Actually, the only time I ever took out a one-iron was to kill a tarantula. And I took a seven to do that.
JIM MURRAY, *The Best of Jim Murray,* **1965**

No Instant Golfer can ever do anything with a two- or three-iron but poke the fire.
JIM MURRAY

Don't move, hole!
LEE TREVINO, hitting an iron at the pin

I'll take anything in the air that doesn't sting.
DAVE MARR, **1968**

If your caddie coaches you on the tee, 'Hit it down the left side with a little draw,' ignore him. All you do on the tee is try not to hit the caddie.
JIM MURRAY, *The Sporting World of Jim Murray,* **1968**

It may have been the greatest four-wood anyone ever hit. It was so much on the flag that I had to lean sideways to follow the flight of the ball.
GARY PLAYER, to the press

The good chip is like the good sandtrap shot, it's your secret weapon. It allows you to whistle while you walk in the dark alleys of golf.

TOMMY BOLT, *How to Keep Your Temper on the Golf Course,* **1969**

I've got the yips – not with my putter, with my wedge.

LIONEL HEBERT, **1970**

I once hit a drive five hundred yards – on a par-three hole. I had a three-wood coming back.

CHI CHI RODRIGUEZ, **1970**

Through years of experience I have found that air offers less resistance than dirt.

JACK NICKLAUS, on why he tees up the ball so high

You must have a good, fluid swing to make that club pay off. If I catch one of my amateur friends playing with a one-iron he had better be putting with it.

TOMMY BOLT, *The Hole Truth,* **1971**

If that's featherin', I'd hate for you to pluck my chickens.

LEE TREVINO, to an amateur partner trying to feather an iron shot, **1973**

I never leave myself a half shot if I can help it. . . If I leave myself a tricky little half shot and don't hit it just right over that water, that dog ain't gonna hunt.

LEE TREVINO, *Golf Digest,* **1974**

In case you don't know very much about the game of golf, a good one-iron shot is about as easy to come by as an understanding wife.

DAN JENKINS, *Dead Solid Perfect,* **1974**

The first yardage stripe is 270 yards. That puts me out before it starts.

MASON RUDOLPH, at a long-driving contest, *Golf Digest,* **1974**

I know this. If I learn to hit that ball dead straight before I starve, I might rule the world.

ROD CURL, **1975**

I only hit the ball about 220 off the tee, but I can always find it.

BONNIE LAUER, *Golf Magazine,* **1977**

Hickory golf was a game of manipulation and inspiration; steel golf is a game of precision and calculation.

PETER DOBEREINER

Tee it high and let it fly, ain't no trouble in the sky.

LARRY MCCARTHY, bartender, San Rafael, Calif., **1977**

It's hard to take a chance when you can't reach the green in the first place.

TOM KITE, on why he doesn't take chances,
Sports Illustrated, **1982**

A big worm popped its head out of the ground beside the ball and I was so surprised I took my eye off the ball.

GREG NORMAN, on why he topped a drive, **1982**

In golf, you're always thinking about how the course is playing, whether the greens are fast or slow or whether the wind is blowing or dying or shifting. All of a sudden you say, 'Aw, just give me a five-iron.'

REX CALDWELL, *Golf Magazine,* **1983**

She was rattling in the locker room, itching to get out.
GREG NORMAN about his trusty persimmon wood driver
before the 1990 US Open

I would much rather be hitting the driver and a nine-iron
out of the rough than hitting a driver and a four-iron out of
the fairway.
JACK NICKLAUS, *Golf Digest,* **1983**

If Jack Nicklaus had to play my tee shots, he couldn't break
eighty. He'd be a pharmacist with a string of drugstores in
Ohio.
LEE TREVINO, *San Francisco Examiner,* **1983**

I've built golf courses and laid the irrigation system just by
teeing off.
LEE TREVINO, *'The Tonight Show',* NCB-TV, **1983**

My goal this year is basically to find the fairways.
LAURI PETERSON, *San Jose Mercury News,* **1983**

The woods are full of long hitters.
HARVEY PENICK, University of Houston golf coach,
San Francisco Chronicle, **1984**

When I first came out on Tour, I swung all out on every tee
shot. My drives finished so far off line, my pants were grass-
stained at the knees.
FUZZY ZOELLER, *Golf Magazine,* **1984**

I have no idea what a persimmon [wood] feels like. I've never
played them and never had any interest in hitting them, even
for kicks.
CHARLES HOWELL III, US pro, twenty-five years after the
introduction of the modern metal wood, *GolfWorld,* **2004**

I had [one] shank – and now you're comparing me to David Duval?
DARREN CLARKE, asked if a shanked four-iron at the PGA Championship meant he was struggling with his game like Duval, *GolfWorld*, **2004**

Who dominates the game today? It's 100 per cent bombers. It doesn't make any difference where you hit it anymore. You just hit it as far as you can. You're hitting it so close to the green, they can't put enough rough out there to make any difference.
JACK NICKLAUS, *Palm Beach (Fla.) Post*, **2005**

I kept wondering what's so difficult about hitting a 1-iron . . . Every time I saw an odd 1-iron, it piqued my curiosity even more. It became an evil obsession.
Club aficionado MIKE MACDOUGALL, fifty-two, who spent four years and $120,000 collecting one- and two-irons,
Palm Beach (Fla.) Post, **2005**

Bibliography

Argea, Angelo, with Jolee Edmondson. *The Bear and I.* New York: Atheneum, 1979.

Armour, Tommy. *A Round of Golf with Tommy Armour.* New York: Simon and Schuster, 1969.

Baker, Stephen. *How to Play Golf in the Low 120s.* Englewood Cliffs, N.J.: Prentice-Hall, 1962.

Ballesteros, Severiano, and Dudley Doust. *Seve: The Young Champion.* New York: Golf Digest, 1984.

Barkow, Al. *Golf's Golden Grind.* New York: Harcourt Brace Jovanovich, 1974.

Bartlett, Michael, ed. *The Golf Book.* New York: Arbor House, 1980.

Beard, Frank. Edited by Dick Schaap. *Pro.* New York: World, 1970.

Beck, Fred. *89 Years in a Sand Trap.* New York: Hill and Wang, 1965.

Bisher, Furman. *The Masters.* Birmingham, Ala.: Oxmoor House, 1976.

—. *The Birth of a Legend.* Englewood Cliffs, N.J.: Prentice-Hall, 1972.

Blalock, Jane, with Dwayne Netland. *The Guts to Win.* Norwalk, Ct.: Golf Digest, 1977.

Bolt, Tommy, with Jimmy Mann. *The Hole Truth*. New York: J. B. Lippincott, 1971.

Bolt, Tommy, with William C. Griffith. *How to Keep Your Temper on the Golf Course*. New York: David McKay, 1969.

Brown, Eric, with Alan Herron. *Out of the Bag*. London, Eng.: Stanley Paul, 1964.

Browning, Robert. *A History of Golf*. London, Eng.: J. M. Dent, 1955.

Campbell, Patrick. *How to Become a Scratch Golfer*. New York: W. W. Norton, 1963.

Casper, Billy. *My Million Dollar Shots*. Grosset and Dunlop, 1970.

Chinnock, Frank. *How to Break 90 – Consistently!* New York: J. B. Lippincott, 1976.

Concannon, Dale. *Nick Faldo: Driven*. London, Eng.: Virgin, 2001.

Cotton, Henry. *The World of Golf*. London: Purnell, 1971.

Davis, William H., ed. *100 Greatest Golf Courses – And Then Some*. New York: Golf Digest, 1982.

Demaret, Jimmy. *My Partner, Ben Hogan*. New York: McGraw-Hill, 1954.

Dobereiner, Peter. *Down the Nineteenth Fairway*. New York: Atheneum, 1983.

—. *The Glorious World of Golf*. New York: McGraw-Hill, 1973.

—. *The World of Golf*. New York: Atheneum, 1981.

Feinstein, John. *The First Coming: Tiger Woods, Master or Martyr*. New York: Ballantine, 1998.

Gallwey, W. Timothy. *The Inner Game of Golf*. New York: Random House, 1979.

Gibson, Nevin A. *Great Moments in Golf*. New Jersey: A. S. Barnes & Co Inc, 1973.

Gladstone, Dr Irving A. *Confessions of a Golf Duffer*. New York: Frederick Fell, 1977.

Gleason, Dan. *The Great, The Grand and the Also-Ran*. New York: Random House, 1976.

Graffis, Herb. *The PGA*. New York: Thomas Y. Crowell, 1975.

Gregston, Gene. *Hogan: The Man Who Played for Glory*. Englewood Cliffs, N.J.: Prentice-Hall, 1978.

Gross, Milton. *Eighteen Holes in My Head*. New York: McGraw-Hill, 1959.

Hackett, Buddy. *The Truth About Golf and Other Lies*. Garden City, N.Y.: Doubleday, 1968.

Hagen, Walter, with Margaret Seaton Heck. *The Walter Hagen Story*. New York: Heinemann, 1957.

Herold, Don. *Love That Golf*. New York: A. S. Barnes, 1952.

Hill, Dave, and Nick Seitz. *Teed Off*. Englewood Cliffs, N.J.: Prentice-Hall, 1977.

Hobbs, Michael, *Great Opens*. New York: A. S. Barnes, 1977.

Hobbs, Michael, ed. *In Celebration of Golf*. New York: Charles Scribner's Sons, 1983.

Hope, Bob, with Dwayne Netland. *Confessions of a Hooker*. London: Stanley Paul, 1986.

Jenkins, Dan. *Dead Solid Perfect*. New York: Atheneum, 1974.

—. *The Dogged Victims of Inexorable Fate*. Boston, Mass.: Little, Brown, 1970.

—. *Fairways and Greens*. New York: Doubleday, 1994.

Johnson, William Oscar, and Nancy P. Williamson. *Whatta-Gal*. Boston, Mass.: Little, Brown, 1975.

Jones, Bob. *British Golf Odyssey*. Monterey, Ca.: Angel Press, 1977.

Jones, Jr, Robert Tyre (Bobby). *Golf Is My Game*. Garden City, N.Y.: Doubleday, 1960.

Keane, Christopher. *The Tour*. New York: Stein and Day, 1974.

Lardner, Rex. *Downhill Lies*. New York: Hawthorn, 1973.

—. *Out of the Bunker and Into the Trees*. New York: Bobbs-Merrill, 1960.

Lema, Tony. *Golfer's Gold*. Boston, Mass.: Little, Brown, 1964.

Longhurst, Henry. Edited by Mark Wilson with Ken Bowden. *The Best of Henry Longhurst*. Norwalk, Conn.: Golf Digest, 1978.

Lopez, Nancy, with Peter Schwed. *The Education of a Woman Golfer*. New York: Simon and Schuster, 1979.

Low, George, with Al Barkow. *The Master of Putting*. New York: Atheneum, 1983.

Maikovich, Andrew J. *Sports Quotations*. Jefferson, N.C. and London, Eng.: McFarland, 1984.

McCarthy, Colman. *The Pleasures of the Game*. New York: Dial, 1977.

McCormack, Mark H. *Arnie*. New York: Simon and Schuster, 1967.

McDonnell, Michael. *Classic Golf Quotes*. London, Eng.: Robson, 2002.

Miller, Dick. *America's Greatest Golfing Resorts*. New York: Bobbs-Merrill, 1977.

—. *Triumphant Journey*. New York: Holt, Rinehart and Winston, 1980.

Morley, David C. *The Missing Links*. New York: Atheneum, 1976.

Mulvoy, Mark, and Art Spander. *Golf: The Passion and the Challenge*. Englewood Cliffs, N.J.: Prentice-Hall, 1977.

Nash, Bruce, and Allan Zullo, with Bill Hartigan. *Golf's Most Outrageous Quotes*. Kansas City, Mo.: Andrews and McMeel, 1995.

Nicklaus, Jack, with Herbert Warren Wind. *The Greatest Game of All*. New York: Simon and Schuster, 1969.

Palmer, Arnold, with Bob Drum. *Arnold Palmer's Best 54 Golf Holes*. Garden City, N.Y.: Doubleday, 1977.

—, with William Barry Furlong. *Go For Broke*. New York: Simon and Schuster, 1973.

Penna, Toney, with Oscar Fraley. *My Wonderful World of Golf*. New York: Hawthorn, 1965.

Peper, George. *Golf's Supershots*. London: Stanley Paul, 1982.

Perry, Paul D. *Billy Casper*. Englewood Cliffs, N.J.: Prentice-Hall, 1969.

Player, Gary, with Floyd Thatcher. *Gary Player*. Waco, Tex.: Word Books, 1974.

Plimpton, George. *The Bogey Man*. New York: Harper & Row, 1968.

Potter, Stephen. *Golfmanship*. New York: McGraw-Hill, 1968.

Price, Charles. *Golfer-At-Large*. New York: Atheneum, 1982.

——. *The World of Golf*. New York: Random House, 1962.

Price, Charles, ed. *The American Golfer*. New York: Random House, 1964.

Puckett, Earl, ed. *Golfer's Digest*. Northfield, III.: Digest Books, 1974.

Rees, Dai. *Dai Rees on Golf*. New York: A. S. Barnes, 1959.

Rice, Grantland, with O. B. Keeler. *The Bobby Jones Story*. Atlanta, Ga.: Tupper & Love, 1953.

Roberts, Clifford. *The Story of the Augusta National Golf Club*. Garden City, N.Y.: Doubleday, 1976.

Robertson, James K. *St Andrews*. Fife, Scot.: Citizen Office, 1967.

Rosaforte, Tim. *Tiger Woods: The Makings of a Champion*. New York: St Martin's, 1997.

Ryde, Peter, ed. *Mostly Golf*. London, Eng.: Adam and Charles Black, 1976.

Sanders, Doug, with Larry Sheehan. *Come Swing with Me*. Garden City, N.Y.: Doubleday, 1974.

Sarazen, Gene, with Herbert Warren Wind. *Thirty Years of Championship Golf*. New York: Prentice-Hall, 1950.

Schaap, Dick. *Massacre at Winged Foot*. New York: Random House, 1974.

——. *The Masters*. New York: Random House, 1970.

Schoor, Gene. *Babe Didrikson*. Garden City, N.Y.: Doubleday, 1978.

Scott, Tom, and Geoffrey Cousins. *The Golf Immortals*. New York: Hart, 1969.

Seitz, Nick, and Bob Toski. *Superstars of Golf*. New York: Golf Digest, 1978.

Sheehan, Larry, ed. *Best Golf Humour from Golf Digest*. New York: Golf Digest, 1972.

——. *Great Golf Humour from Golf Digest*. New York: Golf Digest, 1979.

Skyzinski, Rich. *Quotable Tiger*. Nashville, Tenn.: TowleHouse, 2001.

Snead, Sam, with Al Stump. *The Education of a Golfer*. New York: Simon and Schuster, 1962.

Stanley, Dave, and George G. Ross, eds. *The Golfer's Own Book*. New York: Lantern Press, 1956.

Strege, John. *Tiger: A Biography of Tiger Woods*. New York: Broadway, 1997.

Trevino, Lee, and Sam Blair. *They Call Me Super Mex*. New York: Random House, 1982.

Updike, John. *Rabbit Is Rich*. New York: Knopf, 1981.

Venturi, Ken, with Oscar Fraley. *Comeback*. New York: Duell, Sloan and Pearce, 1966.

Wikipedia: The Free Encyclopedia, wikipedia.org, 2005, 2006.

Wind, Herbert Warren. *Herbert Warren Wind's Golf Book*. New York: Simon and Schuster, 1971.

——. *The Story of American Golf*. New York: Farrar, Straus, 1948.

Wind, Herbert Warren, ed. *The Complete Golfer*. New York: Simon and Schuster, 1954.

Wodehouse, P. G. Edited by D. R. Benson. *Fore!* New York: Ticknor & Fields, 1983.

Wright, Ben, with Michael Patrick Shiels. *Good Bounces and Bad Lies*. Chelsea, MI.: Sleeping Bear, 1999.

Index